Abraham in Arms

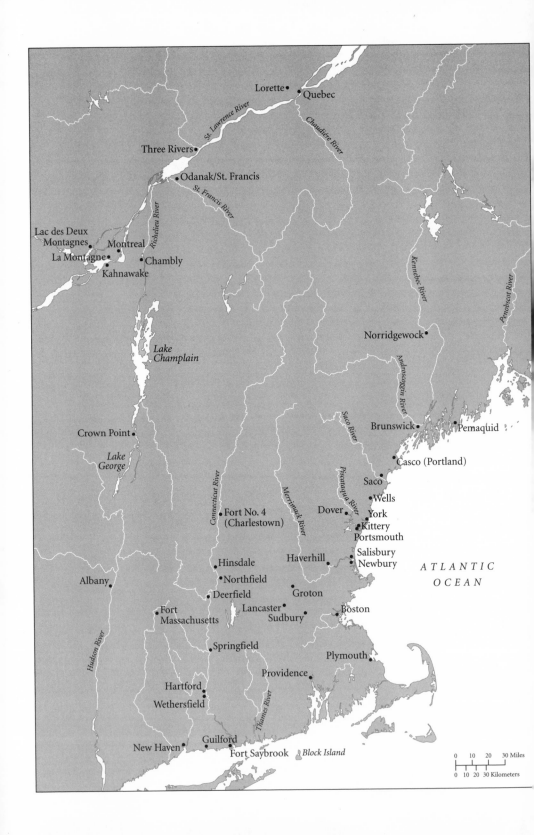

Abraham in Arms

War and Gender in Colonial New England

Ann M. Little

PENN

University of Pennsylvania Press
Philadelphia

EARLY AMERICAN STUDIES

Daniel K. Richter and Kathleen M. Brown, Series Editors

Exploring neglected aspects of our colonial, revolutionary, and early
national history and culture, Early American Studies reinterprets familiar
themes and events in fresh ways. Interdisciplinary in character, and
with a special emphasis on the period from about 1600 to 1850, the
series is published in partnership with the McNeil Center for
Early American Studies.

A complete list of books in the series is available from the publisher.

Copyright © 2007 University of Pennsylvania Press
All rights reserved
Printed in the United States of America on acid-free paper

10 9 8 7 6 5 4 3 2 1

Published by
University of Pennsylvania Press
Philadelphia, Pennsylvania 19104-4112

Library of Congress Cataloging-in-Publication Data

Little, Ann M.
    Abraham in arms : war and gender in Colonial New England / Ann M. Little.
        p.   cm. — (Early American studies)
    Includes bibliographical references and index.
    ISBN-13: 978-0-8122-3965-2
    ISBN-10: 0-8122-3965-2 (alk. paper)
        1. New England—History—Colonial period, ca. 1600–1775.   2. Frontier and pioneer
life—New England.   3. New England—History, Military.   4. New England—Social
conditions.   5. Masculinity—New England—History.   6. Sex role—New England—History.
7. English—New England—History—18th century.   8. Indians of North America—New
England—History.   9. French—New England—History—18th century.   10. New
England—Ethnic relations.   I. Title.   II. Series.

F7.L68   2006
974'.02—dc22   2006042166

Frontispiece: Northeastern borderlands, ca. 1670–1763

For C.P.M.

Contents

Wars of the Northeastern Borderlands, 1636–1763

The Pequot War	1636–37
King Philip's War/Metacom's Rebellion	1675–76 (to 1678 in Maine)
King William's War	1688–97 ⎫ first two Anglo-
Queen Anne's War	1702–13 ⎬ French wars
Dummer's War/Ralé's War/Greylock's War	1723–26
King George's War	1744–48 ⎫ last two Anglo-
Seven Years' War/French and Indian War	1756–63 ⎬ French wars

Introduction
Onward Christian Soldiers, 1678

In 1678 Samuel Nowell preached an artillery election sermon he called *Abraham in Arms,* in which he urged New England men to remember that *"Hence it is no wayes unbecoming a Christian to learn to be a Souldier,* not only a Spiritual Souldier but in the true proper sence of the letter." His warning was timely, and prescient: Nowell preached in the wake of King Philip's War (also known as Metacom's Rebellion), a united Indian uprising that lasted from 1675 to 1676 in southern New England and persisted on the eastern frontier until 1678. Unlike previous Indian wars and threatened uprisings, King Philip's War was not waged by just one Indian tribe or by one leader, as the name implies, but by nearly all of the Algonquians living near the English settlements of New England. From the Narragansett and Wampanoag of Rhode Island to the Eastern Abenaki of Maine, Indians made common cause against English settlers. At the time that Nowell warned his flock that they must be soldiers for their faith and for New England, the war had barely ended in Maine. The eastern frontier was worrisome for another reason—namely, because it harbored another enemy to Protestant New England. Early English explorers and French Jesuits had made competing claims on Maine's waterways, land, and peoples, from the Saco River northeast to the mouth of the Kennebec. Already in this latest war, Maine settlers notified their governor in Boston that they had spied French men among the Abenaki, aiding them in their efforts to drive the English back into the sea. Thus with New England on the brink of more than eighty more years of war with Indians and the French, Nowell urged New England men to be girded for battle, ready to advance and defend the frontier of English Protestant settlement. Perhaps this is why Nowell preached so insistently that military readiness was on a par with spiritual preparedness: after all, *"the Battle is the Lords."*[1]

Nowell's sermon title was significant. The Abraham of the Old Testament resonated deeply with English men in the New World, as he embodied the ideal of the householder-patriarch, at once obedient to God and the unchallenged leader of his family and of his people in war and peace. Also like Abraham, the authority of English men was based on their sex, their religion, and their ethnicity. But over the years of English settlement, Abraham's enemies in New England had manifested themselves with a vengeance. Algonquian and Iroquois peoples threatened the safety of his household and mocked his pretensions to dominate New England: "you dare not fight, you are all one like women," they taunted in battle, and then stripped the bodies of the dead and took English captives alive into the wilderness. Although the English had won both major New England Indian wars (the Pequot War, 1636–37, and King Philip's War), by 1678 they still did not dominate the northeastern borderlands militarily, politically, or economically. Moreover, warfare between the English and Indians was devastating for Indian and English communities alike, characterized as it was by attacks on small settlements, the burning of individual homes and farms, and the constant involvement of so-called noncombatants like women, children, and the infirm. Although victorious over King Philip, English men might still be stung by comments like those of John Wompus, an Indian who judged that English men "had acted all one like children" in the late war, and their inability to protect their homes and families from fire and captivity meant that "New England hath Lost the day & yt is knowne in old England."[2] Furthermore, subordinates within the English community— even within their own families—threatened the governorship of their households and of New England itself. Wives ran away, and daughters taken into captivity in colonial warfare sometimes became baptized Catholics, married French or Indian men, and refused to return to New England.[3]

This book tells stories about the people who lived in New England, New France, and Indian country, from the establishment of the first permanent English colony in New England to the end of the Seven Years' War. It argues that ideas about gender and family life were central to the ways in which these people understood and explained their experience of cross-cultural warfare. In fact, they had a great deal in common when it came to warfare in particular, since in the seventeenth and eighteenth centuries European and Indian cultures were organized around a gendered hierarchy that privileged manhood and reserved politics and war for men almost exclusively. This book is part of a trend in recent scholarship to move away from an emphasis on cultural difference and instead analyze the implications of the many similarities between Indians and Europeans.[4] Questions of similarities and differences in women's lives have been a point of contention for feminist scholars, and many have labored for decades to move beyond the essentialism of early feminist assumptions that the experience of womanhood was universal and transhistorical.[5] Recent important early American women's histories illustrate the dramatically different experiences of Euro-American, African American, and Indian women, as well as signal the ways in which a gendered hierarchy structured the lives of all women and men in the Atlantic world.[6] Despite these differences, some assumptions about gender (and especially about men's roles in their societies) were also strikingly similar in Africa, Europe, and the Americas. It was a universally understood insult throughout the early modern Atlantic world to call a man a woman. Nowhere in colonial America would being called a woman be understood as a compliment or a neutral comment on a man's competence or worthiness.

These important similarities notwithstanding, Indian and European observers in the colonial period focused on their differences when talking or writing about each other, and as the colonial period wore on, they became even less willing to acknowledge their similarities. However, historians must not take these observations at face value. Portraying one's enemies as utterly strange and different—as savage, irrational, weak, or foolish (as opposed to oneself: civilized, rational, strong, and wise)—undoubtedly served the psychological needs and political agendas on all sides, although only English-speaking peoples had the technology and literacy rates that would help spread their version of the truth throughout the North American colonies and across the Atlantic Ocean.[7]

Finally, this book attempts to reconstruct the colonial Northeast as a borderlands whose religious, cultural, linguistic, and geographic boundaries were permeable, fragile, and contested by Europeans and Indians alike.[8] Just as a mythology of difference served the various political agendas of Europeans and Indians in the northeastern borderlands as they embarked on nearly a century and a half of almost uninterrupted warfare, so the nation-states that arose in peacetime hired surveyors, cartographers, and historians to impose boundaries and create a new mythology of difference—one that has created segregated histories for Canada, the United States, and Native America.

Power relations in the northeastern borderlands, as in the wider early modern Atlantic world, were based in large part on gender inequality, an idea that was gaining renewed social and political importance in the first century after Columbus's discovery. Scholars of early modern Europe have identified a major shift in gender politics in the Reformation era, when both Protestant and Catholic religious reformers turned to male heads of household to assert more control in the ordering of society in the face of diminished church authority.[9] At the time of the Columbian encounter, Native American and African cultures also privileged men over women, especially in the realms of political and military leadership. While Indian and African women usually retained more economic power than European women did, all four continents that formed the basin of the Atlantic world used gender as a fundamental tool in the hierarchies that ordered their many and diverse societies.[10] Furthermore, historians of Native Americans have recently argued that the stresses and conflicts that European colonization brought to Indian country may have exacerbated tensions between Indian men and women.[11]

The borderlands of colonial New England, New France, and Indian country are a promising place to understand the workings of gender and power, as it was a place where all families—Native, English, and French—were undergoing rapid changes. Indian families and communities were pressured not just by the changes brought by Europeans in the form of new technologies, trade goods, and political and military conflict. Many Indian communities—some of them otherwise untouched by the European invasion of the New World—were devastated by Old World diseases to which they had no inherited resistance. Indian families were faced with threats on all sides to their traditional ways of life, as they were pressured by the new environmental, demographic, and political realities of the colonial world. Most Native peoples used a variety of strategies to adjust to an increasingly European-dominated politics and economy, such as joining other tribes, living in missionary towns, fighting against European encroachment, or seizing and adopting European captives into their families. Whether they chose to accommodate to or resist European invasion, the colonial world fundamentally altered Indian families.[12] Similarly, with imbalanced sex ratios in the immigrant European population and without the powerful institutions that shaped late medieval and early modern Europe—the manor house, schools, and guilds—colonial Euro-American households were stressed by having to assume a number of social functions for which they were frequently inadequate. In New England, households in tandem with town and colony government—what was known as "household government"—became a legally defined and empowered "second estate" charged with ensuring the proper ordering of society.[13] In the fledgling agricultural villages and towns along the St. Lawrence River, where the sex ratio among French settlers remained extremely imbalanced through the seventeenth century, female religious orders like the Ursulines and the Sisters of the Congregation of Notre Dame attempted to fill the gap in social services by running poor houses, hospitals, and schools in Québec, Montreal, and Three Rivers. French men frequently turned to intermarriage with Indians or English captives, as well as keeping Indian and English servants and slaves to populate their households. However, instead of allowing for the reproduction of an ideal European social order, these *métis* families and families with war captives embodied many of the tensions and instabilities of life on the northeastern frontier.[14]

Because of the many challenges their families faced, these cultures used ideas about gender and family life to explain and justify their political and military conflicts with one another. Time and again, Indian, French, and English people found each other wanting in the particular roles they assigned men and women and the ways they managed their households. No other men were as manly as their men, no other women understood their honorable place in the community like their women, and no other children were being raised properly in the North American borderlands. I must be clear about the nature of my argument: I do not argue that the French, English, and Indian people warred on and killed each other because they hated the ways in which their enemies organized household and family life. Other historians have demonstrated clearly and convincingly that material reasons drove the competition for the conquest of North America— agricultural lands and hunting grounds for furs were in fact the great prize for whoever could dominate New England, Acadia, and the St. Lawrence River Valley militarily and politically.[15] Gender and family differences were, however, central to the language and ideology of conquest and were the key principles upon which theories of difference were constructed in the colonial northeastern borderlands, and the English were especially garrulous in making their arguments. Their justifications for warfare, and for conquering and removing Indians and French Catholics, were not coincidentally developed at the same time that other Atlantic world societies were justifying the mass enslavement and exploitation of African labor for similar material goals.[16]

The historiography of cross-cultural gender relations that informs this book was pioneered by women's historians, many of whom in the past twenty years have shifted to a more theoretical focus on the nature of gendered power. Pathbreaking studies of extraordinary sophistication not only historicized women's experiences by showing how the nature of women's work, their roles in family life, and the ideals of womanhood changed over time; they also opened new doors for considering the ways in which gender and class, or gender and race, worked together to structure power relationships in colonial America and the early national United States.[17] This focus on gender—its historical and cultural specificity, and how it changes over time—has also led to a burgeoning literature on early American masculinity and the ways in which manhood was constructed, experienced, and challenged by others in different places, times, and cultures.[18] This study both draws on and adds to both of these literatures on early American men and women, showing how in one specific region rent by warfare and intercultural conflict we can see the same broad changes that characterized the entire colonial Atlantic world.

At the same time that women's historians were broadening their focus to include evaluations of gender and power, ethnohistorians openly challenged the eurocentric historical narratives of the past four centuries. In the 1970s and 1980s, ethnohistorians urged the profession to abandon its traditional approach to American Indian history, which treated Native peoples more as environmental or meteorological forces rather than as human beings whose decisions were rational and could be explained through traditional historical methodology and anthropological approaches to understanding Native cultures. Native Americans were not the irrational, inscrutable, wild creatures most often described in colonial documents, nor did they simply die off, fade away, or retreat to the margins of colonial society as Europeans and Euro-Americans achieved the demographic advantage. Like women's historians, ethnohistorians insisted that colonial history was unintelligible without a consideration of inter-Indian and Euro-Indian power relations. Through varying strategies of forming trade and military alliances, warfare with Europeans and other Indians, migration, segregation, and intermarriage with Euro-Americans and African Americans, Native peoples chose different paths at different times to preserve and even strengthen their numbers, power, and prestige.[19]

One of the principal aims of this book is to draw together these two rich and fruitful literatures and use them together to interpret the complex world of colonial New England, New France, and the Indian lands that lay between these shifting and fragile borders.[20] By using the insights of gender and ethnohistory together, I depart in significant ways from the 1990s' cultural studies emphasis on difference as an explanatory concept for encounters among New World societies. Although it is true that colonial French, Indian, and English people alike insisted that it was cultural differences that drove their political and military conflicts, historians should read such pronouncements skeptically. While there were in fact great economic, religious, and cultural differences among Indian, French, and English people, what seemed to disturb them even more was evidence of their essential sameness.[21] Most northeastern borderlands people made their living in agrarian-based economies supplemented by hunting, fishing, and trade; all three peoples therefore were fighting for political and military control of the same resources. But perhaps the most important common touchstone of these cultures was the value they placed on masculinity and on men's performance in war and politics. Indian, French, and English men agreed that to be ruled by other men was to be reduced in status—to that of a woman perhaps, or a child, a servant or slave, or even a dog. Because everyone spoke and understood the same gendered language of power, they knew very well that it was not only their sovereignty or their livelihoods that were at stake in seventeenth- and eighteenth-century warfare; what was at stake was their very manhood.

Because of the cross-cultural nature of this study, it also draws on the rich historiography of the new Western history and of the emerging field of borderlands history.[22] Like those early U.S. borderlands historians Francis Parkman and Frederick Jackson Turner, I see the colonial border wars as part of a larger story of North America; unlike my nineteenth-century predecessors, I do not see this story as having such a righteous outcome.[23] While deeply influenced by the new borderlands historiography, this book remains a study of New England fashioned within a borderlands framework—it is not an equally balanced investigation of Canada and Indian country as well. This is in part due to the sources available, which are overwhelmingly English-language sources written and published in New England and London. Widespread literacy and a printing press meant that New England was able to record and publish the first draft of history faster than French or Native North Americans. This book is an effort to examine that first draft of history from a variety of critical perspectives and to help us see its contradictions, complexities, truths, lies, and political and diplomatic calculations.

The strategies of talented ethnohistorians have helped colonial historians read European sources for Native voices, and they have forced us all to be a lot shrewder and more cautious about the bias of our sources generally.[24] I have used Canadian sources wherever possible, although the low levels of literacy there in the colonial period (at least compared to colonial New England) mean that my French sources are overwhelmingly from church and political elites, who frequently had as little regard for their working-class *habitants* as they had for their foes in New England and Iro-quoia. While in a sense this study is burdened by its wealth of New England sources, the advantage they offer is that they reflect a much broader cross-section of New England society than French or Indian sources can. Like many traditional studies of colonial New England, this book relies on offi-cial records like court and probate records, the correspondence of colonial officials, and the published and private writings of ministers and other elites. Boston's own publishers and presses also did their share for the pres-ervation of colonial history, putting into print countless election sermons, captivity narratives, broadsides, and calls to arms. However, colonial New England's relatively high literacy rate means that we have a good number of public and private writings of non-elites—accounts of skirmishes and battles from volunteers and soldiers stationed in outposts far from Boston; petitions from desperate Maine and New Hampshire families destroyed by Indian attacks and captivity; diaries kept by provincial soldiers during the Seven Years' War; and even the letters and private musings of a few Anglo-American women.

Because of the bias of the sources, these war stories told in captivity narratives, dispatches from the front, and histories written by war veterans and civilians alike are all representations of the past rather than necessarily reliable truths. I am indebted to the work of cultural studies scholars who have argued persuasively that every historical source has its own agenda.[25] However, this book strives to do more than just discuss English representa-tions of their enemies and their experiences of war. As unreliable as the sources are, they are relatively rich and numerous in colonial New England, so I hope that I am also uncovering something of the truth of what the experience of war was like for English, French, and Indian peoples alike.

My story begins with the first seventeenth-century encounters between English settlers in southern New England and the different Algonquian-speaking nations they found there, principally the Mohegans, Pequots, Nar-ragansetts, and Wampanoags. Chapter 1 establishes the gendered nature of early Anglo-Indian contact and conflict by describing the essential similar-ity of Indian and English men on two key points: both politics and war were men's occupations, and both were arenas for establishing one's manhood. Both groups believed that to be bested (or, as the English of the time tell-ingly called it, *mastered*) by other men in war meant a possible loss of self-mastery and the prospect of being ruled by other men. Thus, both English and Indian people understood that what was at stake in their struggle for dominion in the northeastern borderlands was their masculine privilege of self-rule. Chapter 2 extends this theme of warfare and gender (particularly masculinity) into the mid-eighteenth century, following the progress of borderlands conflicts throughout New England and into the St. Lawrence River valley, Acadia, Iroquoia, and Abenaki country. It considers one particular aspect of Anglo-Indian warfare, the Native American ritual of stripping dead enemies and live captives, and the English experience as subjects and witnesses of these rituals. English people were disturbed by their own nakedness and by seeing Indians dressed in European-style clothing, transgressions they saw not just as a blurring of ethnic lines but also as a frightful blurring of gender identities as well.

Chapters 3 and 4 shift the focus from masculinity and men's experiences in war to a consideration of Native and English women's experiences in warfare and captivity, which come more to the fore in the late seventeenth and early eighteenth centuries. At this time, the center of conflict shifted from southern New England to its northern and western frontiers because of the French engagement of imperial warfare with England. With declining numbers within Indian families, and French allies willing to pay Indian warriors for English captives, captivity among the Indians—both temporary and lifelong—became a much more common strategy of Indian warfare against the English. Chapter 3 argues that captivity was stressful not just for English captives but also for the Indian households that had to incorporate sometimes several strangers into their families, at least temporarily. Indian women in particular seem to have borne more than their fair share of the burden of integrating strangers into their families, strangers who were utterly ignorant (if not contemptuous as well) of the kinds of work and behavior required of them. Furthermore, this chapter argues that the purpose of the captivity narratives written and published by returned New England captives (or by their ministers) was to show the disorderly nature of Indian family life as a further means of undermining Native sovereignty: weak (or brutish) Indian men, arrogant women (or their opposite and equally distorted stereotype, "squaw drudges"), and unruly children—this evidence of households in chaos was intended to suggest that Indians were unworthy of political sovereignty. Chapter 4 continues this focus on women caught up in the consequences of war by considering the fates of English female captives who never returned to New England, the majority of whom chose to remain with their French Catholic redeemers. Although the French likely modeled their treatment of English captives on the strategies of their Indian allies, this chapter suggests that they were much more successful than Indians at keeping English captives for two reasons: New

France had a cadre of seasoned missionaries, and Canada was desperate for European women and their domestic skills. This chapter also argues that we should see these girls and women as agents, not simply as victims of warfare or fortune, as life in Canada offered them more legal rights in marriage and better economic protections than New England did.

Finally, Chapter 5 continues to analyze the nature of the conflict between New England and New France but returns to explore the relationship between martial prowess and manhood in the mid-eighteenth century during the last two imperial wars. It demonstrates the striking similarity of the gendered language and ideas used by New Englanders to discredit French masculinity and sovereignty in Canada to the language and ideas used to discredit Indian masculinity and sovereignty in the seventeenth and early eighteenth centuries. French Catholicism was described in private writings and published propaganda as even more dangerous than Indian ways— perhaps a reasonable conclusion, given French successes at keeping more of the daughters of New England than their Indian enemies ever did. The colonial encounter changed the political and human geography of New England, but what doesn't seem to change much at all are the ways in which the English and Anglo-Americans saw their enemies, whomever they were. Perhaps the most significant shift in the minds of New England men was their own conception of their manhood. With the shift from wars against local Indian rivals to wars against the French crown, the seventeenth-century ideal of Puritan manhood built closely around family headship, Christian piety, and military prowess in defense of Christian families was transformed into an eighteenth-century imperial masculinity built around more abstract concepts like Anglo-American nationalism, anti-Catholicism, and soldiering for the empire.[26]

Abraham in Arms shows how warfare was central to the political discourse and social and material reality in the northeastern borderlands. Ideas about gender and family life—expressed in language, coercion, force of law, and brute force—saturated these conflicts as French, English, and Indian people struggled to articulate and impose their vision of an ordered society in the rapidly changing colonial world they shared. Although this book ends in 1763, in most of the important ways the struggles outlined here continued for more than a century on the advancing southern and western frontiers of the Ohio and Mississippi river valleys, the Great Plains, Texas, the Rocky Mountains, Oregon Territory, and California. Anywhere in North America where Anglo-American settlements, competing French and Spanish claims, and Indians met, these conflicts continued. If John Winthrop's "City Upon a Hill" became a model for the emerging United States, it was built upon a dark and bloody ground.

Finally, a note on some of the terms commonly used in this book. When writing about English people and their descendants who peopled New England, I use the term "English," although admittedly this word tends to erase some of the important regional, religious, and cultural differences among them. (However, until the American Revolution, this is the term they used to describe their national and ethnic identity.) I also sometimes use the term "Anglo-American" to describe the same people in the later chapters, so as to distinguish New England-born English people from the British regulars and officers who were only used in North American wars beginning in the 1740s. I use the terms "Indian" and "Native American" interchangeably when referring to the original peoples of North America and their descendants in the colonial period. When appropriate, I use the more specific terms to distinguish between the two major cultural and linguistic groups of Native peoples discussed, the Algonquians of the eastern seaboard, and the Iroquois west of the Hudson River. I also try to refer to the specific Indian nation when possible, such as Narragansett, Wampanoag, Pequot, Mohegan, Eastern Abenaki, and Western Abenaki (the Algonquian peoples most often discussed in this book) or the five nations of the Iroquois in this period, which were the Mohawk, Oneida, Onondaga, Cayuga, and Seneca.[27]

The term "New England" here generally refers not just to geography but also signifies lands under significant cultural and political control by the English. I use the term "Canada" to refer to the French settlements of the St. Lawrence river valley and upper Great Lakes, and I use New France when referring to all North American territories claimed by the French, from the maritimes through the Great Lakes, the Mississippi Valley, into the Gulf of Mexico and the Caribbean. Lands controlled and used by Indians I call generically "Indian country." But of course, the point of this book is that the lines dividing these spheres of influence were constantly shifting and contested, so when I am uncertain about the status of a particular place in time, or when I want to generalize about all three regions together, I use the term "northeastern borderlands."

"You dare not fight, you are all one like women": The Contest of Masculinities in the Seventeenth Century

> Come out and fight if you dare: you dare not fight, you are all one like women, we have one amongst us that if he could kill but one of you more, he would be equall with God, and as the English mans God is, so would hee be.
> —Pequot warriors quoted by John Underhill, Newes from America (1638)

Most recent scholars of the Pequot War (1636–37) agree that it was a thinly disguised war of conquest. The Pequots were convenient targets, as they had allied with early Dutch settlements in an attempt to dominate Euro-Indian trade in the region, and therefore over the course of the previous several years the Pequots had alienated their Indian neighbors. Thus, resentful fellow Algonquians like the Narragansetts, the Massachusetts, and the Mohegans were eager to ally themselves with the new European power in the region, the recently arrived English, who had established a number of small plantations on Massachusetts Bay and who were eager to expand into the Connecticut River valley.[1] The English had established a few permanent settlements in the 1620s around the perimeter of Massachusetts Bay, but their numbers began to swell tremendously only in the 1630s as the decade-long "Great Migration" to New England began.[2] With the Pequots weakened by a 1633 smallpox epidemic, and the lucky accident of the murders of a few rogue English traders that were convincingly blamed on the Pequots, the English saw their main chance to take Connecticut.

Throughout most of this short war, the English and their Indian allies engaged in small skirmishes on Block Island and at the new English settlement at Wethersfield, and the Pequots showed themselves capable of effective resistance. Details about even the minor skirmishes in this war were preserved in memoirs by three of the war's English officers: Captain John Mason, Captain John Underhill, and Lieutenant Lion Gardiner.[3] The Pequots had successfully besieged the recently established Fort Saybrook throughout the winter of 1636–37, with Gardiner and only twenty-four people inside—men, women, and children. According to Underhill, who was sent to relieve the fort in early 1637, the Pequots surrounded the fort that spring "and made many proud challenges, and dared [the English] out to fight." Whether they rose to the bait, or just needed to steal or cultivate corn, ten men ventured out of the fort. They came upon three Pequots, but they had fallen into a trap—as they pursued the three Indians, "an hundred more started out of the ambushments" and nearly surrounded the small company. Some were killed, the others fled to the safety of the fort, but the Pequots were not finished with their rout yet. (Perhaps tellingly, Underhill refuses to give a clear number of the dead and wounded.) The Pequots took the dead English men's guns and clothing, and pursued the survivors "to the Fort jeering of them, and calling, come and fetch your English mens clothes againe; come out and fight if you dare." Then the Pequots made their intentions to humiliate English manhood perfectly clear: "you dare not fight, you are all one like women." After all, hadn't the English been led into a trap and beaten badly? Hadn't they fled, leaving their comrades' bodies in the fields to be stripped of their clothing and weapons by their enemies? Underhill reports no English response to this insult, so the Pequots continued, raising the stakes of their challenge: "we have one amongst us that if he could kill but one of you more, he would be equall with God, and as the *English* mans God is, so would hee be." Not only did the Pequots challenge English masculinity by beating them soundly in battle and calling them "women," but in comparing themselves favorably to the *"English* mans God," they challenged English notions of hierarchy. Underhill writes that "this blasphemous speech troubled the hearts of the souldiers, but they knew not how to remedy it in respect of their weaknesse."[4]

As this anecdote suggests, colonial warfare was often expressed as a contest between the Indian and English notions of manhood, and the stakes were high. From their earliest encounters with one another, both Indian and English men claimed to be disturbed by the other's ideas of gender roles, most particularly in the proper performance of manhood. Many scholars have noted that English men who had come to the New World to be farmers were appalled by what they saw as Indian men's laziness and tyranny over Indian women, who labored in the fields while the men pursued "aristocratic" pastimes like hunting and fishing. Alternately, Indian men thought little of the sort of men who would do women's work in the fields, and who even seemed to be proud of it.[5] But there were in fact large areas of agreement in the gender ideologies of Native Americans and the English, in particular in politics and war.[6] For example, Algonquian, Iroquois, and English cultures understood political power as a prerogative of men, and all these societies were characterized by predominantly (if not entirely exclusively) male political leadership. This gendered quality of political power was not incidental, but symbolic of these cultures' shared understanding that men were the natural leaders of society. When Indian men encountered men who farmed and seemed proud of doing women's work, and when English men saw men who allowed women to work the land, each side questioned the masculinity of the other. This was not an innocent moment of confusion brought on by a blinding "clash of cultures"; challenging one another's masculinity was a deliberate political and rhetorical strategy, because in questioning each other's manhood, they questioned each other's right to political power as well. Furthermore, underneath this common understanding of manhood and political mastery is the fact that English and Indians were both agricultural peoples who had need of the same resources: land, principally, but also the ability to keep others off of it, and access to harbors and rivers for easy travel and trade. While both the English and the Indians seized on cultural differences to construct a language by which they might define their enemies and describe their grievances with them, the fact remains that the roots of their struggle were material. English newcomers were rivals for the resources that Native North Americans had enjoyed for centuries. Whether men or women farmed the land was ultimately a matter of culture and aesthetics. Whether English people or Indians would claim and secure land for farming was a matter of life and death.[7]

Accordingly, the conduct of the colonial warfare was especially fraught with challenges to the masculinity of both the English and the Indian combatants. In both cultures, masculinity was defined in part by military success, and political power was often built upon demonstrated military prowess; therefore, men on both sides had something to lose or gain from the outcome of each battle beyond victory for their countrymen and allies.[8] Encounters in warfare and in the discourse on warfare make it clear that both English and Indian men understood their masculinity as a complex thing, built on gender of course, but also encompassing qualities like age and status. Being a man meant not only *not* being a woman, but it also meant being an adult as opposed to an infant, child, or adolescent; for English men it also meant being the head of a household rather than a servant or a slave. Similarly, Indian men put a premium on distinguishing themselves from dogs, useful but servile creatures. Indian men typically shared decision-making within households and kinship groups with adult women, but like English men, they retained almost all control over politics and decisions about war and peace. From the perspectives of both seventeenth-century English and Indian peoples, war was key to the performance of manhood as well as an opportunity to enlarge or protect territorial claims, because manhood and political and economic autonomy were inseparable. Thus, a great deal was at stake when Indian men openly taunted English men for what they saw as their lack of manly courage, or when the English portrayed the Indians as feeble warriors who made great boasts of their bravery but who regularly turned tail on the battlefield. Gender anxieties permeated the wars of the seventeenth century—the Pequot War, King Philip's War (1675–78), and King William's War (1688–97)—as English and Algonquian men on the Atlantic coast of New England fought for political and economic control of the region.

These issues first emerged in early encounters after the first permanent English settlement was established in 1620, when the Indians viewed the English as children dependent upon their fatherly care. The contest of masculinities was vitally apparent in the Pequot War, and the rich documentary records of this war establish many themes in this struggle between men that continued through the seventeenth century and into the eighteenth century: English men became enraged by what they saw as illegitimate "pride" and "insolence" in Indian men; they were humiliated by the open mocking Indian men made of English masculinity; and they were affronted by what they saw as feminized, foolish, or childish Indian men exercising political and military power. Furthermore, the English might have been especially sensitive to displays of Indian mastery, as the history of early English settlements demonstrates that they were in fact weak and vulnerable to famine and disease as they adjusted to the climate and landscape of North America. Indian men, for their part, were equally disdainful of the English, whether enemies or allies: English men, ordinarily stooped in the cornfields like women, looked ridiculous in their military accoutrements, drumming and marching in open fields; they evidently preferred savage attacks on non-combatants to engaging warriors; and they frequently abandoned their dead on the battlefield, leaving them to be stripped and scalped. By the last quarter of the century, as King Philip plotted his uprising against English settlement, Indians had the measure of their English enemy and fought not only to preserve their own independence but also to master the English, as they knew the English intended to master them.[9]

From the start, English and Indian men jockeyed to establish their authority in each other's eyes. Both English and Algonquian Indian men understood political power as an arena of masculine achievement; accordingly, establishing political authority was done with words and actions that conveyed one's masculinity.[10] Indian and English leaders were eager to demonstrate their independence (as opposed to feminized dependence) and the dependence of others upon them as a means of demonstrating that they were the most consequential men around. This kind of symbolic communication is evident in the first encounters between the Plymouth settlers and Native leadership shortly after the arrival of the English in late 1620. No less a leader than Wampanoag (or Pokanoket) Sachem Massassoit gave the English their first lesson in Indian diplomacy. When a delegation from Plymouth paid a formal diplomatic call on the Wampanoag leader, they rendered him a formal salute with their guns and observed Indian protocol by bringing him gifts, including a coat and a chain for his neck. While William Bradford's journal portrays this visit initially as a meeting among dignified equals, it becomes clear that the English were in fact supplicants to Massassoit. Although the Wampanoag Indians had been devastated by the smallpox epidemic that had ravaged coastal New England from 1616 to 1618, at a population of around 1,000 they were still stronger and more numerous than the starving English colony of sixty souls who barely survived their first winter and were ill prepared for spring planting. When the English delegation approached the Wampanoags in March of 1621, the sachem assumed the role of a benevolent fatherly host to the English: "For answere to our Message, he told us we were wellcome, and he would gladly continue that Peace and Friendship which was betweene him & us: and for his men they should no more pester us as they had done." Massassoit established his authority as a recognized leader of the Indians by guaranteeing their future behavior, but perhaps more importantly, he made the English dependent upon his largesse as well, promising to "helpe [the English] with Corne for feed, according to [their] request."[11]

Massassoit continued this performance by delivering a long speech, in case the meaning of his previous message was too subtle for these strangers to grasp: "This being done, his men gathered neere to him, to whom he turned himselfe, and made a great Speech; they sometime interposing, and as it were, confirming and applauding him in that he sayd. The meaning whereof was (as farre as we could learne) thus; Was not he *Massasoyt* Commander of the Countrey about them? Was not such a Towne his and the people of it? and should they not bring their skins unto us?" In the manner of a call-and-response between a Christian minister and his flock, Massassoit's men responded according to the script: "they answered, they were his & would be at peace with us, and bring their skins to us." This call-and-response continued as Massassoit rhetorically established his dominion over "at least thirtie places, and their answere was as aforesayd to every one," his men affirming the truth of his words. The English audience for this performance found the repetition hard to bear: "as it was delightfull [to the Indians], it was tedious unto us." Perhaps they were uncomfortable being under the benevolent wing of an Indian protector, or perhaps they just didn't like Massassoit reminding them of his pride of place in the political order. Nevertheless, Massassoit had made his point. Because of the extent of his power, he could guarantee the safety and security of the English plantation—or, if he pleased, he could doom it. Still Massassoit's performance continued, as "he lighted Tobacco for us, and fell to discoursing of *England,* & of the Kings Maiestie." Once again, he revealed much about Native notions of political leadership as he speculated on the strange spectacle of a King without a consort, "marvayling that he would live without a wife." (King James I's queen Anne had died in 1619.) As the ritual assertion of Massassoit's patronage network showed, being a leader was all about the number of one's dependents. Thus, for a man to call himself a king and not be the head of a complete household was strange to the Wampanoag sachem.[12]

Both Indians and English people believed that it was well for leaders to receive guests kindly and to entertain them generously.[13] This was a function of being a wealthy and powerful leader, as well as a means of extending a patronage network. Although Massassoit was at great pains to assert his devotion to his broad network of supporters, his English guests were not impressed by his hospitality. Not only did they find his performance of his power "tedious," they found him a poor host. "Late it grew, but victualls he offered none," they complained. He did however offer them the honor of his bed, as "he layd us on the bed with himselfe and his wife, they at one end and we at the other, it being onely plancks layd a foot from the ground, and a thin Mat upon them. Two more of his chiefe men for want of roome pressed by and upon us; so that we were worse weary of our lodging then of our journey." The next day the English men were invited to share a very meager meal of two large fish split forty ways by Massassoit and his men. When the English men announced that they would take their leave that day, "[v]ery importunate he was to have us stay with them longer: But wee desired to keepe the Sabboth at home." Perhaps more immediately, they "feared we should either be light-headed for want of sleepe, for what with bad lodging, the Savages barbarous singing, (for they use to sing themselves asleepe) lice and fleas within doores, and Muskeetoes without, wee could hardly sleepe all the time of our being there; we much fearing, that if wee should stay any longer, we should not be able to recover home for want of strength." The next day before dawn, they "tooke [their] leave and departed, *Massasoyt* being both grieved and ashamed, that he could no better entertaine [them]."[14] Was Massassoit really "grieved and ashamed" at the poor hospitality he offered? That is doubtful. Perhaps Bradford's language here was part of an effort by the English to portray Indians as poor, and their leaders as weak and unmanly because of their inability to provide better for their guests. Either way, the English telling of the story ends with Massassoit appearing ridiculous, claiming to control vast reaches of land and men like a king, but then offering his court and guests just a few morsels of boiled fish. Given the hunger in their bellies due to their insufficient planning and hard luck, the English delegation had little cause to criticize Massassoit for his hospitality, especially since their families would be fed only by the largesse of the Wampanoags.

Later in the seventeenth century, the English became even more scathing in their judgment of Indian diplomacy and manhood. Increase Mather consulted *Mourt's Relation* in writing *A Relation of the Troubles which have hapned in New-England*, a history of Anglo-Indian relations published in 1677 in the immediate wake of King Philip's War, which suggests that he believed that Philip's uprising may have been rooted in Anglo-Indian diplomatic relations in the 1620s. (This was a reasonable supposition, as Philip was Massassoit's grandson.)[15] Whereas Bradford and his compatriots were content with ridicule, Mather was ready to see treachery afoot among all Indians, not just the Wampanoags but also their Massachusett neighbors. For example, Mather claims that when Kunacum, the sachem of Manomet (now Sandwich, Massachusetts) was entertaining Captain Miles Standish of Plymouth Colony, two Massachusett Indians came to call on Kunacum. One of the Massachusett, Wituwamet, "took a dagger from about his neck, and presented it to the *Sachim*, and made a speech to him (which the Captain could not understand) boasting of his own valour." Wittawamet then allegedly tried to draw Kunacum into a conspiracy to harm Standish, boasting of "how he had been the death of Christians both French and English and what pittifull weak Creatures they were, that when they were killing, they died crying, and made sower faces, more like children then men." Here the theme of weak and dependent—or childlike—English men reappears, as the Indians let Standish know how little they think of him. Behaving "insolently," one of the Massachusett Indians "jeered at Capt. *Standish*, because he was a man of little stature, and yet a Captain." Mather did not let the Indians have the last word on English manhood, however, as he reports that when Standish and his men attacked the Massachusett Indians, they killed some but others fled to a swamp, where "the Captain dared the *Sachim* to come out, and fight like a man, but in vain." In the end, Mather claims that not only were the Massachusetts easily cowed in battle, "the rest of the Indians were stricken with such terror, and dread of the English, that they left their houses, and betook themselves to live in unhealthful Swamps, whereby they became subject to miserable diseases, that proved mortal to multitudes of them."[16]

Indians had their own stories of these early encounters. As Native peoples lost the demographic advantage to the English through disease and warfare, they liked to remind their English antagonists that once they were weak and the Indians were strong and wealthy. Claiming the role of parental protectors of the English upon their first arrival in the New World became a traditional part of Indian rhetoric when protesting later English incursions into their territory. King Philip himself reminded the English of Massassoit's generosity in lending support to the early Plymouth colonists: "when the English first came, the King's Father [actually his grandfather, Massassoit] was as a great Man, and the English as a littell Child." Like a kindly father, "he constrained other Indians from ronging the English, and gave them Corn and shewed them how to plant, and was free to do them ani Good, and had let them have a 100 Times more Land than now the King had for his own Peopell."[17] This role as the protectors and nurturers of the English became central to Indians' understanding of themselves and their early relationship with the English. Mahomett, great-grandson of the Mohegan sachem Uncas who remained allied with the English through the Pequot and King Philip's War, uses the same language of dependence and fatherly concern for the English in recounting his people's history with the English in his 1736 petition to King George II: "upon the first arrival of the English in his ancestors Territories . . . [Uncas] rece[ive]d and Entertaind them with the highest Forms of hospitality & friend[shi]p," granting them "large Tracts of Land for their new settlements." Upon the breakout of hostilities in the Pequot War, Uncas then "brought over his Tribe to the timely assistance of the English." Although it meant the Mohegans were hated by other Indians, Uncas and his descendants were true to the English. Despite English ingratitude for the services of the Mohegans, the petitioner "Mahomet kept faith with the English, continuing their firm adherence and Services to them in the time of the french war nor was ever the blood of one English man Spilt by any of their Tribe tho much injured and greatly dispossesed all their Dealings with them, but on the Contrary the Mohegans have Shed their best blood in defense of the English."[18] Because Mahomett was petitioning the English king as a dependent subject and asking him to intervene against the incursions of the people of Connecticut, it was important for him to remind the king that once the Sachem of the Mohegans assisted a poor and harassed band of English men and women. Once Indians were strong and could have destroyed the English, thus the English owed the Indians the same protections they were offered. Unfortunately for Mahomett, the subtleties of his moral argument escaped the English sovereign and his government. These arguments for manhood, status, and power in diplomatic councils would be amplified in seventeenth-century conflicts, as both English and Indian men believed that war was a proving ground for men's status and worthiness.

The training and assumptions of the first generation of English soldiers in New England were based on contemporary English expectations of war and its conduct. The sixteenth-century religious wars had inspired some English writings on warfare and its manly glories, especially as it related to the defeat of Catholicism. By the middle of the sixteenth century, writers in English began to describe their twin obsessions, religion and politics, in clearly gendered terms, in large part because of the English and Scottish queens who ruled their warring nations from the mid-sixteenth century. Protestant propagandists readily linked Catholicism to femininity and corruption, in contrast to the manly piety and virtue of Protestantism.[19]

English culture and society became even more masculinized and militarized in the seventeenth century. Continental religious wars dominated European politics and diplomacy for the first half of the century, and at the same time domestic politics were inflamed by many of the same concerns in the years before and during the Civil War. Finally, the New Model Army, supportive of the radical puritan faction, took over Parliament with Pride's Purge in 1648, and the nation's conflict ended in a puritan military dictatorship. Puritans in Old and New England understood that they were in a

Figure 1. These military exercises illustrate the proper use of a firelock (or matchlock) musket (A–D) and a pike (E–M). These almost balletic poses of well-dressed, well-armed men also illustrate an ideal of military preparedness for English men in the 1630s and 1640s. From the Lord Du Praissac, *The Art of Warre; or Militarie discourses by the Lord of Praissac,* translated by John Cruso (Cambridge, 1639), 4–5. Courtesy of the Newberry Library.

pitched battle for Christ against Satan, thus militaristic language and meta-phors abound in puritan pamphlets and sermons of the early and mid-seventeenth century. Puritan preachers saw themselves as leading Christian soldiers into battle, delivering and publishing such bellicose sermons as William Perkins's *The Combate betweene Christ and the Devill* (1602), John Downame's *The Christian Warfare Wherein is first generally shewed the ma-liece, power, and politike stratagems of the spirituall enemies of our salvation,*

Satan and his assistants the world and the flesh (1604), William Gouge's *The Whole-Armor of God or the Spirituall Furniture which God hath provided to keepe safe every Christian Souldier from all the assaults of Satan* (1616), and Thomas Taylor's *Christs Combate and Conquest: or, The Lyon of the Tribe of Judah, vanquishing the Roaring Lion* (1618). Typically in these sermons, pamphlets, and books, Christians were called to defend their faith against the incursions of their enemies, sin and the devil. In *The Christian Souldier, his combat, conquest, and crowne*, Edward Turges warned his readers in 1639 that "whilst thou art reading this *summons* to *buckle* on thy *armes,* and *march* out speedily, it is high time, the *Enemyes* are growne *strong* and *potent* for want of opposition. whilst thou lyest *sleeping* out thy *time* they have almost *entered,* nay they have allready *taken* possession of thy *soule.*" *The Christian Souldier* was published on the eve of the Civil War as a conveniently small volume, three and a quarter by six inches, and an inch thick, the perfect size to accompany all Christian soldiers into battle. *The Souldiers Pocket Bible,* published in the 1640s, was less a Bible than a few relevant verses bound into a tiny volume that included a catechism and several reprinted sermons on the Civil War.[20]

As the English political climate turned from puritan protest to civil war, military metaphors for their religious struggle became reality for the most ideologically committed puritans. John Davenport, who would distinguish himself as one of the most orthodox and longest-lived of New England's first generation of ministers, penned a pamphlet justifying a citizen's militia in the year that Charles I dismissed Parliament. Davenport's *A Royall Edict for Military Exercises* (1629) explains that "that which tends to the Common peace, and safetie, must be practised by all: but the *use of the Bow* tends to the Common peace and safety: *Ergo. The use of the Bow* must be practised by all." Bows and arrows were not literally the only legitimate weapons, however: "every Family is commanded *the use of the Bow* and Arrowes, under a penalty: and masters are bound to teach children, and servants, from seven to seventeen therein. Heere Masters are instructed, not in the use of the Bow onely, but in all weapons, postures, actions necessary or usefull in warre, and not for feare of a penalty, but for love of their Country."[21]

Davenport's sermon introduces a new concern to the old equation of good Christians and good soldiers: good soldiers protect and defend not only their faith but also their families. This new concern for domestic safety and security became a dominant theme in seventeenth-century New England artillery sermons. Davenport argues that "the scriptures fully cleare this in examples: of *Abraham,* having at least 318. men in his house, fitted for warre upon a short warning: of *Moses, instructing the people how to camp by their standards, and under the Ensignes of their fathers house:* of *Joshua,* and the *Judges,* under whom, of *Ruben,* and *Gad,* and halfe the Tribe of *Manasseh,* were foure hundred, forty thousand, seven hundred and three score exercised in warres." Clearly, the responsibilities of a patriarch included providing for the safety and security of his household and community: "A Christian Souldier should have this sword alwayes in readinesse, not as swords are in most houses and hands, hung up by the walls, or kept rusty in the scabberd: but it should be like the sword of *Joab,* ready to drop out of its sheath suddenly, and he should use it against spirituall wickednesse." Again, Davenport stresses the connection between Christian preparedness and military preparedness: "What wil it availe you to know the whole Discipline of *warre?* Doe not the heathen as much? There is more required in you then in other men, in respect to your *Christian* profession."[22] Men coming to the New World in the following decade, with the sure knowledge that the "heathen" awaited them, understood very well that Christian commonwealths might have to be forcibly carved out and defended. Furthermore, they understood that the security of their faith and of their families depended upon them.

The pioneers of the conquest of New England were therefore men and women who were part of a militarized branch of reformed Protestantism, and the wars they waged in North America were part of this larger struggle. The current generation of religious historians has argued convincingly that New England was far from the stereotype of orthodox homogeneity. From the first, New England's religious leaders and visionaries were in conflict with each other, and their disputes frequently led to the settlement of new colonies because they could not coexist. (The earliest settlements in Rhode Island and New Hampshire were founded by refugees and exiles from the Antinomian Crisis in John Winthrop's Boston.) However, the passionate conviction of believers on all sides is further proof that reformed Protestant piety saturated the minds and hearts of most English settlers who composed the Great Migration to New England (1630–40).[23] The migration to America and the defense of their families were infused with sacred meaning for most English householders, and like Davenport, many ministers in New England explored this theme in their sermons and teachings. By the time of King Philip's War, another generation of New England ministers carried on this tradition of militant Christian patriarchy.

For example, Samuel Nowell's *Abraham in Arms* (1678) describes what should be the proper concerns of English men at the end of the seventeenth century: the defense of home and family and the defense of Christ. His conceit unites these concerns in the figure of a well-armed and godly patriarch, literally "Abraham in Arms." Nowell uses two scriptures upon which to build his discourse: Genesis 18:19, "I know Abraham, there is none like him in all the earth, he will command his Family, and his household in the wayes of the Lord," and Genesis 14:14, "And when Abram heard that his Brother was taken captive, he armed his trained Servants, born in his own house, three hundred and eighteen, and pursued them to Dan."[24] Families in danger and families torn apart by enemy capture were especially meaningful themes to New Englanders in the wake of King Philip's War, in which so many English men, women, and children were taken into captivity by the Indians. Furthermore, warfare in the northeastern borderlands was characterized not so much by formal battles but by attacks upon isolated homesteads or villages. The immediate context of Nowell's sermon thus justified his concerns for the safety of religion and family, as English communities had seen both imperiled in the recent war.

Like Davenport and his predecessors in England, Nowell begins his sermon with a familiar claim: "That the highest practice of Piety and practice of War, may agree well in one person. Religion and Arms may well be joyned together; they agree so well together, that the Lord assumes the name to himself, *The Lord is a Man of War.*" He goes to great lengths to demonstrate that just wars are essentially defensive wars, but most New Englanders understood both the Pequot War and King Philip's War, as well as dozens of minor skirmishes with Indians, as defensive actions on their part. Accordingly, military preparedness is *"a Duty which God expecteth of all Gods Abrahams in their respective places."* Civil leaders, military officers, and husbandmen alike bore the responsibility of defending their faiths and families: "It is the duty of those that would be accounted of Abrahams Family to learn of them, when God requires to teach them the use of their weapons, and order of War."[25]

Just as important as the will to teach was the will to instill a godly hierarchy within military ranks, one that reflected the broader ideal of English, and later Anglo-American, social order. Perhaps even more than other aspects of life in puritan New England, "discipline is the life of the work [at arms]. Captains are greatly to blame that are softly men, and do not hold their authority in the field. That which would be no fault, or might be winked at at home, should not be suffered in the Field." Leaders of men had to assert their authority as they did in the home, perhaps even more vigorously, or risk an unprepared and effeminate soldiery. Without a proper chain of command, the manhood of New England was at stake: "Intemperance, Luxury, filthiness, and uncleanness in the world doth so debauch men, they are not like to breed up Souldiers for Christ, to do service for Christ." Nowell had some doubts about the readiness, spiritual and martial, of many young men. "I will tell you how we breed up Souldiers, both in Old England and New," he remarks sardonically. "Every Farmers Son, when he goes to Market-Town, must have money in his purse; and when he meets with his Companions, they goe to the Tavern or Ale-House, and seldome away before Drunk, or well tipled. . . . This makes Youth effeminate and wanton, besides the injury to mens Consciences; this doth make men not so bold."[26]

Nowell seemed to think that a well-trained soldiery was especially important in New England, given the relatively primitive conditions of settlement and a bloodthirsty and heathen enemy. "We have no walled towns, as they have in other places, our Forts and Castles are contemptible," a standing army would be too expensive, and allies were at too great a distance to provide ready assistance in case of attack. Thus, besides "that Hedge which God made about Job . . . it is only that wall of Bones (as one calls it) better than a wall of Stones" that stands to defend New England. And its defense would be required, given the "frequent trouble, we may probably and rationally reckon . . . to meet with from the heathen." Besides the Indians, Nowell also kept watch for "the *French* at this day, not far from us" and predicted the continuation of Europe's religious wars in New England: "*Rome* will have no peace with you, and you ought to have no peace with it, and that *Rome's* Agents are abroad at work is plain." The dangers these enemies posed to New England were very clear: Nowell warns, "we must either learn to defend ourselves, or resolve to be vassals."[27] New England men, like their English forbears, would have to first instill a manly hierarchy within their ranks, then impose their dominion upon their rivals.

Thus, according to the ideal of masculine virtue described by Nowell, significant personal service and sacrifice was expected of English men in the fulfillment of their military duties as part of a trained citizen militia. In New Haven and Connecticut colonies, which were founded on or near land taken in the Pequot War, the drum beats calling the eligible men to the watch measured out the nights and days of the settlers, while walking the watch along the borders of the plantations reminded these men of the literal limits of English settlement. "The state and condition of the place where [they] live[d], by reason of the Indians and otherwise" compelled English men to manage their towns as armed encampments on a hostile frontier. All able men between the ages of sixteen and sixty were required to walk the watch at their turn, patrolling the town and the edges of the settlement for fire, for disturbances, or especially for "any person or persons whom they shall find disorderly or in a suspicious manner wthin dores or wthout, wther English or Indians, or any other straingers whatsoevr." In order to maintain the militia, each man was responsible to keep himself properly armed with "a muskett, a sworde, bandaleers, a rest, a pound of powder, 20 bullets fitted to [his] muskett," or other shot upon penalty of a twenty-shilling fine. Military officers were elected annually, an artillery company was organized, and men of mustering age were required to attend monthly or bimonthly training exercises and present their weapons for inspection there. Despite the fact that many New Haven and Connecticut men saw action in the Pequot War, compliance with these duties was not 100 per-cent—in fact, missing watch duty or militia training was probably the most common offense cited in early New England records.[28] Furthermore, most military historians agree that the quality of soldier produced by these hap-hazard musters was rather poor by professional European standards. Even amidst what English settlers perceived as a hostile frontier, training days frequently were occasions marked more by drinking, carousing, and mis-handling of firearms than serious military drills.[29]

Evidence from seventeenth-century probate records indicates that men of soldiering age were in fact well armed. To be sure, gun ownership rates varied across seventeenth-century New England, according to the de-tail and quality of the inventories, proximity to the frontier, and age of the householder.[30] A survey of York County, Maine, inventories from 1658 to 1678 reveals a rather low rate of gun ownership: only about a third of the men died with guns listed in their inventories. However, the Maine records probably do not reflect accurate householder gun ownership rates for two reasons. First, they seem to include a large number of transients like mari-ners and sojourners, who seem to have owned the contents of a sea chest but little else. Second, the records are not as detailed as other inventories, so guns might be included in phrases like "homelott, dwelling house, and contents," but there is no way to know for sure.[31] In the more rigorously detailed records of southern New England, nearly 80 percent of men's in-ventories in New Haven and Connecticut surveyed show evidence of men keeping arms and the other accoutrements of war. Of the small number of Connecticut and New Haven men whose inventories showed no signs of weaponry, nearly half of these records looked like they described the contents of a sea chest rather than the necessary items for keeping a house and farm; these men were therefore probably mariners, day laborers, or servants rather than householders, and so would not have been required to keep their own arms. Other men who died unarmed were probably either exempt from military service due to age and infirmity, or they were simply very poor.[32]

Furthermore, New England men seem to have held their guns in special regard, as they were one of the very few moveables men mentioned specifically in their wills and designated for a particular male legatee. John Collins of Gloucester, Massachusetts, specified in his will that his eldest son John should have his "great Gun or fowling piece and all the rest of my Ammunition both Sword & bandelieirs," and left his other son James his "Muskett Sword & Bandeliers." Firearms and other tools of war might have been so significant a legacy for fathers to their sons that at least one man specified that his weapons should go to his as-yet-unborn child if it proved to be a boy: John Purkas wrote a will when his wife was pregnant with their third child, specifying "if God give me a sonne wch my wife goeth with all, my mynd is that if my sonne shall live to the age of eighteene yeares, that he shall have my gunne, wch is a fierlocke, and my sowrd and bandaleres and rest," along with his other tools, the house, and land in Hartford. Another Connecticut man, Edward Chalkwell, died without any hope of a male heir. In his short will, his first request was that his friend Nicholas Sension have his "gunn and sword and bandaleers and best hatt," along with forty shillings.[33] Having a gun was therefore significant to English men: it was a mark of prestige and a privilege of their sex.

The symbolic importance of guns to English manhood becomes even clearer when we consider those who did not own guns, and those whose gun ownership was discouraged or prohibited by English laws: English women, Indians, African Americans, and Catholics. The exclusion of these groups suggests that however many householders actually kept a gun in working condition, the ownership of guns was by definition political. By tradition, English women did not own guns; when they were widowed, New England women did not keep their husbands' guns or other weaponry in their houses. Some of the earliest laws on the books in New England were laws forbidding the sale of guns and ammunition to Indians.[34] Gun ownership from the start was reserved for English male heads of households and was thus a symbol of their position at the top of the earthly hierarchy. Promotional tracts urged that each English man bring "Armes, *(viz.)* a sword, Calliver five foot long, or long Pistol, Pikehead: six pound of powder, ten pound of shot, half an old slight Armour, that is, two to one Armour," and "Guns, and powder for the Fort" as well. Only by suitably arming themselves and refusing to trade guns to the Indians "shall Christians and their Cattel be safe and quiet, and severely puting to death all that sell the Indians Guns, Arms, and ammunition, then Indians are sooner ruled, civilized, and subjected." Of course, these laws—after laws regulating sexual activity— were probably the most commonly broken laws throughout New England, as Indians adopted firelock and flintlock muskets as soon as they could get their hands on the weapons. Banning the licit sale of weapons to the Indians made the black market all the more lucrative. No wonder that many English men and women decided that the profits were greater than their fears of Indians using European weaponry against them. Furthermore, when Indians rose up against English rule and enslaved African Americans rebelled against their masters, they understood very well the practical and symbolic value of firearms. Slaves who planned uprisings in New York in 1712, in South Carolina in 1739–40, and in Maryland in 1740 all stockpiled firearms or targeted arsenals as their first objects of conquest.[35]

The militarized culture of seventeenth-century England, the ideological and religious conflicts that shaped the exploration and settlement of the New World, and widespread gun ownership all demonstrate that English men in New England were not strangers to war. It was part of their understanding of themselves as puritans and as men, and their first experiences of warfare with Indians only intensified New England men's identification of war with manliness. Battle accounts, captivity narratives, and quickly published "histories" of Anglo-Indian warfare through the seventeenth and eighteenth centuries constantly evoke gendered rhetoric when describing the conduct of war on the frontier. For example, William Hubbard writes of an attack of Sudbury, Massachusetts, during King Philip's War, comparing "the courage and resolution of the English, though but forty in number," to "*Indian*[s, who] could hardly be discerned from a better man." Similarly, he credits one Captain Holyoke, who if he "had not played the man at a more than ordinary rate, sometimes in the Front, sometimes in the flank and reer, at all times encouraging the souldiers, it might have proved a fatal business to the assailants."[36] Increase Mather writes of "English Souldiers" who "played the men wonderfully" in an engagement in the same war, and commended Connecticut especially for having "acquitted themselves like men and like Christians" in the war.[37]

Military success vindicated English manhood beyond a doubt, but not even defeat could deprive English men of their superiority in the accounts of their exploits written by their countrymen. Through the seventeenth century, Englishness alone remains the final proof of masculine worth. While defeat at the hands of the Indian enemy might temporarily shake the confidence of English men, and failure on the battlefield might deprive them of their homes, families, and lives, most English observers still held that English men were masters of their domain. When the English were beaten badly their conduct as soldiers was still described as "manful" or "manly" beyond reproach. Cotton Mather (son of Increase), in his history of King William's War, *Decennium Luctuosum,* describes the fort at Casco (now Portland, Maine) as "manfully Defended" until its ultimate surrender in 1690 after five days of fighting, although two-hundred English people were lost to either death or captivity. In a 1692 attack on York, he writes that "those *Garrisons* whereof some had no more than Two or Three *Men* in them, yet being so well *Mann'd,* as to Reply, *That they would Spend their Blood unto the last Drop, e're they would Surrender;* these Cowardly Miscreants had not mettle enough to meddle with 'em."[38] Thus English manhood, while in theory built on performance, remained in the eyes of the beholder. English propagandists like the Mathers *père* and *fils* had their reasons for portraying English men as manful even when defeated by Indians. Indian men likely questioned English manhood even when it was victorious.

Indian men also understood war as a male enterprise, one that was central to their understanding of themselves as men. In fact, political leadership and military prowess were probably even more closely linked among Indians than among the English. Algonquian sachemship was tied very directly to proven military success, whereas New England's governors and council members tended to be civilian lawyers and merchants. And among the seventeenth-century Iroquois, war was central to their culture, mythology, and history. In Iroquois "mourning wars," the worth of a warrior was measured by his ability to bring prisoners back home for either adoption or ritual execution. For the Iroquois, like the Algonquians and the English, warfare was also central to the formation of their political leadership. While Iroquois women had the power to choose male village leaders, they did not serve as leaders themselves. They played a crucial role in the adoption or execution of war captives, and they seem to have held sway over several of the most important rituals involving captives. However, Iroquois women's political power apparently did not extend beyond the sphere of the village, and the important decisions of making peace or of making war were reserved for men alone.[39]

While scholars are in more general agreement that Algonquian women

Figure 2. Indian villages from the Great Lakes region to Florida were commonly depicted as surrounded by a wooden palisade, suggesting European interest in their military technologies and readiness. The French siege engine depicted at the lower right of this heavily fortified Iroquois village is almost certainly fanciful. From Samuel de Champlain, *Voyages et Descouvertures faits en la Nouvelle France* (Paris: Claude Collet, 1627). This item is reproduced by permission of the Huntington Library, San Marino, California.

were even more thoroughly shut out of politics (and therefore out of warfare) than Iroquois women, Algonquian women too played key roles in the ritual torture and execution (or adoption) of captives. Furthermore, the hereditary nature of Algonquian leadership meant that the genealogy of their mothers was important to many sachems' claims to rule. By the last quarter of the seventeenth century, a few Algonquian women also rose to sachemship—most notably Awashunkes of the Saconet people and Weetamoo (sometimes called Weetamore) of the Pocasset. Evidence of their leadership

Figure 3. This highly stylized illustration published in John Underhill's *Newes from America* (London, 1638) highlights the circular design of the palisade around the Pequot village by surrounding it with a line of English soldiers firing muskets, backed up by another circle of Indian allies with their bows drawn. This item is reproduced by permission of the Huntington Library, San Marino, California.

entered the English record around the time of King Philip's War. These women, usually called "Squaw Sachems" or "Sunksquaws" in seventeenth-century English records, most likely came to their positions because of a combination of two factors: the genealogical nature of Algonquian political leadership and the severe depopulation their people had experienced due to disease and warfare over the first sixty years of English occupation. Although they led weakened people, their political reach was still considerable. Both English leaders and Philip courted their allegiance before the outbreak of the war—indeed, both women actually warned English authorities of Philip's designs, which strongly suggests that their allegiance could have been swayed to the English for the right price. Benjamin Church

Figure 4. This detail from "Virginae Item et Floridae," an undated map of eastern North America, features cartouches labeled "civitatum Floridae imitatio" on the left and "Civitatum Virginiae forma" on the right, both of which look very much like the palisaded Pequot village fort in Underhill's *Newes from America*. This item reproduced by permission of the Huntington Library, San Marino, California.

worked especially hard to secure the loyalty of Awashunkes to the English, visiting her court several times before and even after the outbreak of hostilities, but apparently authorities in Boston thought too little of these potentially valuable allies to strike the deal. In the end, both women sided with Philip and shared his defeat. According to one account by Increase Mather, Weetamoo, "who was next unto *Philip* in respect of the mischief that hath been done, and the blood that hath been shed in this Warr," met a rather fitting warrior's end. When she was found dead by some English soldiers in August of 1676, she was beheaded and her head "set upon a pole in *Taunton*, [and] the Indians who were prisoners there, knew it presently, and made a most horrid and diabolical Lamentation, crying out it was their Queens head." When Philip was captured and executed, his head was displayed in the same manner in Plymouth. Awashunkes was allowed to keep her head, and even her life after the war. But as Ann Marie Plane has discovered, Awashunkes was stripped of her power and effectively put under the thumb of English government in 1683 by a squalid charge of abetting infanticide—a crime only plebian women were accused of in early New En-

Figures 5–6. When English people fortified their villages in the northeastern borderlands, they borrowed the Indian palisade design, as wood was readily available and wood fences could be put up quickly. This reconstruction of eighteenth-century Fort Number Four at Charlestown, New Hampshire, shows the similarity of English defensive design and the previous Indian examples. Note the spacing of the palisades, like that of the Indian forts, which would reduce the fence's vulnerability to fire in a siege. Photo by author.

gland. Although female sachems remained very uncommon even as Indian desperation and dispersal accelerated in Southeastern New England after King Philip's War, in the eyes of English observers, women's political leadership was just more evidence of how confused Indian societies were about "proper" gender roles, and especially powerful evidence for their belief that Indian people were unworthy of political autonomy.[40]

Indian men's ideas about war are more difficult to discern than those of colonial New Englanders, as scholars must parse the language and interpretations of European observers who were often their immediate foes, and who consistently attempted to aggrandize their own manhood by undermining Indian masculinity. Despite the bias of English narratives, there are consistent similarities that support the notion that war was an important proving ground for Indian men. Like English men, Indian men were proud of being brave warriors and of being known and respected as courageous in battle. Captain John Underhill describes the Indians he fought in an early engagement on Block Island as "able fighting men, men as straite as arrowes, very tall, and of active bodies." English observers recognized that even the vilified Pequot had among them "many courageous fellowes," who in the climactic torching of the Pequot village were "unwilling to come out, and fought most desperately through the Palisadoes, so as they were scorched and burnt with the very flame . . . and so perished valiantly."[41]

The English men involved in the Pequot War were generally impressed by the professed willingness of their Mohegan allies to join the fight, and by their pledges of brave soldiering. Some English reports emphasize the willingness of the allied Indians to put themselves under English command, as in Underhill's discussion of the Mohegan alliance: "These *Indians* were earnest to joyne with the *English,* or at least to bee under their conduct . . . [promising] to be faithfull, and to doe [the English] what service lay in their power." Presumably, this supposed willingness to accept English notions of hierarchy, with English leadership on top, made the Mohegans very appealing allies. In his description of Uncas, Captain John Mason appreciatively reports that the Mohegan sachem predicted "*the* NARRAGANSETTS *would all leave us, but as for* HIMSELF *He would never leave us:* and so it proved: For which Expressions and some other Speeches of his, I shall never forget him. Indeed, he was a great Friend, and did great service." Similarly, William Hubbard reports that one of King Philip's "Captains, of far better Courage and resolution than [Philip], when he saw [Philip's] cowardly temper and disposition, fling down his Armes, calling him *white Liver'd Curre,* or to that purpose, and saying, that he would never own him again, or fight under him, and from that time hath turned to the English and hath continued to this day a faithfull and resolute Souldier in their quarrel."[42] This story told by Hubbard is doubtlessly self-serving in its glorification of the supposedly superior courage of the English versus Philip's cowardice, however it suggests that Indian men valued bravery as a fundamental aspect of a man's character.

The promises of assistance and boasts of bravery from Narragansett allies were looked at much more skeptically by the English and the Mohegans alike, as hinted at above. Nevertheless, they reveal the premium that Native men put on their status as brave, successful warriors. As Mason reports, "The *Narragansett Indians* . . . frequently despised us, saying, *That we durst not look upon a* PEQUOT, *but themselves would perform great Things."* Mason's irritation with such boastfulness might have been enhanced by the snub he had initially received by the Narragansett sachem Miantonomi when Mason first requested free passage through his lands. He reports that Miantonomi told him *"That he did accept of our coming, and did also approve of our Design* [against the Pequots]; *only he thought our Numbers were too weak to deal with the Enemy, who were* (as he said) *very great Captains and Men skilful in War.* Thus he spake somewhat slighting of us." At another time, Narragansett warriors "one by one, [made] solemn Protestations how gallantly they would demean themselves, and how many Men they would Kill."[43] Most English men could not help but hear a rebuke of English soldiery when Indians—even allies—boasted of their own expertise in war. Although Underhill and Mason were very biased reporters, they nevertheless reveal that Indian men saw war as a proving ground as much as English men did.

One very important aspect of Indian men's performance as warriors was their behavior when captured, ritually tortured, and executed. Meeting death as a man and proving oneself worthy of the honor of ritual execution was more revealing of an Indian man's true worth than his performance in battle.[44] A French observer in the 1750s writing about the death of a Mohawk warrior describes the Indian ideal of stoicism and pride in the face of death: "To show his bravery, the Mohawk began to sing, daring his tormentors to do their worst. This bravado seemed more the result of rage than of courage. It did not fail to arouse his tormentors, and the more courage he showed, the more fury was shown by his tormentors. At last he died cursing his executioners to the very end." The goal of this conduct was to inspire the admiration of his Ottawa executioners. "Sometimes savages manifest regret at having killed a courageous man, because they consider him brave.

This is the meaning of the victim's song." The "victim's song," as he styled it, was an overt assertion of masculine bravado: "'I am brave and fearless; I do not fear death. Those who fear it are cowards. They are less than women. Life and death are nothing to the man who has courage. May despair and rage choke my enemies. May I not devour them and drink their blood to the last drop. I have done so many brave deeds. I have killed so many men! All my enemies are dogs! If I find them in the land of spirits, I will make war on them. Now I lament my body; I am coming to death like a brave.'" Coming to death like a brave—rather than a weak woman or a cowardly dog—was of the highest value. "A savage going to his death would not be considered brave if he displayed any feeling under his tortures. This would be a sign of weakness, for which they would scorn him." This was a ritual little understood by most European men, who when honored in this fashion greatly disappointed their Indian hosts. Recall the remarks mentioned earlier by Wituwamet, who disdained Europeans when they faced death by ritual execution, "what pittifull weak Creatures [Europeans] were, that when they were killing, they died crying, and made sower faces, more like children then men." In describing the execution of two English prisoners, the French observer noted above describes a similar scene: "I wish only to say that all the cries, groans, and oaths uttered during these tortures only aroused the mirth of the executioners," perhaps because of the unmanly fashion in which the English men met their deaths.[45]

Indian men were not only contemptuous of enemies who seemed to behave more like women or children than men. They also frequently insulted opponents by calling them dogs, and complained about being treated like dogs by Europeans. Despite the close association between Indians and their dogs, the insult worked because of dogs' reputation for servility. An account of King Philip's War in Maine notes that Indian men peppered some English men with both bullets and insults, "calling our Men *English Dogs* and it was well, if our *English*, in way of Retaliation, did not give them as bad language." Calling someone a dog could also specifically impugn a man's status as a warrior; it was not just a generic insult to his manhood. Another account from King Philip's War relates a prewar council that attempted to solve the conflict through diplomacy. "The indians saied the english ronged them but our desier was the quarell might rightly be desided in the best way, and not as dogs desided ther quarells. the indians owned that fighting was the worst way." While this insult seems to have had particular resonance with Indians, its meaning was well understood by their European enemies and allies alike.[46]

Because of the importance of military success and courage in the face of death for Indian men, they adapted readily to the new challenges of Anglo-Indian warfare in the seventeenth century. As noted above, English plantations passed laws early on to prohibit the trading of guns and ammunition to the Indians, but these laws were notoriously ineffective. Indeed, New England merchants desiring to make inroads into the beaver trade had a direct incentive to assist Indians in procuring muskets, which the Indians were interested in from first sight. (Muskets were vitally important to the beaver trade because they were a consumer good that Indians desperately wanted, not because Indians used them in the hunt.) Bow-hunting is a skill that puts a premium on accuracy and technique, so the switch from the quiet and accurate bow-and-arrow to the noisy, cumbersome, and inaccurate musket was far from inevitable. Matchlock muskets, the most common form of weaponry owned by the early English settlers, were effective when fired in a tight group formation in a formal battlefield engagement, but they were not good for hunting or sniping because they were awkward to load and fire and not known for their accuracy. Flint- or firelock muskets were faster and easier to load and fire, and they were thus preferred by the Indians who recognized their superior performance given the demands of warfare and hunting in the northeastern borderlands. By the time of King Philip's War, great numbers of Indian men owned flintlock muskets or carbines, and their skills in marksmanship were well known among the English.[47]

In military terms, a "parley" (or "to parley," in verb form) is an informal discussion with the enemy, as opposed to a formal diplomatic engagement.[48] Colonial war narratives record a great deal of talking between Indians and English combatants, including a prodigious amount of taunting, insults, and threats. Both sides seem to have found verbal jousting as important as actual combat in establishing and maintaining their pride as warriors and thus their masculinity. As we saw in Massassoit's performance for the early Plymouth colonists, speechmaking and rhetorical assertions of Native men's power were as important to Indians as English men's words were in constituting their authority through the written instruments of deeds, charters, and the law, and the oral culture of politics. Free speech—especially loud, boastful, and proud speech—was a gendered prerogative in early New England; it was clearly linked to political power as only adult English men were granted such liberty. Similarly, speech was central to the conduct of Indian diplomacy and war, and aggressive boasts of masculinity and mastery were common among Iroquois and Algonquian men in the seventeenth and eighteenth centuries.[49] Among the Iroquois, skillful speechmaking was especially prized, given the spirit of consensus upon which Iroquois politics were based. Father Joseph Lafitau, a Jesuit missionary in Canada from 1712 to 1717, notes that those who spoke with "wit and *savoir faire* . . . gain[ed] a great deal of credit and authority." In fact, skillful oratory was so highly valued that Lafitau makes a point of noting that "not considered at all in the qualifications is whether they are of a ranking maternal household; their personal merits and talents are the only things considered." These talents could be turned against enemies and used skillfully to intimidate them. Taunting the enemy with words as well as arrows, harquebuses, and muskets was a common element in Indian warfare before the arrival of European enemies. Lafitau recounts a story from Samuel de Champlain's adventures in which his Algonquian allies spent the night before battle against the Iroquois "singing death songs, boasting of their own tribe's noble deeds and saying, as was customary, many scornful things about their enemies over whom each party promised itself an easy victory."[50]

Because of its importance to Native and English political cultures and constructions of masculinity, this kind of verbal jousting is characteristic of Anglo-Indian warfare through the colonial period and is evident before any shots were fired in the Pequot War. Indeed, accounts of battles are frequently more detailed about exchanges of words between warring sides than of bullets. For example, on the eve of one early engagement the Pequots met Underhill's ships as they sailed up the Pequot (now Thames) River, "running in multitudes along the water side, crying what cheere Englishmen, what cheere, what doe you come for?" Continuing on with their taunts, they asked, "what Englishman, what cheere, what cheere are you hoggerie, will you cram us—That is, are you angry, will you kill us, and doe you come to fight?"[51] This taunting was meant to cast aspersions not only on English soldiers but upon English manhood.

More commonly in English accounts, though, English men and their allies responded energetically in the face of Indian "jeering." In another incident from the Pequot War, Mason reports that the Narragansett allies deserted the English war party just before the climactic engagement of the war. When he asked Uncas, *Where were the Rest of the Indians? They answered, Behind, exceedingly affraid.* Mason then takes his rhetorical revenge for having heard how brave the Narragansetts would stand in battle: "We wished them to tell the rest of their Fellows, *That they should by no means Fly, but stand at what distance they pleased, and see whether* ENGLISH

MEN *would now Fight or not."* Mason felt himself and the manhood of all "ENGLISH MEN" vindicated by the evidence of Indian cowardice, even if in an ally. Similarly, the anecdote that opens this chapter is a prime example of the power of "parley." But sometimes, Indian "parley" was too shaming to provoke any response, as in the anecdote that opens this chapter. When the Pequots taunt Underhill and his men by "jeering at them, and calling, . . . come out and fight if you dare: you dare not fight, you are all one like women," Underhill confesses that these triumphant insults "troubled the hearts of the souldiers, but they knew not how to remedy it in respect of their weaknesse."[52] In these representations of war, the volley of words and symbolic imagery seems just as important as the volley of bullets and arrows that accompanied them.

Perhaps because Indians also valued verbal wit and reveled in insulting their enemies, Mason and Underhill both attached the telling adjectives "proud" and "insolent" to their descriptions of their enemies in the Pequot War—two adjectives that imply that the English officers did not see them as foes who were their equals. After all, "insolent" is a word used to describe an inappropriate display of will in an inferior, and pride—one of the seven deadly sins—was a sore affliction to a society and culture built around a strict hierarchy. Underhill justifies English conduct in the climactic battle of the war by declaring that "so insolent were these wicked imps growne, that like the divell their commander, they runne up and downe as roaring Lyons, compassing all corners of the Countrey for a prey, seeking whom they might devoure." Servants who ran away or stole from their masters were insolent; children who talked back to their parents displayed unseemly pride and were insolent; and apparently, to the English settlers, Indians who fought the expansion of English geographical and political control were proud and insolent as well.[53]

This kind of "parley" continues in representations of encounters between English and Native soldiers in King Philip's War. William Hubbard points to the "insolency of *John Monoco* or *one eyed John*" as an Indian especially deserving of English scorn. When Monoco and his men attacked Groton, Massachusetts, in March of 1676, they "by a sudden suprizal early in the morning seized upon a Garison house in one end of the Town, continued in it, plundering what was there ready at hand, all that day." That night, he was "very familiarly in appearance," calling out to the English captain sheltered in another garrison house, "and entertained a great deal of discourse with him, whom he called his *old Neighbour.*" In this presumptuously familiar mode, Monoco fell to "dilating upon the cause of the War, and putting an end to it by a friendly peace: yet oft mixing bitter Sarcasmes, with several blasphemous scoffs and taunts at their praying and worshipping God in the meeting house, which he deridingly said he had burned. Among other things which he boastingly uttered that night," he claimed to have already burned the towns of Medfield, Lancaster, and promised to burn Chelmsford, Concord, Watertown, Cambridge, Charlestown, Roxbury, and even Boston itself. He then boasted, according to Hubbard, "at last in their Dialect, *What Me will, Me do:* not much unlike the proud *Assyrian* (if his power had been equal to his pride) sometime threatened against *Jerusalem.*"[54]

Why was it important to record this parley in such detail? It almost seems as though Monoco's boasting of his exploits was more disturbing to his English audience (and to his chronicler Hubbard) than the deeds themselves. Only English men in early New England had the liberty to speak the way that John Monoco did; women and children who took such liberties were censured by the courts and their communities for their insolence. Perhaps this is what disturbed Monoco's audience—that an Indian man was assuming the rights that English men reserved for themselves. Even as Hubbard gleefully recounts Monoco's fall, his narrative focuses on Monoco's transgressions as a braggart rather than as a killer, noting that Monoco's bold ambitions were "by the remarkable providence of God, so confounded within a few months after, that he was bereft of his four hundred and fourscore [men] (of which he now boasted) and only with a few more Bragadozio's like himself." Monoco and his "insolent" colleagues paid for their actions against the English, which consequences gave the lie to Indian bravery: "*Sagamore Sam, old Jethro,* and the *Sagamore of Quoboag* were taken by the English and [Monoco himself] was seen (not long before the writing of this) marching toward the Gallows (through *Boston* Streets, which he threatened to burn at his pleasure) with an Halter about his neck, with which he was hanged at the Towns end, *September 26* in this present year 1676." Hubbard makes it clear that he takes pleasure that Monoco is punished for his threatening words, not just for his actions: "*So let thine Enemies perish O Lord,* and such contempt be poured on all them that open their mouthes to blaspheme thy holy Name."[55]

Sometimes parley could even take the place of bullets, especially if the words were uttered in the service of the English. Increase Mather tells the story of "an Indian called *Matthias,* who fought for the English." As English forces closed in on Philip and his men in August of 1676, Mather writes that Matthias secured the surrender of a number of Philip's men with the power of his words alone: "when they were come very near the Enemy, [Matthias] called to them in their own Language with much vehemency, telling them they were all dead men if they did but fire a Gun." It is not clear if Philip's confederates were impressed by what Matthias said, or by the fact that it was from the mouth of another Indian, but Mather claims that these words "did so amuse and amaze the Indians that they lost a great advantage against the English."[56]

Cotton Mather records another gendered "parley" between the defenders of a garrison at Wells, Maine, during King William's War. Of course, this is probably an entirely imaginary encounter as Mather never went anywhere near the frontier during the war, instead preferring to write his hawkish screeds in favor of invading the St. Lawrence River valley from the comfort and safety of Boston. Nevertheless, his representation of frontier warfare reveals the importance of "parley" for the English as a tactic on and off the battlefield, especially exchanges in which the English could highlight the inadequacies of Indian men, whether as rhetoricians or soldiers. Thus, Mather sets the scene of the siege of Wells to emphasize the importance of words as weapons, since the English were heavily outnumbered—fifteen men in the fort and fifteen in a sloop in the bay versus five hundred Indians and French soldiers. The French and Indians stood offshore calling to the English in the sloop: "The Enemy kept Galling the *Sloops,* from their Several Batteries, and calling 'em to Surrender, with many fine promises to make them *Happy.*" This did not deceive the English, who "answered with a just *Laughter,* that had now and then a mortiferous *Bullet* at the End of it," punctuating their laughter with deadly force. The enemy did not neglect the garrison with their verbal parley, and sent "a *Flag of Truce* to the Garrison, advising 'em with much Flattery, to *Surrender;* but the Captain sent 'em word, *That he wanted for nothing, but for men to come, and Fight him.*" Taking up this challenge, "the *Indian* replyed unto Captain *Convers, Being you are so Stout, why don't you come, and Fight in the open Field, like a Man, and not Fight in a Garrison, like a Squaw?*"

Perhaps the Indian's words were inspired by his observation of the women inside the garrison, whom Mather says "on this occasion took up the *Amazonian* Stroke, and not only brought Ammunition to the *Men,* but also with a *Manly* Resolution fired several Times upon the Enemy." Thus what might have been a damning observation by the Indians is redeemed by Mather, who turns the Indian's words around to imply that even English women are better soldiers than Indian men are. The verbal challenges continued, with the Indians alternating between threats and cajolery to get the

English to surrender: "they fell to Coaksing the Captain, with as many *Fine Words,* as the *Fox* in the Fable had for the Allurement of his Prey unto him." Despite their poor numbers, Mather writes that the intrepid English refused to surrender, using only words to fight the Indians. Nevertheless, this was enough to frustrate the Indians, who "fell to Threatening, and Raging, like so many Defeated Devils, using these Words, *Damn ye, we'll cut you as small as Tobacco, before to morrow Morning.* The Captain, bid 'em to make Hast, for *he wanted work;* So, the Indian throwing his Flag on the Ground, ran away." According to Mather's self-serving account, the mere boasting of English men and their challenges to Indian masculinity were enough to repel a force of five hundred men.[57]

While taunts and insults directed at their enemies in battle may have enhanced their military prowess, being left speechless by an enemy was part of the humiliation of defeat. Words failed Increase Mather in his account of King Philip's War when telling of a shameful lack of courage displayed by a group of English men surprised by an Indian attack while on their way to meeting one Sabbath near Springfield. What was really embarrassing was that the Indians were outnumbered by English men more than two to one. Mather confesses his loss of words in telling such a sordid tale: "*O Lord What shall I say when Israel turns their backs before their Enemies?* What shall be said when eighteen English-men well arm'd, fly before seven Indians?"[58] Apparently, Mather could think of nothing to say, or to write, on the subject—he was silenced by the sad performance of the English.

Even away from the heat of battle, Indian and English men challenged each other's fitness in war. After the carnage and destruction that King Philip's War visited upon both the English and Indians, one Indian man, John Wompus, regaled an English married couple in Cambridge with his detailed criticism of English men in war and in politics. Wompus's comments reveal the complex ways in which masculinity was constructed for both Indian and English men: being a man was about more than just *not* being a woman; it was also about assuming the status of an adult and performing the role faithfully and convincingly. After taking a draft of beer from Hannah Meade, Wompus cut himself some tobacco and began to speak his mind on the conduct of the English in the late war. According to Hannah, "[M]uch of his descours [w]as to speake under valewingly of the English in yr warlike attempts agnst the enemy." Wompus even used English stereotypes about Indians in comparing them unfavorably. "[H]ee spake many words in a disdainfull way of the English, both of sd Authrty of sd country & of the people saing yt they had acted foolishly & weekly in manageing they were as the Indians." In comparison, Wompus "fell soe in to discourse what great things hee would doe if hee were to Leade soulders against ytt enemis: & withall spake very disparigingly & contemptuosly of the English persons acting against yee enimis." After comparing the English to the defeated and scattered Indians of southern New England, Wompus then compared them to another weak and dependent population, saying "yt they had acted all one like children . . . [the] English had sent out souldiers all one gren hornes like yt child." Condescendingly, Wompus reassured his English hosts "yt tis no mattr I know what: but I will keepe it private yet New England hath Lost the day & yt is knowne in old England."[59] By comparing English military leaders and their soldiers to "children" and to the desperate, defeated Indians, Wompus challenged their manhood as effectively as if he had called them women. All three categories of people were classified as weak, dependent peoples in late seventeenth-century New England, and that was a status that was directly at odds with being a man.

When it came to actual fighting, the sense each side had of being challenged by the enemy continued not just with words but with actions. Frustration grew on both sides because of cultural differences in warfare—its goals and its conduct—although not because of its importance to defining manhood. From both Indian and English perspectives, the men they fought (and for some, fought alongside) behaved like no other men they had ever encountered: Indian men continued openly taunting English men for what they saw as their lack of manly courage, their foolhardiness for insisting on fighting in large groups in open fields, and their barbarousness in insisting on killing everyone they could rather than engaging in smaller fights and taking prisoners. The English saw the Indians as feeble warriors who made great boasts of their bravery but who regularly turned tail on the battlefield after sustaining only a few casualties. Furthermore, their interest in taking live captives rather than killing as many men as possible was baffling to the English.[60] However, as Anglo-Indian warfare continued through the seventeenth century and into the next, both sides learned from each other and even made adaptations to their new worlds of war. Nevertheless, both sides found it useful to complain about their enemies' tactics.

Initially, different expectations of warfare and of what constituted bravery meant that Indian and English men did not recognize one another's displays of manliness. For example, John Underhill's party first landed on Block Island in 1636 and attempted to engage the Pequots there. Announcing their intentions, the English "beat up the Drum and bid them battell,

[and] marching into a champion field we displayed our colours." Any European army would have recognized this ritual performed by the English as a call to battle, but such a martial display would have seemed strange to the Indians, who did not understand or share the ritualized choreography of European battles. According to Indian notions of war, making a big show of a landing party, marching into an open field, and calling attention to oneself with flags and drums was utter madness—a sure way to get killed fast in battle. Indeed, the response of the Indians to this English posturing was as though to a group of madmen: confused and frustrated, Underhill reports that "none [of the Indians] would come neere us, but standing remotely off did laugh at us for our patience." Unfortunately for the Indians, the English did not wait for an Indian war party to respond. Instead, Underhill writes that they took immediate revenge for what they interpreted as Indian mockery of their manhood by firing on "as many as we could come neere, firing their Wigwams, spoyling their corne, and many other necessaries." He reports gloryingly that "we spent the day burning and spoyling the Countrey" and then the next day set sail for "the *Nahanticot* shore." Once again, they issued a formal call to battle, but once again "we were served in like nature." In this, Underhill seems at once irritated by the Indians but perhaps proud that the English put on such an intimidating display that "no *Indians* would come neere us, but runne from us, as the Deere from the dogges." Once again, Underhill and his men answered this Indian refusal to meet them in battle by "having burnt and spoyled what we could light on." Even when Indians responded to English calls to battle, the English discredited their efforts, as in this report from Mason: "Then [the Pequots] run and met [the English] and fell on pell mell striking and cutting with Bows, Hatchets, Knives, &c, after their feeble Manner: Indeed it did hardly deserve the Name of *Fighting*."[61]

English men were similarly willfully blind to the content and display of Indian valor. William Hubbard demonstrates this in his description of the torture and execution of an enemy Indian by the English-allied Mohegans at the end of King Philip's War. Upon his capture, the enemy Indian had boasted of killing nineteen English men and one Mohegan, so the Mohegans had asked to keep him so that they might execute him ritually. Although he provides a detailed report of the ritual, Hubbard clearly does not understand the proofs of manliness that are being asked of, and delivered by, the doomed prisoner. He reports, "In the first place therefore, making a *great Circle*, they placed him in the *middle*, that all their Eyes might at the same time, be pleased with *utmost Revenge* upon him; They first cut one of his *Fingers* round the *joynt,* at the *Trunck* of his *hand,* with a *sharp knife,* and then brake it off, as men use to do with a *slaughtered Beast,* before they *uncase* him." The torture continued as "they cut off another & another, till they had *dismembred* one hand of all its *digits,* the *blood* sometimes spirting out in *streams* a *yard* from his hand." According to the protocol of Indian executions, this was an ordeal to be borne manfully by both the victim and the torturers, who were to withstand it stoically. The victim would prove his own masculinity and worth as a warrior not just by refusing to cry out, or whimper, or pray for mercy but by laughing, singing, dancing, making jokes, and even asking for greater suffering. Hubbard demonstrates his and the other English men's incomprehension of these values when he reports that this "*barbarous* and *unheard of Cruelty,* the English were not able to bear, it forcing *Tears* from their *Eyes;* yet did not the *Sufferer* ever *relent,* or shew any sign of *Anguish:* for being asked by some of his *Tormentors,* how he liked the War? . . . this *unsensible* and *hard hearted Monster* Answered, he liked it very well, and found it as sweet, as *English men* did their *Sugar.*" A very satisfying answer for the Mohegans, but Hubbard is so unknowing about the importance of grim jollity and even wit in this ritual that he condemns the prisoner's response as proof of his "unsensible," "hard-hearted," and even monstrous nature. Just as in the encounter on Block Island that so vexed Captain Underhill, the Mohegans were probably annoyed by the childish, unmanly behavior of their English allies, crying and turning their heads away from this test of valor, exposing their own weakness and unworthiness as warriors. Indeed, this prisoner was such a model of Indian manhood in his torture and execution that he puts the English witnesses to shame. Hubbard reports, "in this frame he continued, till his *Executioners* had dealt with the *Toes of his feet,* as they had done with the *Fingers of his hands;* All the while making him *dance* round the *Circle,* and *sing,* till he had wearied both himself and them." He stopped dancing only when "[a]t last they brake the *bones of his Legs,* after which he was forced to *sit down,* which 'tis said he silently did, till they had *knockt out his brains.*"[62] Indian men had no use for the emotional displays of European men when they witnessed such scenes, let alone when they were the victims of the torture and ritual execution, and the English men here were clearly disturbed by what they saw as the extreme cruelty of the Indians. As with Captain Underhill's experiences going into battle on Block Island, Mohegan and English men completely misinterpreted each other's performances of masculine worthiness.

Misunderstandings and perceptions of effrontery continued to characterize frontier warfare, but the more careful English students of war developed some understanding of the difference between English and Indian styles of warfare beginning with the Pequot War. For example, Underhill himself apparently understood the Indian preference for smaller war parties versus European-style large engagements. He notes that "the Indian fight farre differs from the Christian practise; for they most commonly divide themselves into small bodies, so that we are forced to neglect our usuall way and to subdivide our divisions to answer theirs." This shrewd tactic necessarily reduced English firepower, as their weapons were most effective when fired in massed formations. Furthermore, Underhill reports that there were among the English "a people that spend most of their time in the studie of warlike policy" who gave advice about engaging Indians in battle. One of the best students of Indians in general and of military strategy in particular was Lion Gardiner, although he claims bitterly in his narrative of the war that his advice was rarely sought out or heeded.[63] For the most part, English and Indians alike claimed to be shocked by each other's conduct of warfare. Each believed that the other's style of fighting was unmanly, sometimes not worthy of being considered proper warfare at all.

Despite the efforts of Gardiner and Underhill to understand Indian warfare, differences between English and Indians styles of war not only continued through the war but marred the relations between the English and their Indian allies. Their frustration with each other's conduct comes out most visibly during and after the climactic surprise attack on the Pequot village also known as the "Mystic Fort." The English guessed that the Indians would expect them to land their army in ships, so they decided to march overland through Narragansett country to destroy the village. The allied forces of English, Mohegan, and Narragansett troops camped about two miles from the village and then arose before dawn to finish the march and make their attack. But, as related above by Mason, most of the Narragansett warriors deserted the raiding party before they made their final approach to the village.

This may have been due to their scruples about attacking the sleeping village, which was in fact populated for the most part by women, children, and the elderly, as the Pequot warriors were away from the village, busy fighting the war. The English and the Mohegans proceeded into the village, firing on anyone in sight and burning every wigwam, and they later boasted that "men, women, and children" perished in the attack.[64] By Underhill's estimates, "there were about foure hundred soules in this Fort, and not above five of them escaped out of our hands. Great and dolefull was the bloudy sight to the view of a young souldier that never had been in Warre, to see so many soules lie gasping on the ground so thicke in some places, that you could hardly passe along." Aware of how shocking such an attack might seem to a European or colonial audience, Underhill acknowledges, "it may bee demanded, Why should you be so furious (as some have said) should not Christians have more mercy and compassion?" Perhaps, he says, but "sometimes the Scripture declareth women and children must perish with their parents." Indeed, the English appeared bloodthirsty, and they reveled in the savagery of their attack: The Pequots "were now at their Wits End, who not many Hours before exalted themselves in their great Pride," writes Mason, "threatening and resolving the utter Ruin and Destruction of all the *English,* Exulting and Rejoycing with Songs and Dances: but GOD was above them, who laughed his Enemies and the Enemies of his People to Scorn, making them as a fiery Oven: Thus were the Stout Hearted spoiled, having slept their last Sleep, and non of their Men could find their Hands: Thus did the LORD judge among the Heathen, filling the Place with dead Bodies!"[65] Despite this total rout, the English themselves were somewhat vulnerable after the attack. They were very low on supplies, had wounded men to care for, and were unsure if they should march to the river to take their leave of Pequot country.

The desertion of their Indian allies vexed the English, while English savagery greatly disturbed even their most loyal allies, the Mohegan. When a party of Pequot warriors arrived and fixed on fifty retreating Narragansett Indians, Underhill writes that the Narragansetts came to him and Mason, "crying, oh helpe us now, or our men will bee all slaine." Of course, Underhill and Mason took this opportunity to rebuke Indian perfidy: "We answered, how dare you crave aide of us, when you are leaving of us in this distressed condition, not knowing which way to march out of the Countrey." But the English decided to demonstrate the superior honor and manhood of English soldiers and officers by assisting the weak, failed Narragansetts. "You shall see," writes Underhill, "it is not the nature of *English* men to deale like Heathens, to requite evill for evill, but wee will succor you." Underhill and thirty of his men rescued the cornered Narragansetts, and in their retreat "slew and wounded above a hundred *Pequeats,* all fighting men that charged us both in reere and flanks." Although not an eyewitness, William Bradford agreed with Underhill's estimation of Narragansett manliness, although he seemed even more insulted by reports that the Indians tried to take the credit for the defeat of the Pequots: "The Narigansett Indeans, all this while, stood round aboute, but aloofe from all danger, and left the whole execution to the English, exept it were the stoping of any that broke away, insulting over their enimies in this their ruine and miserie, when they saw them dancing in the flames." Bradford claimed that the Narragansett warriors taunted the Pequots, "calling them by a word in their own language, signifing, O brave Pequents! which they used familierly among them selves in their own prayers, in songs of triumph after their victories." Thus, English ideas of order and hierarchy were expressed through these reports from the Pequot War. From the English perspective, Indian men as enemies and as allies were brought to heel, witnessing first-hand the superiority of English soldiers and of English manhood.[66]

From the Indian perspective, however, this new English style of warfare was disturbingly destructive. Bradford's claim that Narragansett warriors were gleeful in the face of the Mystic inferno rings false when compared to eyewitness reports of the reactions of other Indians. The scale and the savagery of English warfare was foreign to the Indians, both enemies and allies alike. Mason boastfully reports the reaction of Pequot warriors when they came upon the burning ruins of their village and families: "beholding what was done, [they] stamped and tore the Hair from their Heads." They did not attempt to pursue the retreating English and Mohegan army, because as Mason glibly suggests, the English had "by that time taught them a little more Manners than to disturb us." Yet even their Mohegan allies were disturbed by this English style of warfare. Underhill writes that "our *Indians* came to us, and much rejoyced at our victories, and greatly admired the manner of *English* mens fight: but cried *mach it, mach it*; that is, it is naught, it is naught, because it is too furious and flaies too many men."[67] The price of victory was too high for Indian enemies and allies of the English alike.

The defeat of the Pequots not only secured their immediate lands for English settlement but opened New England's southwestern frontier to exploration and English settlement. Indians who had seen the price exacted of the Pequots for making enemies of the English were willing to placate the newcomers with grants of land. These lands were in turn settled by many of the war's English officers and enlisted men.[68] Thus the war's legacy lived on: because the war had not removed all Indians from the southwestern New England frontier, the Indians and English people of southern New England forged a suspicious coexistence. Indian uprisings remained a clear danger in the minds of the English settlers, and the presence of English men and women in their environment continued to rankle the Indians. Some of the former Pequot War officers became the chief architects of New England's policies for dealing with the Indians and thus repeated many of the same brutalities that characterized English action in the war. Some Indian leaders remembered well the lessons they learned at gunpoint and urged all Indians to live up to the English men's worst nightmares.

Accordingly, the four decades between the Pequot War and King Philip's War were not a time of calm in the northeastern borderlands. Rumors of Indian uprisings, actual Indian plots against the English, and the Anglo-Dutch Wars kept New England in a state of fairly constant military alert. On the southern and western frontier of New England, in Connecticut and New Haven, the colonies settled in the wake of the Pequot War seemed especially vulnerable. In the late summer of 1642, Lion Gardiner was informed of a massive Narragansett-led plot to destroy the English. Gardiner, the builder and commander of Fort Saybrook during the Pequot War, had maintained his Indian contacts and immediately informed New England's political leaders. Waiandance, sachem of the Montauk on the far eastern end of Long Island, had informed Gardiner that Miantonomi, sachem of the Narragansett, was trying to build an Indian alliance to rise up and kill all the English, "man and mother's son." This was the same Miantonomi who lent support to the English in the Pequot War (although the English found his warriors to be of little value) and was still the antagonist of Uncas, the Mohegan sachem.[69]

Although Miantonomi's plan was discovered and foiled by another English-allied Indian, New England authorities decided that they should take no chances with their security and set about creating more formal political and military alliances among their scattered settlements. Previously independent "plantations" joined colonies, and the four puritan colonies (Massachusetts, Plymouth, Connecticut, and New Haven) joined together to form the United Colonies of New England. At their first meeting in September of 1643, the United Colonies reviewed the whole affair and washed their hands of their former ally. Mindful of Uncas's loyalty and his abiding hatred of Miantonomi, the commissioners asked Uncas to "put such a false & blood-thirsty enemie to death, but in his owne Jurisdiccon, not in the English plantacons." In October, New Haven and Connecticut men offered to assist Uncas in hunting down and executing the Narragansett sachem.[70] Still, Miantonomi's death quelled neither Indian nor English fears of being destroyed or reduced to dependence on the other.

Aside from entering into formal political and military alliances, English settlers also used town and colony laws in their attempts to get control of the Indians, so that (in the words of some local authorities) they would no longer suffer the "proud cariage and manifold abuses . . . from the Uncircumcised Heathens round about us." In the 1640s through the 1660s, dozens of laws were passed regulating Indians who entered English settlements or who had any dealings with English people. Indians were prohibited from carrying arms in English towns, and sometimes from entering English towns entirely. The trading of land and liquor between English people and Indians was expressly forbidden in all English colonies. In measures designed to limit Indian mobility, English people were forbidden to sell horses or boats to Indians, and blacksmiths were forbidden to do work for them. Colonies even declared limited wars on local Indians, and English complaints about Indian "abuses" continued.[71] Tensions rose again to crisis proportions in 1669 when rumors of another uprising of Indians on Long Island reached New England. As in the 1642 plot, Pequot War veterans on all sides were involved: former Captain, now Major John Mason, the interpreter Thomas Stanton, Uncas, and the Eastern Niantics. The 1669 plot remained nothing but a rumor, but like most interactions along the Anglo-Indian frontier, it kept both sides in a constant state of readiness for, in Mason's words, "as great a hazard as ever New England yet saw."[72]

By the 1670s, English and Indian men had learned from each other what to expect, although they still criticized each other's tactics. Military historians have traditionally argued that King Philip's War represents a turning point in the "Americanization" of colonial warfare, although the tactical differences between the Pequot War and the later wars of the seventeenth century have probably been overstated.[73] However, the degree to which North American warfare was changing English tactics was a matter of debate and some anxiety. New England writers continued to exaggerate or highlight the differences between English warriors and Indian warriors, if only to reassure themselves and their readers that they were utterly different from the "savages" they fought.

Despite the fact that King Philip's War, even more than the Pequot War, was composed of Indian raids on individual homes and small, isolated settlements, the English still sometimes marched into fields en masse, drummers loudly announcing their intentions, and colors flying. The Wampanoags and Narragansetts would probably have found foolish one "Ensigne *Savage,* that young Martial Spark," memorialized by William Hubbard. "[S]carce twenty years of age, had at that time one bullet lodged in his Thigh, another shot through the brim of his Hat, by ten or twelve of the Enemy discharging upon him together, while he boldly held up his Colours in the Front of his Company."[74] His enemies probably thought he got what he deserved for calling attention to himself in that manner in battle.

Comfortable English civilians like William Hubbard argued strongly that English men should stick to their traditional ways of fighting, as adopting Indian ways was ineffective and possibly even dangerous to the English cause. One Captain Lothrop was responsible for losing an important battle as well as his own life because he "having taken up a wrong notion about the best way and manner of fighting with the *Indians* (which he was always wont to argue for) *viz.,* that it were best to deal with the *Indians* in their own way, *sc.* by skulking behind Trees and taking their aim at single persons." Hubbard judged that "herein was his great mistake, in not considering the great disadvantage a smaller Company would have in dealing that way with a greater multitude . . . which gross mistake of his, was the ruine of a choice company of young men, the very flower of the County of *Essex.*" Adopting the Indian style not only killed Lothrop and his men but also "the twenty slain with Capt. *Beers* men, who betook themselves at first to their Trees" instead of marching in formation. "[H]ad he ordered his men to March in a Body, as some of his fellow-Commanders advised, either backward, or forward, in reason, they had not lost a quarter of the number of them that fell that day by the edge of the Sword. For the Indians, notwithstanding their subtlety and cruelty, durst not look an *Englishman* in the face, in the open field, nor ever yet were known to kill any man with their Guns, unless when they could ly in wait for him in an ambush, or behind some shelter, taking aim undiscovered."[75] Here, Hubbard suggests that English military tactics alone would win the fight without a shot fired, as cowardly Indian men would quail in the face of such a manly display. However, actual military men would have been wise to regard Hubbard's advice with great caution, as he had no firsthand experience with warfare and was a highly ideological chronicler of King Philip's War. His goal was to put as much distance between the English and their Indian enemies as possible, but in criticizing the English for adopting Indian ways he demonstrates that the English and Indians were adapting to North American warfare and experimenting with each other's tactics.

Similarly, Cotton Mather's description of the siege of Wells, Maine, during King William's War suggests that Indian and English men still disagreed about their manner of fighting. Badly outnumbered, an English captain refused to have his forces leave the garrison when an Indian leader taunted him to fight in the open *"like a Man"*: *"What a Fool, are you? Do you think, Thirty men a Match for Five Hundred? No* (sayes the Captain,

counting as well he might, each of his *Fifteen* men, to be as Good as *Two!)*"
Instead, he proposed that the Indians *"come with your Thirty men upon the
Plain, and I'le meet you with my Thirty, as soon as you will."* The Indian thus
answered, *"Nay, mee own, English Fashion is all one Fool; you kill mee, mee
kill you! No, better ly some where, and Shoot a man, and hee no see! That the
best Souldier!"*⁷⁶ Cotton Mather, like Benjamin Hubbard, never saw action
in an Indian war, and he had a strong interest in representing the Indians
and the English as being entirely unlike one another. Here he appears to
deride the Indian's notion of the "best Souldier" as a man who hides himself, mocking Indian manhood by employing a fantasy of broken English.⁷⁷

Officers' accounts of later seventeenth-century wars also provide evidence of some tactical experimentation and of the different kinds of success
Indians and English men met with in their attempts to borrow from each
other. Benjamin Church, in his narrative of King Philip's War, mentions
these tactical innovations without much comment, suggesting that English
men had already incorporated some Indian ways of fighting into their ma-
neuvers. For example, he commonly divides his men into small groups
rather than approaching the enemy in a formal battlefield formation. At
one point, Church argues that *"if they intended to make an end of the War,
by subduing the Enemy, they must make a business of the War, as the Enemy
did."* He then tells his fellow officers that he would *"not lye in any Town or
Garrison . . . but would lye in the Woods as the Enemy did."* Despite Church's
interest in adopting Indian tactics, his narrative suggests that Indian men
were much more adept at creating a successful mix of Indian and European
tactics, especially when it came to the effective use of muskets. In one battle,
Church is surprised by "a Volly of fifty or sixty Guns" issuing from a heavily
wooded area as he and his men marched in an open field. The Indians were
true to their usual reluctance to march into open fields and kept cover in
the woods, but if Church's guess at the size of the volley is correct, they had
adopted the European tactic of firing at once in a sizable, tight formation
in order to maximize the effect of the gunfire. Church then warned his men
not to return fire all at once, *"lest the Enemy should take the advantage of
such an opportunity to run upon them with their Hatche[t]s,"* another traditional Indian tactic. Church tried to answer this Indian assault by borrowing the Indian style of breaking up his men into small groups and scattering
them, but he found that he was too late, as the enemy had already "possessed themselves of every Rock, Stump, Tree, or Fence that was in sight."
The enemy had even "possessed themselves of the Ruines of a Stone-house
that overlook'd them, and of the black Rocks to the Southward of them; so

that now they had no way to prevent lying quite open to some, or other of the Enemy."[78] Church and his men were thoroughly bested by the Indians' combination of both traditional Indian and borrowed European tactics.

By the end of the seventeenth century, men like Church might have been more willing to engage in Indian tactics because an emerging discourse on racial difference began to put more rhetorical distance between Euro-Americans and Native Americans. English people began talking about Native people—and especially Native men—in new ways. Beginning with accounts of King Philip's War, but then increasingly in accounts of the late seventeenth- and early eighteenth-century intercolonial wars, English commentators began to use language that challenged not only the masculinity of Indian men but their humanity. By de-gendering Indian men, Indian men were not just feminized but dehumanized—no longer assumed to be men, but animals, or perhaps even a new, racially identifiable species.[79] In his 1676 *Brief History* of King Philip's War, Increase Mather calls the enemy Indians "wolves" once and compares an Indian to a "dying Beast." However, he still seems to see Indians as essentially human, telling of the loss at one point of "not less then a thousand Indian Souls" and suggesting that he still held out hope for the humanity of Indians. But within a few years, he seems to have changed his mind. In *An Essay for the Recording of Illustrious Providences*, published in 1684, he tacitly compares the ravages of the late Indian war to other destructive forces of nature like land and sea storms.[80] The message of this depoliticization of Indian warfare is clear: Native men are not rational political actors, and the English are not bound to respect them as such.

Mather's son Cotton pushed his father's new ideas about Indians even further at the end of King William's War, with the publication of *Humiliations follow'd with Deliverances* in 1697. In this book, the younger Mather is even more convinced of the providential nature of Indian wars, claiming that they have been unleashed upon New England by a God striving to return his chosen people to the path of righteousness: "Alas, our *Plagues* have been *wonderful!* We have been sorely Lashed, with one Blow after another, for our Delinquincies." Of the many Indian victories over the English, and the many English taken captive, he writes, "We have been *Humbled* by a Barbarous Adversary once and again let loose to *Wolve* it upon us." By dehumanizing the Indian enemy, he delegitimates their claim to political independence. The latest war has been "an unequal Contest with such as are *not a People, but a Foolish Nation.*"[81] Wolves, creatures who are "not a People," but fools—all categories of dependents, not adult men who are husbands, fathers, and masters, not beings with a claim to political autonomy.

In his 1699 publication on King William's War, *Decennium Luctuosum*, Cotton Mather not only calls Indians "wolves" over and over, but he also elaborates on their animal natures by calling them "tygres" or "Fierce Things in the Shape of *Men*," explaining that they live in "dens" or "kennels." Significantly, he uses the word "Tawnies," referring to the color of Indians' skin. Cotton Mather comes to use "tawny" as a substitute noun for "Indian" in this quickly produced history of the latest Indian war. He writes of "a horrible Tawny in the Entry, with a gun in his Hand," a "Tawny Wench [who] violently push'd" an English girl into a river, "Tawny Servants," and so on.[82] This identification of Indians as racially marked would not be complete for at least several more decades, and the next chapter will explore just how unsettled the line between English and Indian remained well into the eighteenth century. Nevertheless, the supposedly "tawny" nature of Indians would be something that colonial Anglo-Americans would attempt to define and fix throughout the eighteenth century.[83]

In nearly a century of warfare, the contest between Indian and English men had seriously weakened the claims of coastal Algonquians like the Narragansetts, Massachusetts, Wampanoags, Mohegans, Niantics, and Pequots to independent manhood. Despite their greater willingness to adapt to the new technologies and circumstances of colonial warfare, Algonquian men could not fight the demographic forces that likely explain the eventual victory of the English: the horrific effects of smallpox and other pathogens on their numbers, and at the same time the tremendous successes that English and Anglo-Americans had in populating New England.[84] But Anglo-American men hardly rested well after three generations in New England. They seemed to have secured southern and eastern New England from serious Indian attacks after King Philip's War, but their northern and western frontiers remained vulnerable, as the French intercolonial wars began almost immediately after King Philip's War ended. Furthermore, the French had proven tremendously successful at creating alliances with Indians, and there were hundreds of thousands of Native Americans in the North American interior who would ally themselves economically, politically, and militarily with the French.

By the end of the seventeenth century, many New England men had discovered a tragic secret of warfare that ministers and political leaders did not talk about in their speeches and sermons, and many civilians did not want to hear about. While warfare was often crucial to English men's collective political sovereignty and private ownership of land in the seventeenth century, it was also an experience that could cast individual men into a frustrating and humiliating dependence. Wounded veterans who survived seventeenth-century wars had no Veterans Administration to appeal to, and those who could not work due to their infirmities were left to beg for the mercy of capricious colonial governments. In addition to applying for release from future military service, many men requested pensions or other cash assistance to support themselves and their families. For example, Samuel Reed of Charlestown, Massachusetts, describes himself in his 1685 petition as "altogether unabell to help my self And Ever sens [King Philip's War] have had pane mor or les . . . for som yeres past: whereby I am altogether disinabelled to worck: which my nesesety calls for in order to the mantanans of my self & famely: I having line in this lame condishon the most part of this last winter." Reed requested an annual pension, while Obadiah Dickenson's 1680 petition requested eleven pounds from the colony. Dickenson explained that "haveing been through many difficulties & straites I have meete withall by Reason of ye Late Captivitie I have Endured with ye Indians togeather with ye destruction of my habitation & Estate." Stephen Greenleafe of Newbury, Massachusetts, was probably lucky to survive a 1695 Indian attack on his town, in which he suffered shots to the wrist and to the belly, "wounds [that] have been very painful and costly to [him] in the cure of them and have in a great measure utterly taken away the use of his left hand, and wholly taken him off from his Imployment this Winter." Greenleafe was awarded forty pounds for his troubles, perhaps (in his words) to serve as "an Encouragemt. to others speedily to relieve their Neighbours when assaulted by so barbarous an Enemy."[85] Such men were already compromised as men because of their inability to continue compulsory military service. Their poverty and disability reduced them to a precarious dependence on the colony for their own and their families' support. Thus while the rhetoric of seventeenth-century warfare celebrated robust Christian soldiers as they marched off to war, the reality was that many of these former warriors endured lives of diminished manhood and independence.

Chapter 2

"What are you an Indian or an Englishman?" Cultural Cross-Dressing in the Northeastern Borderlands

Now if you'll fight I'll get you English coats,
And wine to drink out of their captains' throats.
The richest merchants' houses shall be ours,
We'll lie no more on mats or dwell in bowers.
We'll have their silken wives take they our squaws,
They shall be whipped by virtue of our laws.
—Benjamin Thompson, New England's Crisis (1676)

Warfare on the colonial northeastern frontier was a Hobbesian test of survival: it was nasty, brutish, and often mercifully short. It was also complicated and almost hopelessly confusing: in every war, some Indians fought on the side of the English, although the same allies could be enemies in the next war, and by the 1680s, the English waged wars out of rivalry with the French as well as out of a lust for Indian lands. Each side fought in a manner that confused and enraged the other, if we can pretend for the sake of false clarity that there were only two sides in any war. Each side spent days and weeks tracking the enemy through tangled forests, brambles, and swamps, and each side accused the other of launching attacks that were horrifyingly violent and inappropriately aimed at noncombatants, especially women, children, and the elderly. Furthermore, Indian and English men had different styles of warfare and brought different expectations to battle.[1] Surprise attacks on small parties and ambushes on isolated settlements defined the scale and scope of warfare on the overlapping borders of Native, French, and English settlement.

One scene from a Pequot War (1636–37) battle embodies many of the tensions and ambiguities inherent in Anglo-Indian warfare, a new kind of war against strange enemies. In "a prettie passage worthy [of] observation," Captain John Underhill writes, "wee had an *Indian* with us that was an interpreter, being in English cloathes, and a Gunne in his hand." When this Indian was sighted by the enemy, they challenged him: "What are you an Indian or an English-man?" Surely the Pequot meant by this question: whose side are you on? Are you Indian or English? But in Underhill's telling of the story, masculinity as well as ethnicity was at stake in the answer the Pequot antagonist receives. He reports that the interpreter responded to the challenge by saying, "come hither . . . and I will tell you." Then "hee pulls up his cocke and let fly at one of them, and without question was the death of him."[2] Thus in Underhill's telling, an Indian, temporarily transformed into a real (English) man by English clothes and powerful phallic weaponry, fells an Indian man with his superior display of masculine force.

Underhill's comrade Lieutenant Lion Gardiner, the commander of Fort Saybrook, was similarly confused by his antagonists in another confrontation during the Pequot War. He was alarmed by the appearance of "a troop of Indians within musket shot" at the mouth of the Connecticut River, "laying themselves and their arms down behind a little rising hill and two great trees." In his memoirs of the war nearly thirty years later, he recalls that "presently came three Indians, creeping out and calling to us to speak with us." The Indians approached Gardiner and his translator, Thomas Stanton, warily and were suspicious of everything the English men said, even of their true identities. "They asked who we were, and he answered, Thomas and Lieutenant. But they said he lied." Finally they were assured of the English men's identities, for as Gardiner remembers, "when I spake to them they knew my voice, for one of them had dwelt three months with us." Despite this admission of familiarity on both sides, the theme of confused or mistaken identities continued through the encounter. When the Indians "asked us if we would fight with Niantecut (Niantic) Indians, for they were our friends and came to trade with us," Gardiner replies, "we knew not the Indians one from another, and therefore would trade with none." The Indians continued with their questions: "Have you fought enough? We said we knew not yet. Then they asked if we did use to kill women and children? We said they should see that hereafter." But English men were not the only ones who could dissemble. Gardiner reports that after being "silent a small space . . . they said, We are Pequits, and have killed Englishmen, and can kill them as mosquetoes, and we will go to Conectecott and kill men, women, and children." Were they really Pequots, or Niantics as they had first claimed? Did they originally intend to trade, or to fight? Had they changed their minds because of Gardiner's subtly menacing replies to their questions? Or did they just want to intimidate the English into thinking they were Pequot warriors? (And with so many Algonquian speakers like these allied with the English against the Pequots, cases like this one were even more confusing.)

In this encounter the Indians and English provoked each other with words, but the Indians may have meant to provoke the English with their appearance as well: several of them were dressed in English men's clothing. This is a detail that Gardiner holds back in his narrative until after he reports the Indians' deadly threat. This combination of aggressive parley and English clothing enraged the translator: "When Thomas Stanton had told me [the threat to kill English people], he prayed me to shoot that rogue, for, said he, he hath an Englishman's coat on, and saith that he hath killed three, and these other four have their cloathes on their backs." While Gardiner demurred to fire on the Indians dressed in English clothing, the cultural cross-dressing had evidently angered Thomas Stanton, the man whose job it was to interpret the Indians.[3] This is no doubt because the clothing was evidence of the Indians' claims of having killed English men, but it also may have reflected English men's discomfort about the blurring of English and Indian identities, and of their concerns that Indians might successfully masquerade as English men, as "real" (English) men. In a war that was so confusing, with an enemy that seemed constantly to defy all expectations, having an enemy looking from a distance like one's own army presented a problem from a practical military perspective. But beyond the practical complications, the use of English clothing by Indians, and of Indian garments by English people, held deeper and sometimes more troubling meanings for Indian and English people alike.

This scene from the Pequot War was only the beginning of more than a century of anxiety over the appropriation, use, and display of English garments seized by Indians, and of English people being put into Indian dress. This anxiety was especially acute in war, but the rapid and widespread adoption of European-made cloth and clothing gained through trade or diplomatic connections meant that there were many different reasons a Native man or woman would appear in English garb. Cultural cross-dressing became a recurring theme on the colonial New England frontier, one that had different meanings and was put to different uses by English people and Indians alike throughout colonial America.[4] Like understanding a foreign language, understanding clothing requires translation too, as it can be expressive of the subjectivity, emotions, and social position of the wearer.

Both the English and the Indians had long taken clothing and other items from the bodies (dead or alive) of their vanquished enemies, but this practice took on new meanings in colonial America. For the English, being stripped of their clothing and made over as Indians or witnessing cultural cross-dressing by Indians was a disturbing, even a deranging experience, as they feared the blurring of identities such practices implied. Wearing apparel taken from their enemies had different meanings for the Indians: they sometimes did it to mock the English, sometimes perhaps to honor them, and sometimes to celebrate their victories on the battlefield. All of these uses and their meanings implied an intimacy between captive and captor, victim and victor, that made sense within the Indian understanding of war. Of course, this intimacy, this blurring of ethnic and cultural boundaries, was precisely what the English found so offensive and fearsome.[5]

Furthermore, the use of the term "cross-dressing" is intentional, as English people were disturbed by cultural cross-dressing because it blurred not just ethnic boundaries but gender identities as well. In the eyes of the English, ethnicity in the seventeenth century was a mutable phenomenon, and they feared that Indians might claim the privileges of Englishness as long as they dressed and performed the part. Similarly, gender was understood not as a fixed biological or chromosomal identity in the early modern period but as one that was constructed from a variety of gestures, words, behaviors, and material goods—most especially clothing and adornment.[6] Before Enlightenment classification and nineteenth-century scientific racism, clothing was read as representative of bodily truths, signifying the ethnicity, class, and gender of the wearer in the early modern period.[7] When English men saw Indian men dressed in their clothing, they saw an impersonation not of a genderless Englishness, but of gendered English men. Indian men wearing or brandishing plundered English clothing could also be interpreted as a mockery of English manhood. Similarly, when English men and women were stripped of their European-style clothing and put into Indian garments, they feared taking on what seemed to them the androgyny of Indians manifested in their dress and gender roles.[8] Most of the New England evidence involves Indian and English men, offering the historian an opportunity to focus on the challenges to English masculinity posed by cultural cross-dressing.

The meaning of cultural cross-dressing changed over time. In New England, seventeenth- and early eighteenth-century English men and women were much more threatened by the prospect of Indians transforming themselves into English men and women. But by the middle of the eighteenth century, after a century of disease, warfare, and the seizure of their lands, and the defeat of their French allies, Indians no longer posed the political and military threat they once had to English conquest. After the Seven Years' War (1756–63), New England was no longer the volatile frontier it had been, and it ceased to produce the stream of war correspondence, captivity narratives, and histories of its Indian wars that kept its presses busy through most of its colonial history. Anglo-Indian warfare shifted southward and to the west, and Anglo-American soldiers, officers, and war captives in these new borderlands had the same experiences described earlier by New Englanders. These people then took over the production of the kinds of texts that no longer suited New England and cut and fashioned them for their own purposes.

Both Indians and English people invested dress and adornment with a great deal of symbolic power and understood them as markers of both ethnicity and gender. The production and use of woolen and linen cloth was especially significant from the English point of view, as apparel made from woven cloth was uniquely European, and thus on the Anglo-Indian frontier it was powerfully expressive of European identity. Renaissance England was a society in which clothing was a commodity rich in real and symbolic value. Cloth production was central to its economy, clothing was a costly and treasured possession, and livery was commonly offered as a wage supplement to household servants and apprentices. Furthermore, clothing marked gender, rank, age, and status; on the Anglo-Indian frontier, amidst a people who did not produce woven cloth, it marked ethnicity as well. But clothing was not only symbolic or expressive of the identity of the wearer, it was potentially transformative, as emancipation from servitude was commonly marked with a new suit of clothes, and boy actors on the Elizabethan stage were turned into women by their costumes.[9] Here was the pleasure and the danger inherent in clothing: it could obscure or transform identities. If clothing could turn bound people free and boys into women, perhaps it could turn Indians into the English and the English into Indians, at least temporarily.

In colonial British America cloth was an item of great economic and cultural value, perhaps even more than in Old England. English women produced little cloth domestically until the later seventeenth century, and it was a mode of production never adopted by northeastern Indians in the colonial period.[10] In one seventeenth-century New England colony, probate records over forty years attest to the importance English householders placed on cloth items. They paid a high price for them, too, as the appraised value of clothing and cloth items was, on average, more than ten percent of the total value of an estate. Given this kind of capital investment, all but the meanest households had the same basic inventory of linens, aside from personal clothing: sheets, pillow biers (cases), blankets, napkins, towels, and tablecloths. Wealthier colonists sometimes had more specialized linens, like damask tablecloths, an embroidered "cubbard cloth," a "drinking cloth," and even a set of "childbed linen." Humbler households clearly aspired to increasing their stores of cloth, as spinning wheels, flax, cards, and wool and linen yarn appear in their inventories.[11]

Wherever English people went in North America, they took yards and yards of cloth with them. Even amidst the trials and privations of war, clean and sweet bedding was of utmost importance to the health and goodwill of English soldiers during the Seven Years' War. One English officer complained to General Jeffrey Amherst that he was of late "Obliged to have all the Men's bedding Wash'd, & put two Nights in the River, it was in so filthy a way, it could not be given to the Men; as yet, they all lie on the Boards in their Blankets, which I have done to prevent disorders coming among the Men, for certainly so dirty a place I never came into." Not having cloth or clothing was as great a hardship as the want of food and drink, as Joanna Cotton indicated in her 1697 letter about the hardships of King William's War (1688–97) for the people of Salisbury, Massachusetts: "These great rattes scarsety of bread and war which hath continued so long that thay are afraid to setle a man least that starve him, [and] severall talk of remouving[. T]he cry of the hungri is very great some nay many have neither meate drink nor cloath."[12]

Cloth and clothing were not only valuable for marking English identity on the frontier. Personal clothing was also valuable for marking other distinctions among the English in the New World. In fact, it was one of the only means by which colonials might be judged in such a mobile and fluid society. Associations with important people back in England might be exaggerated and letters of introduction forged, so appearance counted for a great deal. Clothing marked colonial bodies as bound or free, English or (in the absence of woven cloth) Indian, and through its cut and fashioning, as a child or adult. Fine cloth was necessarily imported cloth, which made it not only costly but also valuable as a signifier of class status. In the seventeenth century, New England authorities tried to control the use and display of fine fabrics and clothing through sumptuary laws, but these laws were rarely enforced. By the end of the century, fine, fashionable clothing could be worn by any and all who could afford it. Old-timers railed against the rise of "strange and fantastick Fashions . . . Naked Backs, and bare Breasts . . . powdered Foretops and Topgallants," all of this attire "not becoming the Christian, but the Comedian Assembly, not the Church, but Stage-play, where the Devil sits Regent in his Dominion."[13]

Those on the lowest rungs of society knew that the right clothing—or the wrong clothing—spoke powerfully. Even in the eighteenth century, American-made cloth was coarse compared with imported cloth, and it was frequently considered good enough only for undergarments, or to outfit servants and slaves. Indentured servant William Moraley offered a description of his ragged apparel as proof of his utter destitution in 1729: "I was dress'd at that time in a very odd Manner. I had on a Red Rug Coat, with Black Lining, Black Buttons and Button Holes, and Black Lace upon the Pockets and Facing; an old worn out Tye Wig, which had not been comb'd out for above a Fortnight; an unshaven Beard; a torn Shirt, that had not been wash'd for above a Month; bad Shoes; and Stockings all full of Holes." His scruffy appearance had attracted the attentions of a procurer of indentured labor. No wonder, then, that he was inveigled to bind himself to a Philadelphia-bound ship master for a shave and two pints of beer. Another traveler to Philadelphia who preceded Moraley by just a few years, Benjamin Franklin, agreed that clothing could be the making or the unmaking of a man or woman in this New World. In his autobiography Franklin remembers that during his journey, "I cut so miserable a Figure too, that I found by the Questions ask'd me I was suspected to be some runaway Servant, and in danger of being taken up on that Suspicion." When he arrived in the city he was self-conscious, "still in my Working Dress, my best Cloaths being to come round by Sea. I was dirty from my Journey; my Pockets were stuff'd out with Shirts and Stockings."[14]

Perhaps most importantly, clothing also marked bodies as male or female. Thus English people viewed cultural cross-dressing as a blurring or obscuring of gender identities as well as ethnicity.[15] In the chaos of struggling seventeenth-century settlements, English colonists sometimes tolerated women wielding a greater (although still limited) measure of economic power and independence than they had claimed in England.[16] But because a gendered hierarchy was central to the structure and functioning of colonial society, church and civil authorities worked together to punish men and women whose behavior blurred gender boundaries or challenged the patriarchal order.[17] Clothing as an outward manifestation of a bodily truth could either disrupt or maintain the gendered social order. For example, Thomas/

ine Hall was presented before the Virginia court for sometimes claiming to be and dressing as a man, and other times claiming to be and dressing as a woman. Depending on Hall's outward appearance, he or she would engage in either traditional men's labors or women's work. Various community members testified that they knew he was a man, or that she was surely a woman. Several examinations of Hall's genitalia yielded inconclusive results, so Hall was sentenced to broadcast his or her indeterminate gender status by wearing both breeches and an apron.[18] The choice of breeches and an apron was not incidental, as they were two of the most gendered items of contemporary European apparel. Breeches were the ultimate symbol of adult manhood, as both women and very young boys wore gowns. Cloth aprons were equally symbolic of womanhood, as they were practical garments associated not only with women but with women's domestic responsibilities.[19]

Both Algonquians and the Iroquois also used dress and adornment to denote status and gender, and English observers were intensely interested in describing and in attempting to decode Indian styles of self-presentation.[20] Thomas Morton, a sympathetic reporter of Native ways, notes that although Indians did not dress themselves in woven cloth, they used their attire to communicate social distinctions like age, status, and gender much as the English. His description implicitly draws parallels between English and Indian dress, noting that Indians wore skins and other bodily adornments in such a way as to preserve their modesty and to mark gender and age differences. "Every male after hee attaines unto the age, which they call Pubes, wereth a belt about his middell, and a broad peece of lether that goeth betweene his leggs, and is tuckt up both before and behinde under that belt." With these "breechclouts," Native men girded their loins for the same reasons that English men used shifts and codpieces: "this they weare to hide their secreats of nature; which by no meanes they will suffer to be seene, so much modesty they use in that particular, those garments they always put on." In addition to this, the men usually wore a deer skin around their waists. The women, on the other hand, used two deer or bear skins sewed together to cover their nakedness. Morton emphasizes the dignity of women so generously covered: "[The skins are] so lardge that it trailes after them, like a great Ladies trane, and in time I thinke they may have their Pages to beare them up." Once again, Morton emphasizes the natural modesty of the Indian women: "if any of their women would at any time shift one, they take that which they intend to make use of, and cast it over them round, before they shifte away the other, for modesty, being unwilling to be seene to discover their nakednesse, and the one being so cast over, they slip the other from under them in a decent manner, which is to be noted in people uncivilized, therein they seeme to have as much modesty as civilized people, and deserve to be applauded for it."[21]

Nevertheless, many European observers focused on what they saw as the essentially androgynous features of Indian costume, both before and after Native peoples adopted European cloth and clothing. They note that men and women alike had "no apparel but skins, except they have it from the English or French," although like Morton they note that the skins were fashioned and worn differently. Seasonal variation on dress was accomplished by turning garments inside-out: "in winter they wear the hair side inwards, in summer outwards." Children typically were "continuall[y] naked until they be about five or six years," but in some tribes little girls wore an apron over their waist and hips from a very early age. Elderly men wore deerskin leggings year-round, but in northern New England winters, all men wore them for warmth. Upon the beginning of the Euro-Indian trade, Indian men and women alike adopted the use of European-made men's coats and shirts, as well as cloth and blankets for cloaks. European breeches were universally unpopular with Indian men, who found them uncomfortably constraining. Aside from eschewing trousers, Europeans typically noted that Indian men did not wear hats or beards, which also seemed to enhance their androgyny: since men as well as women went "bare-headed with long hair; sometimes you shall not know the men from the women but by their breasts; the men having no hair on their faces."[22]

While English men found the absence of hats, beards, and breeches striking on Indian men, Indians engaged in other forms of body fashioning to express their role and status within their communities. The symbolic power of hair was one important aspect of denoting status. Hairlessness was associated with powerlessness, perhaps because baldness was associated with babies and old men. Thus, boys were not allowed to grow their hair long or to dress it elaborately as warriors did, with shells, beads, feathers, animal skins and fur, and bones. Women's hairstyles also changed with major life passages. Long hair on women was a marker of sexual maturity and marital status: marriageable girls wore long bangs, but upon marriage women cut their hair and wore a head cover until it grew out again. Older women wore coiffures as complicated as the warriors', while mourners advertised their grief by cutting off their hair. Body painting and tattoos also were important adornments, without which Indian costume was incomplete. William Pote, Jr., taken in Nova Scotia in 1745, describes the elaborate

Figure 7

Figures 7–10. John Simon's mezzotints of the "Four Indian Kings," after the paintings by John Verelst, commemorated the Indians' visit to England and appearance at Court. All of the men are shown wearing a combination of English and Indian garments and styles, which was typical of Indians in the northeastern borderlands in the eighteenth century. Three of the kings (Figures 8–10) are shown bare-legged (and bare-chested), wearing principally an English shirt, a blanket wrap, and moccasins; this was a popular hybrid style of dressing among Indian men and women alike. But Hendrick (Tee Yee Neen Ho Ga Row), identified as the "Emperour of the Six Nations," is shown almost fully clothed in the European style (Figure 7), with a shirt, coat, trousers, stockings, and heavy leather shoes with buckles. His greater conformity to European men's style of dress was perhaps intended to illustrate his rank over the other Indian men, whereas the other men's styles of dress link them to older depictions of Indian women and men as androgynous and substantially "naked" compared to Europeans. This item is reproduced by permission of the Huntington Library, San Marino, California.

Figure 8

grooming his captors engaged in before their triumphant arrival in Québec with their canoes full of war captives: "This morning our Indians Painted themselves in an Extraordinary manner, and Trim'd up their hair and painted ye Indian prisoners, and made great preparation for their appearance at Québec." But it wasn't just their own hair the Indians prepared for the journey, as Pote reports: "they Fixed Poles in ye middle of as many Connews as they had scalps, and hung up their Scalps on ye Top of ye poles. When we arrived Near Québec, there was almost a Continuall Coohooping, one Sort to Distinguish ye Number of prisoners, another ye No, of Scalps and ye other ye Number they had killed."[23]

Accordingly, when English captives were taken their captors often

Figure 9

tried to "Indianize" their appearance by cutting their hair and beards and painting their faces in the Indian style. After being captured in Haverhill, Massachusetts, in 1708, Joseph Bartlett met a similar fate en route to Montreal when he says that his captors "cut the hair from one side of my head—greased the remainder and my face, and painted the latter." Because he was a young man of twenty-one or twenty-two at the time of his capture, Bartlett was apparently given the stylized haircut and markings of an Indian warrior. After William Pote's capture, he reports that he was brought to an uninhabited island by his captors where, he reports, "ye Indians told me to pull of my shirt and wash it, for I must appear Before ye [French] General ye Next day, at this place, they Cut ye Indian prisoners hair and shaved them and painted their faces In ye manner of their own, and had a great

Figure 10

Desire to serve [me] in ye Same manner." However, he writes, "I pleaded so much against it, and told ym I was not of their Complexion, and it was more Convenient, I should Be in ye fasion of ye French, there fore they Let me go as I was quite out of Mode." Another captive he met in prison in Québec was unable to resist a similar fate: "one of ye Prisoners yt was taken at Serostogo yt gives us a Verey poor account of ye a fair yt happened with ym ye Indians had Cut his hair, a la mode des Sauvages, and painted his face." After Robert Eastburn was taken by Indians in western Massachusetts in the 1750s, he was made over as a proper Indian man. First, he says, his Indian master "insisted that I must be shaved, and then he would let me alone (I had at that Time a long Beard, which the Indians hate) with this

Motion I readily complied, and then the *Indian* seemed content." Next, an Indian "painted me, and put a Belt of Wampum round my Neck." Eastburn explains Indian men's antipathy to hats even as he complains about the inconvenience: Even on a four-mile march, "our Heads were not allowed to be covered, lest our fine Paint should be hid, the Weather in the mean Time very cold, like to freeze our Ears." Resisting a haircut had deadly consequences for one captive, according to Thomas Brown, who told the story of another English captive taken during the Seven Years' War who refused to submit to a hair cut, "upon which [the Indians] prepared to burn him." After he spent some time being burned at the stake, the Indians cut his Achilles tendons and forced him to run around until he threw himself into the fire to end his agony.[24]

Although English observers noted and commented on the various aspects of Indian dress and adornment, they still used the word "naked" to signify Indian difference. Although it seems contradictory to describe the apparel worn by "naked" Indians, this paradox had its ideological uses. Like the oppositional binaries "savage/civilized," "heathen/Christian," and "fair/tawny," the distinction of being either "naked" Indians or "clothed" English people was a marker of difference noted by many English commentators in the colonial period. Even commentators and publications that emphasized the modesty of the Indians suggested that this modesty was relative. The title page of Thomas Morton's *New English Canaan* has a very suggestive engraving: a nude (from the waist up) couple, a kind of Adam and Eve emerging from the swirls and flourishes of a baroque Eden. Nakedness was a highly suspect state in the minds of the English because of the reformed Protestant obsession with original sin. Adam and Eve were not ashamed of their nakedness until they ate from the tree of knowledge and were banished from the Garden of Eden. Thus, in the minds of the English nakedness was a sign of insolence, of a refusal to admit sin, and of a rejection of God's laws.[25]

Benjamin Thompson evokes this notion of Indians as undressed and therefore uncivilized people when he calls King Philip's army "a ragged regiment, a naked swarm / Whom hopes of booty doth with courage arm." Benjamin Church, in his account of King Philip's War (1675–78), relates a story about trying to apprehend an Indian prisoner: "but the *Indian* having no Clothes on slip'd from him, and ran again." According to Church, the Indian's nakedness was both a symbol and a tactic of cunning savagery and amorality. Once again, Church and his prey "skuffled and fought pretty smartly, until the *Indian* by the advantage of his nakedness slip'd from his hold again." When help finally arrived for Church, "twas so dark" that his rescuer "could not distinguish them by sight," so he felt the writhing bodies, "the one being clothed, and the other naked" and thereby determined which one he should kill. Church also gives an account of Philip's ignominious death as the great Wampanoag sachem ran for his life from the English "without any more clothes than his small breeches and stockings." After he was shot down in a swamp, some of Church's men "took hold of him by his Stockings, and some by his small Breeches, (being otherwise naked) and drew him thro' the Mud unto the Upland, and a doleful, great, naked, dirty beast, he look'd like." When Abenakis raided her Dover, New Hampshire, home in 1724, Elizabeth Hanson described the thirteen Indians as "all naked." In fact, the nakedness of these Indians proved even stranger when she discovered that they carried with them "old Beaver-Skin Match-Coats, which the *Indians* having hid (for they came naked as is said before)." Stranger still, she learned that "they were used more for Food than Rayment: Being cut out in long narrow Straps, they gave us little Pieces, which by the *Indians* Example we laid on the Fire till the Hair was singed away, and then we eat them as a sweet Morsel, experimentally knowing, that *to the hungry Soul every bitter thing is sweet.*"[26]

For all of their efforts to draw distinctions between themselves and the Indians, English observers and recorders ended up affirming the symbolic importance of clothing and adornment in both cultures. English captivity narratives and accounts of colonial wars reveal that Native people were equally invested in the significance of dress and understood it as a signifier of ethnicity, which is why stripping bodies (dead and alive) was such a prominent feature in warfare and the taking of war captives. In both Algonquian and Iroquois cultures, war captives were most often brought into Indian villages to be adopted into new families. Highly ritualized torture and eventual execution awaited some adult male captives, but for the most part, captives were put through a series of ceremonies and ordeals designed to bring them into the fold of their new Indian families.[27] When Joseph Bartlett arrived at the Iroquois village that ultimately adopted him, they confined him for a while. He reports that "I believe they held a counsel whether to burn me or not. But God, who hath the hearts of all in his hands, spared my life." God did not spare him some ritual torture, however, as "the Indians that took me . . . permitted a squaw to cut off one of my little fingers, and another to strike me severely with a pole." Soon after they "bound up my little finger with plantain leaves, and gave me some roasted pomkin to eat." Next came the introduction of the captives to the whole village: "Here there came together a great company that filled the wigwam, which was nearly forty feet in length, where they sung and danced a greater part of the night, as many at a time as could stand from one end of the wigwam to the other. In this manner they danced round their fire." Dancing too was a means by which captives were brought into their new community, as dancing and singing were important skills in Native villages. Bartlett reports, "they often invited me to dance; but I refused them from time to time. However, they pulled me up, and I went around once with them."[28]

In Bartlett's account of the elaborate and extended ceremony, he provides evidence that stripping and redressing were central to the adoption of captives into new families and communities. Captives were not just thrown into Indian villages and expected to make their own way; they were given to specific families and sometimes assigned the identities of dead or captured family members with the expectation that they would fulfill the missing person's function in the family. "One of them took me by the hand, and, after a lengthy speech, gave me to an old squaw, who took me into another wigwam. . . . An English woman, who belonged to one of the French nuns, came in, and told me I need not fear, for I was given to this squaw in lieu of one of her sons, whom the English had slain; and that I was to be master of the wigwam." Bartlett, who had been provisionally stripped of his English clothing and dressed by his captors back in Massachusetts, was once again stripped and redressed by his Indian mother. "After a little crying and whimpering, she made me put off my Indian stockings and my blanket, and gave me others; and she warmed some water, and washed the red paint and grease from my face and hands." It was important for Bartlett to be dressed not just in any Indian style but in the style his Indian mother preferred, perhaps in the very garments of her dead son. The taking of war captives seems to have been especially central to Iroquois warfare in the post-contact period. Daniel Richter has argued that the taking of captives was not just the result but rather the purpose of what he calls "mourning wars."[29]

The account of Father Pierre Millet, who was captured at Fort Frontenac in 1690 by another Iroquoian tribe, the Oneidas, suggests that stripping the captive was such an important part of the adoption ritual that it was supervised by tribal elites. Millet wrote that he was informed by a man he identified as "the Chief" among his captors that "they should not allow me to be stripped" immediately, "but that they should take me, with all my clothes to their village," implying that he would be stripped only at the appropriate time and place. Once the chief left, as he recalls, "some of the others demanded, pulling off at the same time—my belt, another took my hat, a third my cassock, and a fourth my shirt. Finally the rest pulled off my shoes and stockings." He was left naked except for "only my drawers, which were even demanded by some who said they had dreamed of them, but my conductors opposed themselves to these observers of bad dreams, and saved me from the hands of those who wished to kill me at once."[30] Although the chief's orders did not carry the day, his reassurance to Millet implied that stripping was part of a planned ritual, one that was perhaps reserved for ranking members of the group.

Some captives were stripped and redressed more than once. After Thomas Brown was badly wounded while on a scouting expedition from Fort William Henry in the winter of 1757, he was taken up by French-allied Indians who, he writes, "stripp'd off all my Cloaths, and gave me a Blanket. And the next Morning, they cut off my Hair and painted me," and tattooed the back of his hand "with Needles and Indian-ink." Despite the elaborate transformation he had already undergone, it was only the first of many during his four-year captivity. When he arrived at the Indians' village, he reports that "the Men and Women came out to meet us, and stripp'd me naked" again. Soon afterward Brown was taken in by the French, but then reclaimed by Indians who "came and took me with them to *Montreal* again, and dressed me in their Habit." Brown's journey as a captive was much longer than most, as he eventually found himself taken into a community of Indians on the Mississippi River and was given an Indian mother. "I liv'd with her during the Winter, and was employed in Hunting, dressing Leather, &c. being cloath'd after the *Indian* Fashion." When he joined another party of Indians, he was once again "stripp'd by the *Indians*. and dressed after their Manner."[31]

Many captivity narratives suggest that being dressed in Indian garments meant adjusting to what English people perceived as a lower standard of comfort and warmth. They were "sometimes . . . pinched with the Bitter *Frost*, without Rags to cover their Nakedness," according to Cotton Mather. John Gyles, taken as a boy from an English settlement in Maine in 1689, spent six years as a captive on the St. John's River. In his narrative, he reports that Indian apparel nearly cost him his life on a winter hunt: "We had not travelled far before my Moose-Skin: Coat (which was the only Garment that I had on my Back, and the Hair was in most Places worn off) was froze stiff round my Knees like a Hoop, as likewise my Snow-shoes & Shoe-clouts to my Feet!" His frostbite was so severe that he reports losing all of the skin off of his feet and ankles, as well as his toenails and one toe.

When Hannah Swarton was taken from Casco Bay in 1690, Cotton Mather reported that she was "pinched with Cold, for want of Cloathing, being put by them into an *Indian Dress,* with a sleight Blanket, no Stockings, and but one pair of *Indian-Shoes,* and of their Leather Stockings for the Winter: [Her] Feet were pricked with sharp Stones, and prickly Bushes sometimes; and other times Pinched with Snow, Cold, and Ice, that [she] travelled upon, ready to be frozen, and faint for want of Food." Despite their complaints, captives were probably not dressed poorly compared to their captors, since the goal was to integrate them fully into their new families and communities. In fact, William Pote, Jr., reports seeing a captive English girl who had received rather lavish Indian apparel: "Ye Girl was Drossed after ye manner of ye Indians with a great quantity of wampom which ye Indians Call Extraordinary Embellishment."[32]

The stripping and reclothing of both male and female captives was central to Indian adoption rituals, but even the garments themselves—both the English clothing and Indian apparel they put on the captives—may have held special significance for the Indians. Scholars have written about the rituals of warfare in different Amerindian cultures and have identified ceremonies in which defeated warriors are honored through the ceremonies of their torture and execution. Ritual cannibalism was central to these ceremonies, as it was an opportunity for the victors to celebrate their courageous lives and honorable deaths. It was an opportunity to celebrate and literally to partake of the strength of their enemies. Aztec captors went further with this symbolic—or sympathetic—identification with their slain captives by wearing their flayed skins for twenty days.[33] Perhaps the swapping and sharing of clothing with the English captives held similar meaning on the Anglo-Indian frontier: like sharing a skin, it was an act that bound the captive and the captor together in an intimate embrace.[34] Of course, this kind of blurring of identities was precisely what worried the English.

The symbolism of being stripped and redressed might have been obvious at the time to European captives, or perhaps their understanding of its significance deepened with their knowledge of Indian beliefs and rituals. In any case, redeemed captives seem to have enacted a similarly transformative stripping and redressing upon their return to Euro-American communities. Many captives report feeling very self-conscious about their appearance upon leaving Indian captivity, and they were eager to reestablish their identities as English people through their clothing. John Gyles was eventually purchased by a French family with the assistance of a Franciscan priest. Because of his youth and the length of his captivity, he made a successful transition to living with the Indians, and was trained in all of the skills Indian men were expected to master. Nevertheless, he claims that he rejoiced at the opportunity to leave Indian society. When called into a cabin "where many well rigg'd Gentlemen" had assembled to negotiate his sale, he remembers attempting to "hide my self behind the Hangings, for I was much ashamed; thinking of my former wearing Cloaths, and of my living with People who could rigg as well as the best of them." He recalls being "dress'd up in an old greasy Blanket, without Cap, Hat, or Shirt, (for I had no Shirt for the last six Years, but that which was on my Back when I was taken)," which had certainly been stripped away, and which in any case he would have long since outgrown. He remembers that his new master "kindly receiv'd me" and gratefully reports that "in a few Days Madam made me an Oznabrigs Shirt and French Cap, and a Coat out of one of my Master's old Coats; then I threw away my greasy Blanket and Indian Flap, and look'd as smart as———."[35] In the mind of redeemed captives, being restored to Euro-American civilization necessarily meant being restored to European-style clothing and grooming—a legacy of the ceremony of being stripped and redressed by the Indians.

Gyles's story suggests that while cultural cross-dressing was considered dangerous principally because of the blurring of gender and ethnic identities, it could also erase or obscure European signs of class status and among officers, their military rank. Upon the surrender of Fort Massachusetts to the French and their Indian allies in 1747, the Reverend John Norton commented on the good quarter offered by the French general: "[contrary to Indian practices] we should all be allowed to keep our Clothing." Although the English despised their French rivals for North America, they appreciated the fact that the French shared their notions of fashion and warmth. Norton remarks that while he was imprisoned in Québec, "the Jesuits and some unknown Gentlemen, understanding I was short on it for Clothing, sent me several Shirts, a good winter Coat, some Caps, a pair of Stockings, and a few Handkerchiefs, which were very acceptable." When ransomed to the French, William Pote, Jr., also remarked gratefully that his new captors understood his need for European-style clothing, not just to preserve his cultural identity but also to distinguish himself as an officer among the enlisted men. Shortly after his arrival at the prison in Québec, he was visited by "mr marain ye Generals Son that took me, and Called me out from among ye sailors, and asked me if I had Lived with ym Ever Since I had been In Prison. I Told him yes at which he seemed Exceeding angrey, and asked ye prison keeper ye Reason of our Being Treated with So much Indiferance." How could his jailers have failed to note his status as an officer, and thus have housed him together with the common sailors? "I Told him I supposed I Could give him a Sufficient Reason, and that was our Being Naked and appearing In Such a Miserable Condition, as we had ye misfortune to be put In ye hands of ye Indians, and striped of all our Cloathing." Clothing displayed not only ethnicity and gender but status as well. Marain, sharing Pote's horror, "did me ye honour, as to speak In my Recommendation to ye prison keeper, and whent to his Lordship ye General and brought an order for us to be put forthwith, with ye two Capts. affore mentioned, where we had a Genteel Maintanance mr Southerland and my Self."[36] The "misfortune" of being stripped by the Indians meant that his French captors could not immediately read his status among the other prisoners.

Another captivity narrative suggests even more strongly that the ceremony of being stripped and redressed remained significant to captives after they rejoined European society. Thomas Brown, who was serially stripped and reclothed in the many stages of his journey from western Massachusetts to the St. Lawrence River valley and eventually to the Mississippi River, illustrates the effectiveness of this Indian ritual when he was picked up by a trader and brought back to Montreal to live with a French family. He complains that he was forced to labor in the fields, as he writes, "for my Victuals and Cloathing; I fared no better than a Slave." Like most French families harboring English captives, he reports that "the Family often endeavoured to persuade me to be of their Religion, making many fair Promises if I would: Wanting to see what Alteration this would make in their Conduct towards me, one Sunday Morning I came to my Mistress, and said; *Mother, will you give me good Cloaths if I will go to Mass?* She answered, *Yes, Son, as good as any in the House.*" Perhaps it is not coincidental that Brown asked for clothing if he proved his willingness to share the family's beliefs. After four years with the Indians, he may have come to associate being stripped and reclothed as a badge of submission, or of belonging, or both. In any case, the good clothes were only one symbol of his improved station in the family. "She [gave me the clothes], and I rode to Church with two of her Daughters; in giving me Directions how to behave, they told me, *I must do as they did.* When we came Home, I sat at the Table and ate with the Family, and every Night and Morning was taught my Prayers."[37] Brown writes approvingly of the treatment he received after putting on his new clothes and agreeing to go to Mass.

While Brown's narrative illustrates the enduring importance of stripping and redressing for captives, it also suggests why English people found these practices alarming: they worked. Less than half of all English captives taken from 1675 to 1763 returned home again to New England. Many captives perished during their captivity, a few were killed by the Indians, and a large number disappeared entirely from the historical record after being taken into captivity. But an alarmingly large number voluntarily remained with their French or Indian captors—nearly a third of all female captives and twelve percent of males.[38] These "white Indians" or adopted French Catholics, many of whom explicitly rejected the entreaties of their English families to return to live under English government, were proof of the hazards of the Anglo-Indian frontier. Cultural boundaries were blurred and crossed, and sometimes English men, women, and children never came home again.[39]

In a world as disordered by war, privation, and isolation as colonial America, cultural cross-dressing had no stable or fixed meaning, even in the same time and place and even if witnessed by the same observers. The context in which Indians and Europeans acquired each other's clothing and accessories was crucial to its interpretation.[40] Sometimes clothing served as an agent of diplomacy, and European-style clothing was first associated with high-ranking Indians. William Bradford recalls in his journal that on the occasion of their first visit to Massasoit, sachem of the Wampanoag, delegates from Plymouth colony "gave him a suite of cloaths, and a horsemans coate, with some other small things, which were kindly accepted, but they found but short commons, and came both weary and hungrie home." Despite this early resentment of what the English perceived as a stingy reception on the part of the Indians, gifts of cloth and clothing to high-status Indians became a common element in the rituals of frontier diplomacy. Boston merchant John Usher recommended to the New England Company in 1692 that "presentts of Laced Coates, Shooes, stockins, hatts & shirts with a small Sword and beltt be given to the Sachems. . . . as from the King," as tokens of respect for their dignity and power. During King Philip's War, Pequot leader Robin Cassicinamon was personally rewarded for his loyalty to the English with the gift of a shirt, on top of the twenty yards of cloth Connecticut Colony gave to Cassicinamon's followers.[41]

Throughout King Philip's War, Connecticut gave gifts of cloth and English coats not just to cement alliances with high-status Indians but to reward demonstrations of loyalty to the English. While the English might have perceived these gifts as securing Indian obedience to English political and military goals, Indian allies seem to have retained substantial bargaining power over the price of their cooperation with the English. For example, the English paid their Indian allies to deliver captive enemy Indians into their custody. Over the course of the war, the price of an Indian captive went up substantially: in September of 1675, Connecticut agreed to pay four yards of cloth for every enemy captive delivered to the English. Less than six months later, friendly Indians were entitled to two coats for every child or adult captive, and one coat for "suckling children."⁴² Thus, while the English might have read their clothing on Indian bodies as a sign of political submission in these circumstances, the Indians might well have read this as proof of their success in driving a hard bargain.

Clothing could also signify Indian cultural submission, as in the case of Indian converts to Christianity. When Sachem Ben Uncas, son of the great Mohegan sachem Uncas and ally of the English through the seventeenth century, "declared that he doth embrace the Christian religion," the Connecticut Assembly requested that the governor "procure for the said sachem a coat (made in the English fashion,) and a hat, and also a gown for the said sachem's wife" at the public charge.⁴³ Becoming a Christian meant dressing the part. Through the colonial period, English missionaries encouraged Indians in New England's "praying towns" to dress as the English did as a sign of their conversion to Christianity. In 1674, Daniel Gookin asserted that Christian Indians were easily identified "by their short hair, and wearing English fashioned apparel." In order to entice Indian parents to apprentice their children in English households, in 1660 the United Colonies of New England offered them one coat annually for every year their child remained in service "with godly masters, such as will engage to teach them to read well, and bring them in Christian nurtriture." In these cases, English magistrates and missionaries read the acceptance of European clothing (rightly or wrongly) as an outward sign of the Indians' conversion to English culture as well.⁴⁴

Although clothing played an important role in Anglo-Indian diplomacy and English missionary work, Natives did not wait for the English to bestow cloth and clothing upon them. By the time of permanent English settlement in New England, Europeans had been long involved in trading with the Indians there, and from the first Indians showed great interest in cloth, woolen blankets, coats, and shirts in particular. They actively sought cloth and clothing from European traders, so that most cloth and clothing used by Indians was probably acquired by trading wampum, furs, venison, and other Indian trade goods sought by Europeans. Indians wearing European clothing might have been signaling their interest in continued trade with Europeans and Euro-Americans or their interest in comity and coop-eration on the frontier.[45]

Just as the Indian use of European cloth and clothing was not always perceived as threatening by the English, so too there were circumstances in which English colonists deemed their use of Indian garments appropriate or even superior to their European equivalents. One example of this is the use of moccasins and snowshoes both in captivity and in English settle-ments. For English war captives, their transition to Indian society was marked first by the stripping of English shoes and the donning of Indian moccasins. This was practical as well as symbolic, as moccasins were widely respected as superior for back country travel. Upon their capture in Deer-field, Massachusetts, in 1704, the Rev. John Williams, his wife Eunice, and their children were all stripped of their shoes and "in the room of them" were given "Indian-Shoes, to prepare for [their] travel." William Pote, Jr., reports that his captors "took my shoos from me & Gave me a pair of Dear Skin mogisons such as they wear them selves, and Told me they was better and much Preferable to shoes to march in." An English captive seized in New Hampshire the same year recalled that losing his European-style shoes and receiving moccasins was part of a ceremonial ritual: "[The Indians] sang and danced round me, after which one of them bid me set down, which I did; and then they pull'd off my Shoes and Buckles, and took them from me." Then, "the next Day the Indians gave me a Pair of their Shoes, so that I travel'd with abundant more Ease than when I wore my own Shoes."[46] Apparently, some Indians planned ahead for such exigencies: a scout that came upon an Indian war party in New Hampshire in 1724 reported that the warriors each carried with them "a great many spare *Moggasons,* which were supposed for the supplying of Captives that they expected to have taken."[47]

The repeated iteration of the superiority of moccasins was perhaps in-tended for a reading audience far from the Anglo-Indian frontier, as by the eighteenth century most English colonists were probably very familiar with moccasins and the advantages they offered. English captives and observers of colonial warfare did not see wearing moccasins as a threat to their identi-ties, as they had adopted Indian footwear for their own use and even at-tempted to manufacture their own moccasins and snowshoes. The fact that they were made of leather, like English shoes and boots, probably made them more familiar than Indian skins in place of woven clothing. The En-glish were happy to defer to Indian expertise in the matter, as on the remote frontiers of English settlement especially, poor footwear could doom traveling armies or fleeing captives. A dispatch about a failed expedition to the Kennebec River in Maine in January of 1722 puts sole blame for its failure on the low quality of footwear supplied by Massachusetts Colony. On a mission to seize Father Sebastien Ralé at his highly successful mission at Norridgewock, Colonel Johnson Harmor and Captain Joseph Heath reported that French Jesuit was tipped off about their intended "visset," and their slow-moving army was unable to surprise him. Harmor and Heath claimed that they would have been successful "if wee had not been greviously Clog'd with ye Provinces Moginsons & snow shoos, which are a wild cheat. And therefore we take this oppertunity to Intreat you to move the Govtmt to prepare good materials & Imploy ye Four Hostages to make a quantity of good Indian snow shoos & Moginsons."[48] Apparently Massachusetts Colony was impressed enough with moccasins to attempt making its own, but Harmor and Heath thought that New England officials ought to get the benefit of the craftsmanship of Indian prisoners of war. They were doubtlessly eager to place blame for the failed expedition on anything but their own leadership. Nevertheless, their letter reveals that English colonists shared common ideas about the quality of Indian footwear.

Thus, English use of Indian footwear and the use of cloth and English-made clothing in Indian apparel were commonplace by the end of the seventeenth century, although as noted above, Indians did not tailor or wear these items like English men and women. In 1674, John Josselyn explained, "since they have had to do with the English they purchase of them a sort of Cloth called trading cloth of which they make Mantles, Coats with short sleeves, and caps for their heads which the women use." Mary Rowlandson reported spending her time in captivity in 1676 knitting stockings and sewing shirts at the behest of her Indian masters and mistresses, including a shirt and a cap at King Philip's own request.[49]

After more than fifty years of trade, diplomacy, and war in New England, Indian use of European-made cloth and clothing had many meanings, but these items were commonly understood to be valuable possessions that both Indians and English people invested with great significance. In fact, their many meanings made them even more fraught and dangerous commodities. Scholars of praying towns suggest that by the last quarter of the seventeenth century, English clothing was not a reliable indicator of "friend" Indians or foes. Rather than containing the bodies of praying Indians in English clothing, the English began containing their bodies spatially either on bounded land or in prison camps during King Philip's War.[50] Because English cloth and clothing were so popular and worn so widely by

New England Indians, English men and women could distinguish their allies from their enemies only by confining Christian Indians within strictly defined geographical limits. What did an Indian man in an English man's coat or an Indian woman in an English shirt mean in 1680? He or she could be a praying Indian or a wartime ally loyal to the English, an active participant in colonial trade, an enemy wearing a trophy stripped from a defeated English man, or any combination of these things. Of course, the possibility that the Indian was an enemy wrapped in the garments of a slain or captive English person was what the English found most alarming. What was perhaps even more disturbing was the fact that by the end of the seventeenth century, the English had no way of knowing for sure what their clothing on Indian backs signified in terms of political loyalties, religious affiliation, or warlike intentions.

By the eighteenth century, captives recorded Indian interest in their clothing and cloth items without surprise, demonstrating the importance that both English and Indian peoples put on these goods. Upon her capture by the Abenakis in 1724, Elizabeth Hanson noted that the Indians' first move, after killing one of her children, was "rifling the House in a great Hurry, . . . [they] packed up some Linnen, Woolen, and what other Things pleased them best." In a negotiation for the return of an English captive in Maine the same year, European-style clothing played a crucial role in making the deal: "Having had some talk about the Price they thro' much persuasion let the Captive come to us and having given him some Victuals we sent him back again with a Jackett & pair of breeches to shew them. They liked them very well and sent the Captive to us again." Next, "the Commander sent over a red Coat which they took a great fancy to, so that when the Captive went with it to them he with our persuasion got his Master to come within sight of ye Garrison. At last the Captive being advised by our Commander proffer'd to give his Master to the value of five and twenty Pounds which was their lowest Price." The Indians initially agreed to the deal, but negotiations broke down later. In the end, the Indians kept the coat, "whch is all they have rec'd for they never came to us." In fact, Indian use of European cloth and clothing became so widespread that at least one captive in the 1750s was stripped and then reclothed by his new Indian mother in a European shirt: Robert Eastburn recalls, "I shewed the old *Squaw* my *Shirt* (having worn it from the Time I was first taken Prisoner, which was about seven Weeks) all in *Rags, Dirt,* and *Lice*; she said it was not *good*, and brought me a new One, with ruffled Sleeves (saying that is good) which I thankfully accepted."[51]

Cloth or clothing seized as a spoil of war or as the result of Indian captivity was interpreted very differently throughout colonial Anglo-America than clothing given as tribute or in trade. Despite the fact that English treatises on warfare had long recognized plunder as the right of the victors, the English were outraged when Indians claimed the same rights on the battlefields of colonial America.[52] One of the anecdotes that begins this chapter is a perfect illustration of how the English reading of Indians in English clothing could change according to how it was thought to have been acquired: in Gardiner's tale, only when the English men understand the coats to be the spoils of war does the translator Stanton urge Gardiner to "shoot that rogue, for . . . he hath an Englishman's coat on." When confronted by Indians who had taken English clothing by force, the English saw cultural cross-dressing not as a sign of submission, but variously as a sign of insolence, of mockery, and of outright rebellion against English pretensions to rule America. Moreover, English colonists were concerned about the symbolism of their captives dressed in the Indian fashion. Just as they sometimes saw Indians in European clothing as submissive and accepting of English culture, they feared the same cultural submission they read in English people dressed in Indian garb.[53]

Accordingly, for both Indians and English people, clothing was part of the discourse on status and power on the frontier. A scene from Mary Rowlandson's captivity narrative demonstrates that she was fearful that losing her clothing meant losing her status as an elite English woman. When an Indian woman holding a baby demanded that Rowlandson "give her a piece of [her] apron, to make a flap (presumably, a diaper)," Rowlandson told her, "I would not." Rowlandson apparently saw the request as inappropriate and believed herself to be in a position to refuse it. What could this Indian woman want with her apron? Although Indian and English women's roles were similar in that they were both responsible for preparing food, looking after their households, and child care, there was one great difference between them: Indian women performed agricultural labor, whereas English men were the farmers, a fact that appalled English commentators and led them to denigrate both Indian women as too rough and masculine, and Indian men as too feminine. Rowlandson's cloth apron was symbolic of her status as an English woman who did not do field work and of her roles as a wife and mother with a household to manage. To yield it not just to another woman but to an Indian woman who would allow it to be soiled by an infant was an outrage to English womanhood. Yet Rowlandson was no longer the mistress of her own household; she was now the servant of another woman. When "my mistress bade me give it," she writes, "still I said no." The woman with the baby then "told me if I would not give her a piece, she would tear a piece off it: I told her I would tear her coat then." Only when her mistress swings "a stick big enough to have killed [her]" (but misses) does Rowlandson relent and hand over the apron.[54] No doubt her mistress was irritated by her disobedient and selfish servant.

English men too were fearful of what Indians meant when they took their clothing. In his epic poem of King Philip's War, *New England's Crisis,* Benjamin Thompson makes it clear what English men thought was as stake in war with the Indians. He takes on the voice of Philip exhorting his warriors:

> Now if you'll fight I'll get you English coats,
> And wine to drink out of their captains' throats.
> The richest merchants' houses shall be ours,
> We'll lie no more on mats or dwell in bowers.
> We'll have their silken wives take they our squaws,
> They shall be whipped by virtue of our laws.[55]

In other words, Indian men are determined to become the masters of our households, and they'll achieve this first by putting on English clothes. Then, they'll presume to drink our wine and sleep in our beds with our wives. Having taken over our households, they will put all English people under the lash of their laws. Thus dressing like English men was merely the first step in a monstrous plan to master the English. While Thompson's poem reflects more English paranoia than Indian reality, there are hints that Thompson's fears were coming true on the far reaches of the frontier. Think of Thomas Brown, who when he put on a French suit "rode to Church with two of [his mistress's] Daughters" and then at dinner "sat at the Table and ate with the Family, and every Night and Morning was taught [his] Prayers," as though he were a dutiful son. Or, remember Joseph Bartlett, who after his Indian mother stripped and redressed him to replace her dead son "was to be master of the wigwam." These men took on the privileges of French and Indian manhood respectively because they dressed the part. What was to stop Indian men from claiming the same privileges when they put on English clothing?

The symbolic importance of clothing for Indians and English anxieties about this symbolism fed on each other, especially in the experience of warfare on the New England frontier. English observers and recorders of these wars focus on two aspects of cultural cross-dressing: first, the fact that English bodies—dead or alive—were stripped of their European clothing is noted and commented on again and again, in manuscripts as well as published records. Second, English commentators fixate on the uses to which Indians put this clothing. Sometimes the seized clothing was worn immediately, sometimes it was stored, and sometimes it was displayed ritually by other means.

Since "nakedness" was a marker of savagery, it was disturbing for English people to be reduced to "Adam's livery." Increase Mather, in his rhetorically florid *Brief History* of King Philip's War, remarks time and again that the insult of death was almost matched by the insult of nudity. When the Indians "barbarously murthered both men and women," he writes, they set to work "stripping the slain whether men or women, and leaving them in the open field as naked as in the day wherein they were born."[56] As noted above, clothing was central to the identities of the English colonists. Naked bodies were bodies out of context, bodies stripped of their Englishness and de-gendered. It may seem odd to suggest that English people perceived stripped bodies as de-gendered. Simply knowing the sex of a body was not enough to put it in its place; clothing provided the social and cultural context that made gender a useful category for structuring society. Recall the case of Thomas/ine Hall: clothing was the means by which the Virginia court made Hall's gender identity readable to the community. Since Hall's genital identity was inconclusive, so must his or her costume be. Thus, when English people were taken away from their farms, families, and faith by captivity or death, their tattered garments were literally the remnants of their claim to civilization, their identities as English men and English women.

Significantly, for English people both death and captivity on the Anglo-Indian frontier began with nakedness as the Indian victors stripped the bodies of the defeated and captured. English people were disturbed whenever Indians stripped their bodies of clothing, whether they were stripped as captives or as bodies killed in war.[57] The erasure of ethnic and gender identity implied in the stripping of clothing is repeatedly, almost obsessively, noted in reports of both published and manuscript accounts of Indian attacks. This stripping is described by survivors as almost as painful and obliterating as death itself. When Lancaster, Massachusetts, was sacked in February of 1676 in an early attack in King Philip's War, Mary Rowlandson reports that she saw a townsman attacked by Indians, who "knocked him in the head, and stripped him naked, and split open his bowels." When her brother-in-law "fell down dead" in the same attack, "the Indians scornfully shouted, and holloed, and were presently upon him, stripping him of his clothes." She writes of her increasing horror at the scene, finding one English colonist "chopped into the head with a hatchet, and stripped naked, and yet crawling up and down." During her twelve weeks of captivity, she was appalled to discover that an Indian who had been kind to her kept "bloody [English] clothes, with bullet holes in them" in his wigwam.[58]

English colonists continued to be horrified at the stripping of bodies that had fallen into the hands of Indians. While some bodies were scalped, another practice that outraged the English, stripping seems to have been a much more common phenomenon.[59] Increase Mather's *Brief History* of King Philip's war is similarly replete with mentions of stripped corpses and captives: in the late summer of 1675 in western Massachusetts, more than sixty English soldiers bringing a shipment of supplies were surprised by Indians who "stripped them of their clothes, and so left them to lye weltring in their own blood." At Kittery, Maine, two English men were killed and stripped by Indians, and when a party of English men went after their naked bodies, they too were fired on and many of them killed and wounded. In April 1676, half a dozen captives were taken from the town of Sudbury, Massachusetts. The Indians "stripped them naked, . . . caused them to run the Gauntlet," tortured them, and eventually executed them. The following month, one Captain Turner was shot and "fell into the hands of the *Uncircumcised,* who stripped him, (as some who say it affirm) and rode away upon his horse," leaving Turner to die of his wound. In an assault on Groton, Massachusetts, the previous month, "a parcel of *Indians*" set upon four English men as they left the garrison to fetch some hay. In the attack, "one of them [was] slain, stript naked, his body mangled, and dragged into the high-way, and laid on his back in a most shamefull manner." William Hubbard emphasizes the savagery of the attack by reiterating it and describing further abuses of the corpse: "This assault of theirs was managed with their wonted subtlety, and barbarous cruelty: for they stript the body of him whom they had slain in the first onset, and then cutting off his head, fixed it upon a pole looking towards his own land." The Indian mania for stripping and humiliating English bodies was not limited to those found on the fields of battle either, according to Hubbard: the Indians "dug up out of his grave" an English man who had been slain the week before, "cut off his head and one leg, and set them upon poles, and stript off his winding sheet." Stripping English bodies remained a prominent theme through the seventeenth century: some captives taken during King William's War were told "that when they came to this [Indian] Town, they must be Strip'd & Scourged, and Run the *Gantlet*," according to the Indian custom.[60]

Reports of Indians stripping English bodies continue through the colonial period. In King William's War and Queen Anne's War (1702–13), when the capture and trade of English captives reached its peak, English men, women, and children alike were stripped whether they were killed or taken captive. The Reverend John Williams noted that "at my going from the *Wigwam*, my best Clothing was taken away from me." The possibility of losing one's clothing in war, whether alive or dead, was something that English people had learned to expect. Nakedness was a condition familiar in war, although writers of captivity narratives continued to highlight it in outraged detail. A petitioner from Maine begging relief from the Massachusetts authorities after a 1751 Indian attack noted that he and his wife "saved themselves by getting down the cellar, which they had but time to do without putting on their Cloaths to Cover their Nakedness." Immediately after his capture in 1745, Nehemiah How saw an English man shot along the shore of a river; "some of the Indians swam over the River, & bro't the Canoe over the River, scalp'd & stript the dead Man." When Henry Grace was taken by the Mi'kmaq in the 1750s, he reports, "they took away my Hat, and began stripping me of every thing I had in the World." Robert Eastburn, taken in western Massachusetts about the same time, complains that the Indians "stripped me of my Cloathing, Hat, and Neckcloth (so that I had nothing left but a Flannel Vest, without Sleeves)." He lost even this vest a few days later, to an Indian and a French ally who, he recalls, "immediately assisted the *Indian* to strip me of my Flannel Vest, before mentioned, which was my All." James Derkinderin witnessed an attack in Nova Scotia in 1759, where the Indians "stripped" not just the dead but "dying men."[61] The stripping of English bodies by victorious Indians became common in colonial warfare, but it never lost its power to horrify the surviving English men and women who looked on.

That the loss of clothing was experienced as a loss of gender identity and status is most apparent in the descriptions of Indians stripping defeated English soldiers. The vision of Indians stripping the bodies of dead English men, taking not just their clothing but their weapons and armor as well, was a particularly disturbing aspect of English defeat. From their very first engagements with Indians, English soldiers were confident that their clothing and equipment was powerful and enviable. During the Pequot War, Underhill reports that a company of English soldiers were spied by Pequots "lying in ambush," who nevertheless "gave us leave to passe by them, considering we were too hot for them to meddle with us." What made the English "too hot" to bother with? Underhill claims that the English were too intimidating to attack because they were "compleatly armed, with Corslets, Muskets, bandileers, rests, and swords (as [the Pequots] themselves related afterward) did much daunt them."[62] Both Indian and English men understood that war was an arena for masculine achievement or humiliation, thus when vanquished in battle, the English had already been bested in one test of masculine worth. But bereft of their clothing, armor, and weapons, they were stripped of all proof of their manhood. What could be more insulting than to see the accoutrements of their masculinity on the bodies of their conquerors?

A story from King Philip's War illustrates the special regard Indians had for the wearable spoils of war and the meaning such plunder held for both the victor and the vanquished. After Benjamin Church's men had killed King Philip and taken many Narragansett prisoners in 1676, Church reports that one of Philip's ranking officers absented himself from their camp in the middle of the night. Church grew concerned when this man, Annawon, did not return for quite some time and began to worry that he would attempt an attack or escape. Annawon returned, however, "coming with something in his hands, and coming up to Capt. *Church*, he fell upon his knees before him, and offered him what he had bro't." In this posture of ultimate submission, Annawon showed further deference to Church by "speaking in plain *English*." He said, *"Great Captain, you have killed Philip, and conquered his Country, for I believe, that I & my company are the last that War against the* English, *so suppose the War is ended by your means; and therefore these things belong unto you."* He then rendered Church a tangible token of his triumph over Philip, and "pull'd out *Philips* belt curiously wrought with *Wompom*, being Nine inches broad, wrought with black and white *Wompom*, in various figures and flowers, and pictures of many birds and beasts." Either Annawon or Church must have put it on the English man, as Church remembers that "when hung upon [his] shoulders" this magnificent item "reach'd his ancles." Furthermore, Annawon presented him "another belt of *Wompom* . . . wrought after the former manner, which *Philip* was wont to put upon his head; it had two flags on the back part which hung down on his back: and another small belt with a Star upon the end of it, which he used to hang on his breast; and they were all edg'd with red hair, which *Annawon* said they got in the Muhhogs [Mohawks'] Country."[63] Nothing was more symbolic of Philip's wealth and status as a great sachem, or of his manhood as a great warrior, than his wampum belts. The ritual performed by Annawon is a reversal of the image of the stripping endured by English captives and dead soldiers: laying the wampum belts upon Church was a sign of his and his peoples' submission to the greater warrior, just as stripping defeated English bodies of their clothing was a means of enforcing their submission to their Indian masters.

These encounters from the Pequot War and King Philip's War embody many of the tensions and ambiguities inherent in Anglo-Indian warfare when Indians dressed as English men: English colonists feared that clothing may have had the power to turn Indians into English men, and vice versa. The story that introduces this chapter—when Underhill's Indian ally was successfully transformed into a virile sniper by virtue of an English coat—may have been heartening to the English, but the fact was that this mutability was also threatening. After all, Indian men could put on convincing performances of English masculinity to horrify or humiliate English observers. In her captivity narrative, Mary Rowlandson remembers being fooled by a company of soldiers, "nearly thirty, all on horseback. My heart skipped within me, thinking they had been Englishmen at the first sight of them, for they were dressed in English apparel, with hats, white neck cloths, and sashes about their waists, and ribbons upon their shoulders." When they drew nearer, she realized she had been deceived, as "there was a vast difference between the lovely faces of Christians, and the foul looks of these heathens." And when the Reverend Shubael Dummer was killed in an attack on York, Maine, in King William's War, Cotton Mather claims that when "one of the Tawnies, chose to exhibit himself" to the dead man's children, he did so as "[*A Devil as an Angel of Light!*] in the *Cloaths,* whereof they had Strip the Dead Body of this their *Father.*" Mather's description of this ghoulish masquerade may have been his own fantasy, as a more immediate primary source reporting Dummer's death does not mention such a spectacle. Nevertheless, his version of Dummer's death reveals the continuing English obsession with Indians seizing English clothing.[64]

Another worry for the English was the fact that their French enemies were investing in clothing to make their ally Indians more effective warriors. Cyprian Southack, after a reconnaissance cruise of the coast of Maine during Queen Anne's War, warned the governor of Massachusetts that the French had lately "been at soe Great Charge in Getting in all the Indians from Shanctio, Menness & Cape Salles & all the Placess Agesant & in Cloathing of them In Expection of the English Attacking Port Royall." But when intelligence informed the French that the English had no intention of attacking Port Royal, "in Mounth of June hee will send sume of those Indians this sid[e of] the baye to Due us Sume Mischeife." After all, they were suitably equipped for battle. After Samuel Whitney and his son were attacked and taken into captivity in 1751, Whitney informed the Massachusetts governor and Council that his captors were handsomely rewarded when they delivered the English to the French in Canada: "the said Indians when they came to Canada were new Cloathed, had New Guns given them with Plenty of Provisions as an Encouragement for their exploit." While we can't know precisely what kind of clothing the Indians claimed as their reward for loyalty to the French, it seems reasonable to assume that the French were simply doing what the English did for their Indian allies—courting their favor with European cloth and clothing. The lure of good clothing was so strong that it could make captured English people allies of the French as well. Captive Thomas Brown criticized two English men who decided to ally themselves with a French officer who rewarded their loyalty by giving "those two Men who promis'd to go with him, a Blanket, a Pair of Stockings and Shoes."[65]

The power of English men's clothing and armor was so great that English women might also successfully impersonate English manhood. Images of cross-dressing women, and of women masquerading as soldiers in particular, were familiar figures in English pamphlet literature and popular ballads in the seventeenth and eighteenth centuries. Stories about these "warrior women" circulated quite broadly. For example, the story of Hannah Snell, who first dressed in men's clothing and enlisted as James Gray to fight on the Loyalist side against Bonnie Prince Charlie and then sailed around the world with the British Navy, was first published in a 1750 pamphlet in London and then was immediately picked up by British magazines and a Boston newspaper that very year.[66] These stories implied that because they put on men's clothing, women might not only fight alongside men as equals; they might even best them in the contest for manly virtue. The introduction in the 1750 pamphlet outlining Snell's story begins with a claim by the author that acts of military prowess by men were all too uncommon: "In this dastardly Age of the World, when Effeminacy and Debauchery have taken Place of the Love of Glory, and that noble Arbor after war-like Exploits, which flowed in the Bosoms of our Ancestors, genuine Heroism, or rather an extraordinary Degree of Courage, are Prodigies among Men." Thus, "how much rarer," especially in an "effeminate" age, "and consequently how much more are they to be admired among Women?" In a 1746 broadside called *The Female Volunteer,* the actress

Margaret Woffington is depicted "in the Habit of a Volunteer" as she chides the defeated British Army for their failure at Falkirk. Because British men retreated "before a Scrub Banditti! Who scarce could fright the Buff-Coats of the City," she calls for British women to take up arms in defense of the nation. "You'll think this no unnat'ral Transformation: / For if in Valour real *Manhood lies,* / All Cowards are but Women in Disguise."[67]

Of course, these warrior women were not put forth as serious enlistees on behalf of the English nation; their absurdity is what made them popular entertainment. Like the victorious Pequots taunting the defeated English men at Fort Saybrook by screaming "you are all one like women," these stories and ballads were meant to humiliate cowardly or defeated men by implying that even women could be better soldiers than the present lot. If cowardly men were women "in disguise," as *The Female Volunteer* claimed, or stripped of their manly disguise on the battlefields of New England, then brave women with the right clothing might successfully impersonate men.[68] New Englanders seem to have been familiar with this genre of literature and with the manner of the fight. In an attack on Wells, Maine, during King William's War, the English were badly outnumbered: fifteen men were inside the garrison, and another fifteen in a sloop in the harbor. In his account of the fight, Cotton Mather claims that "the *Women* in the Garrison" made up for the shortage of manpower and "took up the *Amazonian* Stroke, and not only brought Ammunition to the *Men,* but also with a *Manly* Resolution fired several Times upon the Enemy." In a 1706 surprise attack on an English settlement in New Hampshire, local minister Jabez Fitch reported in the same Mather-esque language that "the Garrison which stood near had not a Man in it at that time." No matter: "the *women* assum'd an *Amazonian* Courage, and put on the Habit of men, and acted their part so manfully, that they frighted away the Enemy." Another version of this 1706 attack elaborates on the women's technique: "the women, who assumed an Amazonian courage, . . . put on hats, with their hair hanging down, and fired so briskly that they struck a terror in the enemy, and they withdrew without firing the house, or carrying away much plunder." Once again, manly attire—as much as their briskly fired muskets—made all the difference.[69]

Even when English colonists did not witness the stripping of their compatriots or see Indians wearing the clothing, the Indians still angered them with other displays of English clothing procured in war. After a successful attack on the fledgling settlement at Wethersfield, Connecticut, in 1637, the Pequots used the symbolic imagery of English clothing to boast of their accomplishments as they sailed their canoes down the Connecticut River past Fort Saybrook. Underhill reports that the Pequots claimed nine English lives and "two maids captives." Then, "having put poles in their Conoos, as we put masts in our boats, and upon them hung our English mens and womens shirts and smocks, in stead of sayles, and in way of bravado came along in sight of us as we stood upon *Seybrooke* Fort." It was another English humiliation, and this time the use of the clothing was not at all functional but purely symbolic. With the mocking use of clothing as pretended sails, the Indians succeeded in displaying their latest victory, in calling attention to their war captives, and in intimidating the English: "Seeing them passe along in such a triumphant manner, wee much [feared] they had enterprised some desperate action upon the *English*." Some of the English, provoked by this display, stupidly fired on the Indian flotilla and "grazed not above twentie yards over the Conooe, where the poore maids were." Fortunately, "it was a specially providence of God it did not hit them." This ritual of displaying items taken from captives was apparently widespread geographically and temporally. Nehemiah How relates a similar incident in which his Abenaki captors displayed an even more personal remnant of their defeated foes in the 1740s: "We got into the Canoes, when the Indians stuck up a Pole about eight Feet long with the Scalp of David Rugg on the Top of it, painted red, with the Likeness of Eyes and Mouth on it: We sail'd about ten Miles, and then went on Shore; and after we had made a Fire, we boil'd a good Supper, and eat heartily."[70]

Even with the end of the Seven Years' War, the use and exchange of clothing in the northeastern borderlands were too complex to interpret in just one way. Clothing was vitally important on the New England frontier because it both fixed and disrupted ethnic, cultural, and gender boundaries. Because both Indian and English communities were structured according to hierarchies of gender, performing manhood successfully was a large part of the contest between Indian and English men for the political and military control of New England, and Indian men were very adept at exploiting English fears about their own manhood. Clothes may have made the man— and being stripped may have exposed his inadequacies—but clothing was just one thing that might be captured or shared in the northeastern borderlands. As we will see, family and community ties were even more central to successful "conversions" across cultural, religious, and linguistic borders in colonial America.

Chapter 3

"Insolent" Squaws and "Unreasonable" Masters: Indian Captivity and Family Life

> *My Master intended now to kill us; and I being desirous to know the Reason, expostulated, that in his Absence I had been diligent to do as I was ordered by him.* Thus, as well as I could, I made [his mother-in-law] sensible how unreasonable he was. Now, tho' she could not understand me, nor I her, but by Signs we reasoned as well as we could.
>
> —*Elizabeth Hanson,* God's Mercy Surmounting Man's Cruelty *(1729)*

For English families, being taken captive by Indians in frontier warfare was objectively a terrifying experience: their homes invaded by strange enemies, they usually witnessed the killing of some of the adult men, and then the horrifyingly brutal murder of a toddler or two. Wives and mothers, suckling infants, and children who were old enough to keep quiet when they were told to usually survived the initial attack. Before they left their homes, their families had already been devastated if not entirely destroyed by the enemy, and the hardships of the forced march to an Indian village—sometimes a several weeks' or months' journey without adequate food or clothing—would only serve to emphasize the precariousness of their lives on the New England frontier. Over the nearly ninety years from the beginning of King Philip's War (1675–78) and end of the Seven Years' War (1756–63), losing a family member to the wars of the northeastern borderlands was an experience that afflicted at least a thousand families and was witnessed by thousands more.[1]

Despite this brutal introduction to life among the Indians, or perhaps because of it, most captives who lived to publish their stories almost immediately identified their Indian captors as their "masters," rhetorically putting themselves under the household government of whichever Indian man seemed to be the leader of the raiding party that took them captive. We might expect this of the English children taken by Indians, who would have looked up to their captors as surrogate parents: John Gyles, taken at age eleven from his parents' home in Pemaquid, Maine, wrote of his "Indian Master," explaining retrospectively that "the Indian that takes and will keep a Captive is accounted his Master, and the Captive his Property till he give or sell him to another." But even Mary Rowlandson, the pious, proud wife of a prominent minister and a woman who bitterly resented her captivity, deferred rhetorically to her Indian captors by calling them her "masters," even at one point calling one of them "the best friend that I had of an Indian."[2] Why were English captives of all ages, both sexes, and of different rank in their English communities so eager to call an Indian "master" when the English typically were confused by what they saw as the disorderliness of Native families? Was it simply the psychological adaptation known today as Stockholm syndrome, the sympathetic identification with one's captors that might have served them well as a strategy for survival? Or was it their assumption as English people that Indian families—like their own—should have one head of household, and that that household head must be a man?[3]

Indians who took English captives must also have been more than occasionally frustrated by the experience. Besides coordinating a journey home with large numbers of women and children while avoiding attack or capture by English avengers, it was not easy integrating English people into their families, even temporarily. English people did not know what to eat, how to march, how to work, or that they should stop their endless crying and complaints. From the Indians' point of view, English women were especially lazy and had to be repeatedly instructed in the most basic tasks of Indian women's work. Having them in their wigwams and longhouses was sometimes infuriating, and conflicts over captives sometimes erupted into Indian family feuds. The literature on captivity has focused on the English who were adopted by their new Indian families, but by the end of the seventeenth century most captives were probably taken almost exclusively for financial gain and to cement Native alliances with the French and were never invited to remain with their Indian captors. With the opening of the first imperial war between Britain and France in 1688, most English captives were redeemed from the Indians for a set price as soon as they could be marched to Montreal or Québec. Most of those who remained in Canada converted to Catholicism and joined French families, not Indian families.[4]

Through the narratives of English civilians captured from their homes and families, we can examine captivity from both the English and the Indian points of view. Because the English people taken into Indian captivity were already familiar with a hierarchy to structure family life, they used this understanding of the ordering of households to understand and interpret their experiences in captivity, mapping their expectations of family life onto their experiences in their new Indian families. Furthermore, the evidence also suggests that Indian families used their expectations of family life and work roles to guide their treatment of captives. Indians expected English captives to behave like Indians as everyone struggled to integrate these strangers into their families, and they were frustrated with their captives when they did not take to the work or family roles assigned to them.[5]

But captivity was not simply a situation comedy of errors in the wilderness—in fact, few of the players ever had much more than a hunch as to what was happening in these blended temporary families. Indians had direct political and economic goals in taking and ransoming captives, and very real political intentions guided the way English people told their stories of captivity and shaped their portrayal of Indian families. While English captives in their own retelling of their ordeals appear eager to identify their "Indian Masters" and defer to their authority, they also held these Indian men to the ideal standards of English headship and inevitably found them wanting. Instead of providing for their families, these Indian masters were sometimes failed hunters and let their families go hungry; instead of managing their households as steady patriarchs, they sometimes let their "squaws" rule the roost; instead of controlled temperaments and rational demeanors, some of them were "naturally of a very hot and passionate Temper" and quite "unreasonable" in their conduct toward their subordinates. In short, in accounts published by their English former captives, Indian men were portrayed as inferior men, men incapable of exercising proper household government. Just as European colonists in North America were interested in Indian gender roles, so they were also fascinated by their family lives. The English believed that understanding Native American family life was an important key to dominating Indians politically and economically. The moral of the story for the English audience of captivity narratives was: if Indian men could not control their wives and children, how could these failed men be expected to govern themselves properly? Thus, captivity narratives served to justify the English conquest of the northeastern borderlands, as they argued implicitly that Indian men were incapable of self-rule.[6]

The political uses of the captivity narratives produced in New England in the decades from 1675 to 1763 reached beyond the English conquest of New England. Captivity narratives emerged as a distinctive Anglo-

American genre of literature at the end of the seventeenth century, in the very decades that African chattel slavery became fully established in English mainland colonies like Maryland, Virginia, and South Carolina. Slavery was of course legal in New England and many New Englanders owned Native and African slaves, although the institution was never central to the economy of the region as it was in the nascent slave societies to the south. Nevertheless, this discourse contrasting Anglo-American liberty versus servitude or slavery among the Indians is fascinating to read alongside the dramatic distinctions being invented in the southern colonies between liberty and slavery, and acted out in white and black. As Edmund Morgan noted thirty years ago, American slavery and American freedom were no paradox: Virginians discovered the true value of liberty only because they lived in a world defined by the slavery of the many for the enrichment of the few.[7] The stories of English people reduced to slavery among the Indians gave the readers of captivity narratives a taste of the savage inequalities of the colonial world. Like colonial Virginians, New Englanders were not inspired to tear down the barriers between the English and Indians, or between slavery and freedom. Rather, these stories seem to have convinced Anglo-Americans that they needed to protect their liberty and preserve their privileges at all costs, so long as those costs were borne almost entirely by Indians and Africans.

Early modern English and colonial Anglo-American households were ideally ordered according to the "great chain of being" that articulated humankind's role in society at large as well as its relationship to the divine. Puritan New England was especially committed to this vision, and its colonies were built around a hierarchy based on sex, age, rank, and status. In an address to his fellow travelers on the *Arabella* as it embarked for Massachusetts Bay in 1630, John Winthrop articulated a deeply held belief in the necessity and goodness of earthly hierarchies: "God Almighty in His most holy and wise providence hath so disposed of the condition of mankind, as in all times some must be rich, some poor, some high and eminent in power and dignity, others mean and in subjection."[8] As Winthrop's words illustrate, men and women of his era believed that all just authority on earth emanated from God, who reigned supreme. Since God had delegated his authority on earth to Adam, men were to rule over women, children, servants, and slaves. This ordering of households was not a private matter but one of crucial importance to the functioning of society as a whole: family order was the basis of all order. Political theorists, preachers, and pamphleteers alike used the metaphor of the state to describe the functions of the family, and metaphors from the family to describe the functions of the state. Thus, the family was often described in the seventeenth century as "a little commonwealth," and kings as fathers of their people.[9] Even in the antimonarchical uprisings of the seventeenth and eighteenth centuries, the state and the family remained intertwined in their functions and in the imaginations of the people, and these images were manipulated for political gain. Alongside the rise of Lockean individualism as a competing model for conceptualizing the relationship between the state and its people, corporate and familial imagery nevertheless still saturated political discourse at the end of the eighteenth century. Anglo-Americans in the 1760s and 1770s revolted against their "Mother country" and described King George III as a bad father in order to demonstrate his unfitness to be king. French revolutionaries also constructed their monarch as a failed father and indulged in pornographic fantasies of the queen, both of which had the effect of undermining the legitimacy of Louis XVI's rule.[10]

Accordingly, New Englanders were constantly judging one another's households and their fitness to rule them. Family historians have long argued for the central importance of the colonial family because of the absence or primitive state of development of other social institutions in colonial America. Colonial families were the sites of economic production as well as schools for intellectual development, vocational instruction, and religious teaching. They also were centers of discipline and penal correction, and they filled the role of social service agencies and hospitals by providing care for the very young and the very old and by foster parenting orphans and servants. Ideally, these families were strongly patriarchal because of the many roles the family played in grounding the social order. While the Chesapeake and other colonies to the south struggled to establish a patriarchal social order because neither their English migration nor their African slave importation was family-based, the migration of whole families to New England meant that these colonies were able to achieve more nearly the English ideal.[11] More recently, women's historians have demonstrated that the hierarchical nature of the colonial family did not serve all of the interests of each family member equally, and that they were therefore prone to disorder and breakdown even in relatively stable New England. Wives held dangerous opinions about religion and politics, and refused to keep their contentious views quiet; they sometimes lashed out at their husbands publicly, humiliated them with beatings or adultery, or they ran away. Children were regularly disobedient and frequently embarrassed their parents with their disorderly behavior. Servants and slaves were probably the most rebellious family members, perhaps understandably so because they stood to gain little or nothing for all their labor. New England magistrates were not reluctant to investigate disorderly families and attempt to restore the proper, patriarchal order of households with the force of law. The roles that people played in their families were the roles that people played in their communities at large, so the state saw a clear interest in helping male heads of household regain control of their mouthy wives, rebellious children, thieving servants, and runaway slaves.[12]

This obsession with family life was nothing new in North America. The English puritans who established their colonies in New England had long been at war (sometimes literally) with what they saw as the corruption of sexually incontinent aristocrats and Catholic clergy on the one hand, and the social and sexual libertinism of radical Protestant sects on the other. Like many bourgeois European Protestants, they believed themselves to be part of a moral crusade to enforce patriarchal family values.[13] In America, English puritans attempted to create ideologically and religiously conformist communities, and they regularly banished believers of different stripes— Quakers, Baptists, and the so-called Antinomians most frequently, but they feared similar invasions of Brownists and Familists as well. Central to puritan critiques of these sects was the fear that their leveling religious views— most particularly, their emphasis on the equality of all believers before Christ, and the fact that some of these sects allowed women preachers— necessarily meant that their families were insufficiently governed by patriarchal authority. Puritan propaganda in Old and New England emphasized the licentiousness and sexual danger these groups represented—Baptist preachers were portrayed as having base motives for the practice of adult baptism as whole-body immersion (presumably the temptation to see women in their wet shifts), and Quaker women were feared as spiritual scolds because they had the authority to preach. Other less well-known sects were suspected of encouraging group or open marriage among their believers.[14] Thus, the puritan obsession with family order among the Indians was an extention of the ways in which they judged other English people and themselves. Their writings about Indian family life reflected their fears about English family life, and were similarly shaped to gain rhetorical and political advantage over their foes.

With the endemic disruption of warfare in the northeastern borderlands from 1675 to 1763, English people suffered not just the fact of Indian attack on their families, but also the political and economic disorder that followed in its wake. The English saw Indian warfare and captivity as their world turned upside-down and inside-out, a total assault on the hierarchy that ordered all godly families and communities. Cotton Mather's *Decennium Luctuosum,* published at the end of King William's War (1688–97), makes this argument luridly explicit as it urges New England to *"observe* the Loud *Calls* of Heaven to *All Ranks of men. . . . Hear ye the Rod"* that has been administering the *"Strokes* of Heaven" to the English settlements there. While the Pequot War and King Philip's War were characterized by attacks on both English and Indian noncombatants, King William's War was the first frontier war to consist almost exclusively of attacks on English households and thus yielded large numbers of English captives. Dozens of settlements on the northern New England frontier were hit, from Haverhill, Massachusetts, up to Dover and Oyster Bay on the Merrimack River, and nearly as far north as English settlement extended, up to the Pemaquid Peninsula. For once, perhaps Mather's overblown rhetoric was somewhat justified: New England had been severely damaged by a full decade of Indian attacks, and dozens of adults and almost a whole generation of frontier children were still held in captivity.[15]

As suggested by his evocation of the "rod" that administers "strokes" to punish and humiliate, Mather uses explicitly violent and sexualized imagery to suggest that these Indian attacks were a rape of New England. "There has been a *voice of God* unto all the Countrey in that *Indian Rod,* which hath been used upon us." Aside from rods, Mather describes the many swords wielded by combatants on both sides of this earthly and spiritual war: the *"Sword of the Wicked,"* the *"Sword of Justice,"* and the *"Sword of the Spirit"* are all at work in Mather's text. While his use of these rods and swords is metaphorical, he makes it clear that this metaphor has reached into the lives of many English households and threatens to master all of New England. *"Men of Wisdom, in all Ranks* of men, will *Observe,* and See, and Hear, the meaning of this *Rod;* inasmuch as *all Ranks* of men have smarted under it; yea, it has fetch'd Blood from *all Ranks* of men among us. We will a little particularize 'em."[16]

In "particularizing" the abuses of the Indians, Mather begins at the top of the New England social hierarchy and works his way down, describing the humiliations that have raddled each rung of the ladder. By doing this, he symbolically reconstructs the social hierarchy even as he catalogues the damages it has sustained in a decade of Indian attacks. First, he notes that "Two of our MINISTERS, have been *Struck down,"* and that "some *Rich men"* too have been "reduced . . . to such Necessity, that within Less than One year, they have come to *Beg their Bread."* On the next rung down from the elite, Mather describes the "abundance of *Poor men,* who have been by this *War* plunged still into deeper *Poverty."* Stripped of their lives and their fortunes, English men can no longer fulfill their roles as the protectors, providers, and spiritual guides of their homes and families. And when English men lose the prerogatives of their sex, disorder follows as naturally as night follows the day. "The Straits, the Wants, the Cares of *Widows,* and *Orphans,* or of those that have had many mouths to Feed, especially in our Exposed Frontiers; None can Express them, None can Conceive them, but They, (Nor *They!*) who did Endure them all."[17]

Moving down the hierarchy of English families and communities, Mather considers the particular troubles of women on the frontier: "How many *Women* have been made a *prey* to those *Brutish men,* that are *Skillful to Destroy?* How many a *Fearful Thing* has been suffered by the *Fearful Sex,* from those *men,* that one would *Fear* as *Devils* rather than men? Let the *Daughters* of our *Zion* think with themselves, what it would be, for fierce *Indians* to break into their Houses, and brain their *Husbands* and their *Children* before their Eyes." Like English men, English women too were similarly deprived of their gendered prerogatives and responsibilities as wives and mothers when Indians attacked. But English women as captives continued to suffer more directly under Indian despotism: on the one hand, they might "*fail* and *faint* in the Journey" away from their homes, which might mean that "a Tawny Salvage" would "come with Hell fire in his Eyes, and cut 'em down with his Hatchet." What might be even worse than rape or cruel murder, captive English women might meet with "some Filthy and ugly *Squaw's* to become their *insolent Mistresses,* and insolently to abuse 'em at their pleasure a thousand inexpressible ways." Mather's message is clear: captivity not only disrupted the order of English family life, it also imposed a foreign and ungodly order on English captives. In English accounts of Indian warriors, "insolent" is not a word the English use to describe legitimate authority, only to imply the misappropriation of authority by subordinates: servants and slaves were insolent when they talked back to their masters, and children were insolent when they defied their parents' will. Thus Mather's use of the term "insolent" to describe Indian women's behavior is intentional, implying that unlike the (ideally) tidy, virtuous, and submissive English goodwives, Indian women wielded authority in their own homes and families. Mather's pen stutters on the word, repeating it twice in near succession: "*insolent Mistresses,* and insolently to abuse 'em."

This presumptuousness makes them "Filthy and ugly," monstrous women whose abuses are in the end "inexpressible."[18]

Aside from attacks on the sex- and class-based ordering of English households and communities, Mather writes that Indian warfare and captivity deny the respect due to the aged and the care due to the very young. He expresses outrage that *"Young Indians* have with grievous Flouts and Wounds, Butchered many of our *Old English men.* The *Gray Hairs* of our *Old men,* have been Dyed Red with their own Blood; and their Carcases have been thrown unto the *Swine,* to mangle them." Conversely, Indian adults show no mercy to English children: either they *"Dash'd out the Brains of our Little Ones,"* or they "hideously whipped [them] unto Death," or "brought [them] up in a vile Slavery, till some of them have quite forgot their *English Tongue,* and their *Christian Name,* and their whole *Relation."*[19] With youth not respecting age, adults turning against children, and the living denying respect to the dead, the Indian disruption of the English social hierarchy was devastatingly final.

Although propagandists like Cotton Mather publicized the real and imagined horrors of English captivity among the Indians, Native families were also severely affected by warfare in the northeastern borderlands. Despite English insistence to the contrary, Native men and women in the colonial era were very much like Europeans in that they organized their economy and society according to divisions of sex, age, and status, and this organization was reflected in Native family structure and organization. Iroquois and Algonquian gender roles and family systems were almost identical, in that women did the farming, gathered foodstuffs, medicinal plants, and firewood, preserved and prepared all food, made many household items (such as baskets, pottery, and gourd containers), dressed and fashioned skins for wearing apparel, and managed early child care, among sundry other common tasks. The men busied themselves seasonally in fishing, hunting, and trapping, and often in war. While Native women seem to have had more sway in village and tribal affairs than European women did, the men were still in charge of politics, diplomacy, and war. Because their work provided upwards of 75 percent of the calories consumed by their families, ethnohistorians have argued that Native women's economic importance translated into greater political influence (if not formal political roles) than that of European and Euro-American women in colonial America. Indeed, Iroquois women held separate "women's councils" to discuss tribal affairs, elite women had some formal power in choosing sachems, and matrons played an important role in the torture and/or the adoption of captives into their families.[20] But we must be careful about the logic of the argument that economic importance translates into political influence; after all, English women's labor was very valuable and central to the functioning of their families, but this never translated into any formal political influence for them. (This point is explored more in Chapter 4).[21] For despite their political roles, Iroquois women were still shut out of most of the political decision making and all of the offices of Native rule. As for Algonquian women, we saw in Chapter 1 that Algonquian politics were thoroughly dominated by men; the few "squaw sachems" who appear as tribal leaders in the late seventeenth century seem to be evidence of the ravages of disease and warfare on southeastern New England Indians rather than signs of Native women's traditional role in tribal politics.[22] A seventeenth-century French missionary reports that "some women who have their own voice in these matters, and who make decisions like the old men" were present in Oneida war councils he had observed, suggesting that among the Iroquois political power was shared with a few elite women. Another French observer of the 1750s addresses the question of women's role in politics directly, comparing Iroquois and Algonquian traditions. Overall, though, he remains skeptical of the degree to which women were actually powerful: "[Men] undertake no war and make no treaty without first holding council among themselves. . . . Regarding these councils, Dr. Franklin has observed that, as the people do not know how to write, the women learn by heart the discussion carried on. He says that women as well as children attended these councils. I am not completely in accord with that except for the Iroquois." He had himself never seen an Iroquois village council, "but I have seen them in council with the French. Then the women did not attend. The tribes in the north, west, and south are not accustomed to introduce women into their councils in any way. If that were true, it would be inconsistent with the scorn they have for women." After all, he remarks, "perhaps no nation in the world scorns women more than these savages usually do. The bitterest insult that can be offered a savage is to call him a woman."[23]

Although many Native women in the post-contact period were probably almost as politically marginalized as English women, what impressed English men and women about Indian families was women's power and influence in their families. There is good evidence that both Algonquian and Iroquois women were central not just as producers and caregivers but as decision makers in their families as well. In the more mobile Algonquian communities, women probably made key decisions as to when it was time to make seasonal moves to or away from the planting grounds. They also transmitted use-rights to agricultural plots to their descendants in the female line. In the more settled villages of the Iroquois, the matrilineal organization of Iroquois kinship groups meant that women were powerful within the longhouse. Lineage was traced through the female line, and members of a nuclear family belonged to the same *ohwachira*. In theory the Iroquois were also matrilocal, which meant that young husbands moved into the longhouse and the kinship group of their brides' families. However, matrilocality might not always have been the rule, as there is some evidence that high-status men stayed with their kin groups after marriage, whereas husbands from lower-status families would have been likelier to join their wives' kin, especially if the women were of a more prominent lineage. In fact, even though historians differ in their assessments of Native women's power, they agree that status was just as important as sex in governing Algonquian and Iroquois communities. Thus, we must not mistake the privileges of some elite women as representative of the experience of all Native American women.[24]

One arena of Indian life in which both Algonquian and Iroquois women clearly were major decision makers was in both the torture and adoption of captives, ceremonies that blurred the boundaries between warfare, politics, and family life. Parties of women—usually older women— commonly greeted captives upon their arrival at an Indian village or fort, and these women seem to have had a strong role in deciding which captives would live and which would die in ritual torture and sacrifice, which would be tortured or maimed just a little (by comparison), and which would be adopted and by whom, and what their roles in their new families would be. From the beginning, English observers noted that Indian women were official recorders of the missing and the dead in war. Increase Mather tells the story of an old Pokanoket woman in 1621 who successfully demanded tribute for her three sons, whom she said had been abducted by the early explorer Thomas Hunt. Mather describes her patronizingly as being bought off cheaply for her troubles, "withal giving her some trifles, she was satisfied," but the fact that the English also brought home with them a lost English boy "al bedecked with *Peag*" (wampum, also known as wampumpeag) suggests that this was in fact a kind of exchange of captives in which the woman played a central role in articulating Indian grievances against the English and in negotiating the return of the English boy. Indeed, it might have been her decision to release the captive alone, as a tale from Queen Anne's War (1702–13) nearly a century later suggests: Samuel Butterfield was allowed to serve the "Squaw Widow" whose husband he killed. She and she alone spared his life, as the annalist who records his story suggests that she acted against her tribe's will in suffering him to live.[25]

A French observer in the 1750s noted with horror the key role Ottawa women played in the torture of English captives: Two captives were bound to saplings and then bounced up and down over hot coals. "During this atrocity, of which only savages seem capable, the victims were surrounded by the tormentors, who sang and urged them to defy death. This suffering was yet only the prelude to a greater torment which would make humanity shudder, and is reported only to show the barbarity of the savages. Yet it is a proven fact that men do not always invent and carry out the most cruel tortures. This task is very often left to the squaws, as they are thought more ingenious and subtle in inventing tortures." He describes the women "heating rifle ramrods red-hot, and pushing them into the tortured captives' nostrils and ears. Before this, they burned various parts of the body with firebrands." Children too were encouraged to partake of the ritual, by shooting "arrows into the thighs and arms of the victims, after an interval of a few moments. The savage women came back and burned their victims' fingertips in pipes full of tobacco, then cut off their noses and ears. I must stop here and not bring to light all the even more atrocious things that the most barbarous of imaginations could invent."[26] This kind of power exercised over foreign men fed European stereotypes about Native savagery in general, and in particular, it stoked European fears of Indian women's unnatural power.

Like Indian women, Indian children were viewed by Europeans as having too much liberty and not enough family discipline. English travel narratives that discuss Native family life always remark upon how "very Indulgent they are to their Children," as John Josselin noted in 1674. Dartmouth College founder and missionary to the Indians Eleazar Wheelock put his school in an English town because the Indians' "'great Fondness for their Children' was incompatible with the birchen government necessary to 'humble them, and reform their Manners.' 'Here,' he admitted, 'I can correct, & punish them as I please, . . . but [among their own families] it will not be born.'" In short, as Cotton Mather himself put it, "they are out of measure *Indulgent* unto their Children, there is no Family-Government among them."[27]

The corollary to these very strong wives and mothers and undisciplined children was weak men. Because many of their occupations took them away from their villages, Indian men seemed lamentably peripheral to European observers. When they were on a hunt or in a war party, they were away from their families sometimes for days or weeks at a time. Furthermore, different ideas about marriage also seem to have made Indian men look less important to family life. Indian husbands and wives divorced much more commonly and easily than European men and women, a fact that led Europeans to judge all Indians as sexually promiscuous. (The occasional polygamy of high-status men reinforced this conviction, but for the most part, female promiscuity was of greater concern to the Europeans.) Matrilineal family organization among the Iroquois also seems to have contributed to the perception of Iroquois men in particular as weak or feckless fathers, as maternal uncles seem to have played a parental role as much as, if not more than, the biological fathers of children. The importance of kinship rather than a patriarchal nuclear family made the chain of command difficult for English observers to discern.[28] All of these facts led Europeans to see and portray Indian men as ineffective governors of their households and families.

Even English observers who usually portrayed Native peoples as noble and attractive were appalled by the cheerfulness with which Indian men assumed the role of cuckold to their supposedly bossy, whoring wives. Thomas Morton, the "governor" of the interracial frolic at Merrymount who wrote admiringly of Algonquian people and their culture, could not refrain from making a Native man look foolish for showing off a fair-eyed child as his own. "The colour of their eies being so generally black, made a Salvage (that had a younge infant whose eies were gray,) shewed him to us and said they were English mens eies," apparently not distressed by this indication of his wife's sexual infidelity. Morton then writes, "I tould the Father, that his sonne was *nan weeteo,* which is a bastard, he replied *titta Cheshetue squaa,* which is hee could not tell; his wife might play the whore and this childe the father desired might have an English name, because of the likenesse of his eies which his father had in admiration, because of novelty amongst their Nation." Thus Morton mocks the Indian man for apparently wanting to commemorate this bastardy by giving the child an English name, instead of divorcing his wife and avenging his honor on her or her lover.[29] These portrayals of Native family life seemed to confirm what English people had believed all along: that people incapable of governing their families properly clearly could not be trusted to govern themselves properly. The English believed that like unruly servants, disobedient children, runaway slaves, and mischievous wives, Indians had to be put under English household and civil government, since Indian men clearly could not (or would not) govern them appropriately.

And that was only in the best of circumstances. The Native families discussed here are very difficult to evaluate considering the extremely stressful circumstances they were in: aside from the usual disruptions of warfare (injuries, famine, forced relocation, and so on) and the hazards of using such highly ideological primary sources as English captivity narratives, Indians taking captives in raiding parties were in flight from possible capture or death at the hands of the English. Thus the Native families presented here were not functioning as they would in a more stable time and place. While captivity narratives are highly problematic sources for learning about Native family life, they can give us great insights into the different expectations of family life that both the Indians and the English applied to one another in these temporarily "blended" Native-captive families.

The theme of family destruction was central to the way the English understood Indian captivity as well as a defining feature of the dramatic structure of captivity narratives. Captivity narratives most often begin with a surprise attack on the English home and family by hostile Indians, a theme with two variations that reflect the sex of the author and the different work spaces men and women inhabited: men's narratives usually begin by describing an Indian attack that begins in the fields where they work, and women's narratives typically begin with a description of Indians invading their homes. Remembering the beginnings of his boyhood captivity in 1689, John Gyles wrote that he and his father and brothers were surprised by the Eastern Abenaki shortly after their noon meal in or near their fields of "English Hay" and "English Corn." "The Yelling of the Indians, the Whistling of their Shot, and the Voice of my Father, whom I heard cry out, What now! What now! so terrified me." Jemima Howe's narrative begins with a description of a Western Abenaki attack on her husband and other men while they were on their way home from "hoeing corn in the meadow" near Hinsdale, New Hampshire, in 1755. Her husband, Caleb Howe, was hit by a bullet and scalped, unfortunately surviving overnight only to die the next day. Nehemiah How (no relation), taken in October of 1745 during King George's War (1744–48), was captured when he left the fort to cut wood. And despite the fact that Henry Grace was a British Regular assigned to guard men while they harvested wheat in Nova Scotia, he too was taken captive by the Mi'kmaq. Sometimes men were taken by surprise at night, but most raiding parties seemed to prefer daylight for their ambushes on English men at work.[30]

The openings of most women's narratives locate them in female work spaces, and many further suggest that they were vulnerable because the men were in the fields or traveling. Mary Rowlandson opens her captivity narrative with a dramatic rendering of the 1676 attack on the Lancaster garrison and her household in particular: "The bullets flying thick, one went through my side, and the same (as would seem) through my bowels and of my dear child in my arms. One of my elder sister's children, named William, had then his leg broken, which the Indians perceiving, they knocked him on the head. Thus were we butchered by those merciless heathen, standing amazed, with the blood running down to our heels." What was worse for Rowlandson is that her husband was away from home, "and to add to my grief, the Indians told me they would kill him as he came homeward."[31] Similarly, Elizabeth Hanson begins her narrative by explaining that after "sculking in the Fields some Days," an Abenaki raiding party seized their opportunity "when my dear Husband with the rest of our Men, were gone out of the Way." She writes, "[they] came in upon us . . . all naked, with their Guns and Tomahauks came into the House in a great Fury upon us, and killed one Child immediately, as soon as they entred the Door." Sometimes the women were alone in their houses because the Indian attack had already widowed them or driven away their husbands. For example, in a narrative from King William's War, Hannah Duston is described as being driven from childbed alone after her husband and children made a lucky escape. In another narrative from the same war, Hannah Swarton writes, "I was now left a *Widow.*" Jemima Howe's narrative makes it even clearer that the presence of Indians meant that English family life was torn apart. While her husband lay slowly expiring from his wounds, their Western Abenaki attackers made their way to Bridgman's Fort where Howe and other women awaited their husbands' return from the fields. "They had heard the enemies guns, but knew not what had happened to their friends. Extremely anxious for their safety, they stood longing to embrace them, until at length, concluding from the noise they heard without that some of them were come, they unbarred the gate in a hurry to receive them; when lo! to their inexpressible disappointment and surprise, instead of their husbands, in rushed a number of hideous Indians, to whom they and their offspring became easy prey." With the literal substitution of Indians for English husbands, the women's lives were going to change dramatically, as Howe's narrative explains: "They had nothing to expect, but either an immediate death, or a long and doleful captivity."[32]

Since many adult women were taken into captivity with some of their children, they were not entirely deprived of their status as mothers; in fact, many women captives were surprised and grateful for the consideration Indians showed for their very young babies, giving them time and assistance in nursing them. However, motherhood in captivity had limited powers, as most of them lost children not just to disease and death but suffered their children being sent away to other Indian families and communities. Women's narratives usually credit the Indians with showing great "Humanity and Civility" toward them and their nursing infants by carrying their babies on the march and even saving their babies' lives. Elizabeth Hanson credited a pap made of walnuts, water, and cornmeal with saving her newborn's life after her breast milk dried up, a recipe recommended by the women in her temporarily adopted Indian family. Susanna Johnson endured childbirth on her journey to Canada just a day after her capture from Fort Number Four in New Hampshire. When she went into labor, the Indians responded immediately to assist her, she writes: they "signified to us that we must go on to a brook. When we got there, they shewed some humanity, by making a booth for me." They allowed her husband and younger sister to attend her, and when the babe was born (and named Captive), Johnson reports that the Indians allowed her to rest the entire day and fashioned a bier upon which she was carried for several days as she recovered. And even the perpetually ungrateful Mary Rowlandson admits that she and her wounded child were given a horse to ride for the first several days of her journey in captivity, a luxury few of her captors afforded themselves. It was not only the women who were grateful for the consideration the Indians showed for the needs of themselves and their children. In his narrative, the Reverend John Norton tells a story similar to Johnson's of a Mrs. Smeed who went into labor shortly after her capture in 1746. The war party of both French and Indian soldiers accommodated her needs, as well as the needs of the other women with small children, in captivity: "some of the French made a Seat for [Mrs. Smeed] to sit upon, and brought her to the Camp, where, about ten o'Clock, she was graciously delivered of a Daughter, and was remarkably well." Norton baptized the child, who was named "CAPTIVITY." Then "the French then made a Frame like a bier, and laid a Buck Skin and Bear Skin upon it, and laid Mrs. *Smeed*, with her Infant, thereon; and so two men at a time carried them. They also carried *Moses Scott's* Wife and two Children, and another of *Smeed's* Children. The Indians also carried in their Canoes, Br. *Simon* and *John Aldrich* and *Perry's* Wife, down the river about ten miles." To be sure, this accommodation of motherhood was in part self-serving, which the captives came to understand by the time they were brought to Canada and sold to the French. Susanna Johnson reports that after her delivery of Captive, "my master looked into the booth, and clapped his hands with joy, crying two monies for me, two monies for me." The French did not discount the bounty they paid for every English captive on account of age, so most Native raiding parties took care to preserve the lives of all captives who had survived the initial attack and the first few days of the march.[33]

This discourse on the value of motherhood is not unanimous in all captivity narratives, although it is a strong theme in women's narratives. One very popular narrative by a New England minister portrays Indian captivity as a literal assault upon English motherhood. In Reverend John Williams's *The Redeemed Captive, returning to Zion* (1707), the slaying of exhausted pregnant women by French-allied Huron, Western Abenaki, and Mohawk attackers becomes a motif in his relation of his journey as a captive from Deerfield, Massachusetts, to Montreal. His own wife, Eunice, just weeks out of childbed, was killed en route to Canada. Then on a single page, he writes of the slayings of five pregnant women by the Indians and then the cruel abortion and death of another woman, Mary Brooks. Suffering greatly, Brooks's Indian master allowed her to consult Williams one night. The minister reports that she told him, "by my falls on the Ice yesterday I wrong'd my self, causing an Abortion this Night, so that I am not able to Travel far; I know they will kill me to day." He describes her as a model of piety even in her miserable state: "*I am not afraid of Death,* I can through the Grace of God, chearfully submit to the Will of God. Pray for me (said she) at parting, That God would take me to Himself. Accordingly," he affirms, "she was killed that day." Williams's contrarian views on the treatment of pregnant women might have reflected the harsh realities of the desperate wintertime flight from Deerfield, which was attacked on February 29, 1704. (Almost all other captives—including Johnson, Hanson, and Norton—were taken in the late summer or early autumn.) Or, it might have reflected his own bitterness at the devastation of his family in the attack, as aside from his wife, he lost his daughter Eunice forever when she was adopted by the Kahnawake Indians and remained among them for the rest of her life.[34]

Aside from Williams's narrative, the most gruesome accounts of captivity were most often written by people who never experienced it themselves. Cotton Mather's catalogue of frontier atrocities in King William's War reads like a rusticated *Foxe's Book of Martyrs,* as he amplified the theme of family destruction, and in particular, the slaughter of young English children. In his telling, English babies and children (variously) had their eyes popped out, their brains bashed out, and their bodies either chopped to pieces or hung up in trees. Mather emphasized the inversions of rightful authority that went with these attacks on English families, noting that one Indian perpetrator who was "once a Servant of a *Christian Master* in *Boston,* was become the Master of [a] *Little Christian."* In one undoubtedly entirely imaginary scenario, he writes that after a 1690 attack on Wells, Maine, the Abenaki "fell to Dividing the Persons and Plunder, and Agreeing, that such an *English Captain,* should be Slave to such a one, and such a Gentleman in the Town should serve such a one, and his *Wife* be a *Maid of Honour,* to such or such a *Squaw* proposed, and Mr. *Wheelwright* (instead of being a Worthy Counsellor of the Province, which he *Now* is!) was to be the Servant of such a *Netop."* Mather's basic understanding of the effects of warfare in the northeastern borderlands was that it inverted English hierarchies, turning servants into masters, captains into slaves, and wives into ladies' maids.[35]

Because English men, women, and children alike had suffered the severe disruption of their families and the inversion of their social positions, they began their journey into captivity as people out of context, stripped of central parts of their identities. Rowlandson writes, "All was gone, my husband gone . . . my children gone, my relations and friends gone, our house and home and all our comforts within doors, and without, all was gone (except my life) and I knew not but the next moment that might go too." Later in her narrative, Rowlandson revisits this theme: Using the royal "we," she writes,"we had husband and father, and children, and sisters, and friends, and relations, and house, and home, and many comforts of this life: but now we may say, as Job, *Naked came I out of my mother's womb, and naked shall I return."* Susanna Johnson's family all survived the attack on their household and were all taken into captivity together, but she dreaded being separated from her extended family. "When the time came for us to prepare to march, I almost expired at the thought. To leave my aged parents, brothers, sisters and friends, and travel with savages, through a dismal forest to unknown regions," was too much to bear.[36] What was an English man without a wife—was he still a husband? Could he still claim the prerogatives of a male head of household? What was an English woman without a husband or children? Was she still a wife and mother? And who were the newly motherless and fatherless children of the frontier—to whom did they belong?

Perhaps it is understandable then that English men and women taken into captivity were eager to identify an Indian, always a man, as their "Indian Master." This evocation of the master-servant dyad was not entirely an inappropriate understanding of Indian family hierarchies, given the existence of servants and slaves in Indian families and communities. English captives did not identify their Indian masters after careful study and reflection on their place in their new families, however, but rather assumed for themselves the status of servitude based on their understandings of English household government. While some new captives were expected to take on the role of servants in Indian households and communities, captivity among the Indians was not the equivalent of being a European prisoner of war. As we have already seen, different captives enjoyed—or suffered— different fates. Some were adopted by their Indian families permanently, some joined Indian families only temporarily until they could be sold to the French, and some were ritually tortured and executed.[37] Some were probably expected to play the role of a servant, although evidence from their own captivity narratives strongly suggests that a rough egalitarianism prevailed in these fleeing wartime bands. If captives were expected to walk tens of miles a day with little refreshment, so was everyone else. If captives were expected to gather firewood and forage for food, so was everyone else. If the Indians had a successful hunt and prepared a feast, captives were expected to feast with them. This was as true of captives who were sold quickly as of those who were intended to be adopted permanently—in wartime, the members of the group needed to be able to work together for survival and a successful escape.

The English captives were correct in assuming that they were no longer in charge of the households they joined, however. English men in captivity were no longer in control of their fates, were not sources of spiritual and moral authority, and could no longer claim the economic privileges of being a head of household. English women in captivity were unable to keep their children close to them, and they were no longer mistresses of their own households with the liberty to decide how they spent their time and at what tasks they would work. Children in captivity did not suffer as much of a change in status in captivity as their parents did, because they were already household subordinates in their own families. They were all effectively reduced to what they believed was the status of a servant, so it is no wonder they went looking for a master.

For the most part, authors of captivity narratives use the term "master" quite un-self-consciously; furthermore, they usually have admiring things to say about their masters when they first introduce them in the text. Although she is an extremely proud and elite English woman, Mary Rowlandson first uses the term "master" when she describes threats from some of the Indians that "your master will knock your child on the head." But she soon begins calling Quinnapin "my master," explaining with some pride that he was a very high-status Wampanoag, "a sagamore, and married King Philip's wife's sister." Elizabeth Hanson was also eager to claim an important master, writing that the "Captain" of the Indians was her master. She was pleased with his consideration of her and her infant, as she was just fourteen days out of childbed when she was taken: "my Master, would mostly carry my Babe for me, which I took as a great Favour of God that his Heart was so tenderly inclined to assist me." He helped both her and her six-year-old son at stream crossings and other difficult passages, "in all which he shewed some Humanity and Civility more than I could have expected." Susanna Johnson writes that "my master . . . was as clever an Indian as I ever saw; he even evinced, at numerous times, a disposition that showed he was by no means void of compassion." Some of them explain— probably because of the benefits of hindsight—that this is their understanding of the Indian tradition. For example, Johnson, who wrote her narrative with more than half a century of hindsight, provides a helpful explanation that "according to their national practice, he who first laid hands on a prisoner, considered him as his property."[38] Stephen Williams, the son of Reverend John Williams, was taken at the age of ten in 1704, and his captivity narrative written in adulthood names his Indian "master" on the first page. John Gyles, taken in 1689 at age eleven, was also eager to identify an Indian master.[39]

Occasionally English captives were given mistresses instead of masters: for example, Joseph Bartlett was given to a woman he called his Indian mother, or mistress after his capture in 1708. Jemima Howe was given to "an old squaw, whom the Indians told me, I must call my mother." After her new mother's death of smallpox soon after, she writes, "our family [consisted of] three persons only, besides myself, viz. my later mother's daughter, whom therefore I called my sister, her sanhop, and a pappoose." She then assumes she belongs to her sister's *sannup*, or husband, and begins to call him her "master." Perhaps her Western Abenaki sister inherited her, but it is Howe's English assumptions that put her under the household government of her adopted brother-in-law. This would reflect the clear preference that English people express for naming a master rather than a mistress.[40]

It might not be too surprising that English women and children would look for an Indian master, as they were people who generally lived under the household government of husbands and fathers. But English men, too—even high-status English men—used the term "master" to describe the Indian man who seemed to direct their fates. For example, Nehemiah How, captured in 1745, readily identified a man as "my Master." The Reverend John Norton, captured the following year, identifies Indian men in the raiding party that captured him as masters of the English. The proud Reverend John Williams refers repeatedly to a man he calls "my Master." And even Increase Mather, in his rendition of the captivity narratives of both men and women, refers repeatedly to their Indian masters, as did his son Cotton Mather in his vituperative rants about the cruelty meted out to captives.[41] The notion of Indian mastery in captivity was acknowledged by all English writers of captivity narratives.

At first, submitting to Indian masters and sometimes complimenting them on their "civility" and "humanity" seems to reify the Indians' power over English captives. But as captivity narratives go on to describe life among fleeing Indian bands and wartime Native communities, the term "master" serves to undercut the presumed authority of these Indian heads of household. We will consider the ways in which English people represented their Indian families, and suggest that the experience of taking in English captives was difficult for their Native captors. Warfare and captivity brought English and Indian families into intimate contact with one another, an intimacy that was challenging for English and Indian peoples alike.

Earlier, we saw some of the elaborate rituals Natives employed in the process of adopting captives into their families and communities. Although many captives underwent these elaborate rituals of being tortured, stripped, redressed, and given new names and families, a smaller proportion of captives experienced permanent adoption into Indian families by the end of the seventeenth century. By the 1690s there was an established commerce in captives between the French in Québec and Montreal and their Indian allies, with a fixed bounty offered for male and female captives. From the opening skirmishes of King William's War in 1688 until the end of the Seven Years' War in 1763, the goal of most Native raiding parties was to get captives not for adoption into their own families but to redeem them for a price in Canada. The repeated disruptions of the Native economy caused by these seventy-five years of almost continuous hostilities meant that traditional trade relations with both the French and the English were largely suspended. Indian men had no one to buy the venison they hunted and furs they trapped, and because war and corn cultivation share the same seasons, Native women's fields were frequently spoiled, abandoned, or laid fallow. Accordingly, Native men and women traded in the commodity they could harvest in wartime and for which there was a ready market among the French: captives.[42] While a few of the captives discussed here were meant to be permanently adopted by their Indian families, most spent less than a year away from home—just until their Native captors could get them to market in Québec or Montreal, and then they were sent back home again, usually aboard ship to Boston. In some of the narratives, it is clear that Indian families had no interest in keeping the captives permanently, as the captives never underwent the kinds of transformative rituals described earlier (except for being stripped of some of their English clothing and shoes). Of course, even those writers who underwent adoption rituals (like John Gyles and Joseph Barrett) ultimately returned to New England society, and English men and women, boys and girls, who remained permanently with their adopted Native families left few records reflecting their point of view. Given the highly ideological nature of captivity narratives, what follows is at best a guess as to the actual experiences of both the English captives and their Indian families. I argue with more confidence the political intentions and effects that such stories had on the English colonial project.

After the surprise and savagery of the attack on themselves and their families, one of the first observations English people in captivity made about life with the Indians concerns the offensive and/or meager fare given to sustain them. While English captives sometimes interpreted the poor quality of food the Indians gave them as a personal insult, it is clear from their own accounts that the Indians were simply sharing what they had with their captives. And because the raiding parties were frequently themselves undernourished and on the run from possible capture, they were unable to provide much in the way of food. Even when they returned to their communities, the disruptions of war in a colonial economy based on agriculture and trade often meant that the starving times extended for months, and even years. Because of the seasonally mobile lifestyle of coastal Algonquians in New England, the Indians did not save and store vast quantities of provisions—usually just enough to winter over from the harvest and hunt of the autumn to the return to the planting grounds and coastal fishing of the spring. But the seasons of war were also spring, summer, and early autumn. This meant that the women's fields didn't get planted, or sowed fields had to be abandoned to enemies to harvest or burn. Furthermore, men who would have spent their time hunting, fishing, or trapping game to trade to the English or the French were in raiding parties or in battle, thus taking away from time spent on activities that would sustain their communities economically as well as nutritionally. Even if Native men had furs or venison to trade, war meant that trade relations were disrupted, not to mention dangerous. European allies sometimes had trouble distinguishing between "friend Indians" and the enemy, and by accident of nationality, near neighbors and trade partners might find themselves across enemy lines when war broke out. In the mid-eighteenth century, with the appearance of the British Army and Royal Navy in North American wars, rivers and harbors were blockaded, and forts that had served as trading posts became checkpoints on the frontier. Many Indians, not just those immediately involved in frontier warfare, sustained their communities on what they could gather, plunder, or trade on the black market, but warfare was almost always profoundly disruptive to the local and regional economies.[43]

Nevertheless, one of the most striking and consistent features of colonial captivity narratives are the loud complaints English people make about eating among the Indians.[44] Describing the Indians as having inferior provisions—whether by choice or privation—evoked a stereotype that would have been very clear to most colonial readers, that of the poor Indian. From the very beginnings of English contact with Native Americans, English explorers and writers described North American Indians as poor because of their simple material culture, their lack of urban centers, and their refusal to hoard possessions because of the Native emphasis on reciprocity and gift-giving as a way to maintain community and diplomatic ties. Compared with the fantastic treasures of the Aztecs and Mayas plundered by eager Spaniards, the simplicity of Indian life to the north disappointed English observers. As William Cronon has argued, constructing the Natives as poor was a crucial step toward depriving them of their lands. After all, with such a rich environment at their disposal, didn't their poverty suggest a lack of initiative? According to the English labor theory of value articulated in the anti-enclosure pamphlets of the Levellers and True Levellers (known as the Diggers), shouldn't a people committed to extracting and saving wealth from the land have the first opportunity to work it? English men and women in America might well ask, since the land was a common treasury for all, what right did "lazy" Indian men (always hunting or fishing, like pretended aristocrats) have to monopolize it? The fact that Indian women cultivated the land meant that their work was only selectively visible and rarely acknowledged by the English.[45]

The stereotype of Indian poverty was confirmed enthusiastically and amplified by writers of captivity narratives. Mary Rowlandson's narrative should be famous in its own right for its catalog of frontier dis-gustatory novelties: a few spoonfuls of parched corn, broth from a boiled horse's leg, the fetus of a pregnant doe, a handful of groundnuts or acorns, stews made from maggot-infested bones. Despite a week of near starvation, Rowlandson writes, "it was very hard to get down their filthy trash," but by the third week in flight with her captors, she regarded food that "formerly my stomach would turn against" rather "sweet and savory to my taste." Indeed, she relished feasts of bear-and-groundnut stew, or bear-and-pea stew, surely the best fare she met with in captivity. This acceptance of Indian foods in the face of starvation is also a trope of the genre. Recall Elizabeth Hanson's shock to see that her Abenaki captors preferred to eat rather than wear the "old Beaver-Skin Match-Coats" the Indians carried with them. Aside from beaver skins, Hanson and her children ate what the Abenaki gathered on the run, "Nutts, Berries, and Roots, they digg'd out of the Ground, with the Bark of some Trees," as well as the occasional squirrel or beaver. Hanson reports that she and her children were not given the choicest morsels of beaver; her captors allowed her only "the Guts and Garbage for my self and Children: But not allowing us to clean and wash them as they ought, made the Food very irksome to us," for except for "emptying the Dung . . . in that filthy Pickle we must boil them, and eat them." One of the most food-obsessed captivity narratives is surely Jemima Howe's, who describes eating "crusts and crumbs of bread" out of a greasy swill pail at a French house and saving untasted a precious morsel of bread for one of her hungry children. At each reunion she has with her scattered captive children, she describes the appearance of one of the babies as "greatly emaciated, almost starved." This child even ravenously bit her in the cheek "like a starved and mangy puppy, that had been wallowing in the ashes."[46]

These complaints aside, most English captives affirmed that Native people shared their food equally with their captives. Nevertheless, their stories still confirm the stereotype of poor Indians, since sharing such foul fare generously seemed but a small favor to the English. Stephen Williams remembered a feast of "moose's paunch and bones," stewed "without cleansing of it, for what was on it served for thickening the broth." By comparison, the dried moose meat he was given the following day tasted like "the best victuals I ever eat." John Gyles recalled a somewhat more plentiful diet of "Fish, Wild-Grapes, Roots, &c." among the Maliseet (Eastern Abenaki) in the 1690s, but he still called it "hard Living to me." Henry Grace had an easier time in captivity too, in part because the French allies of his Mi'kmaq captors during the Seven Years' War provisioned them with "salt Beef, Pork, and Pease, and Indian Corn." Despite this relative bounty, Grace complains about the preparation of Indian cuisine, calling it "filthy and wretched. They eat their Meat sometimes raw, and sometimes they would fling it upon a Fire, till it was a little warm" or "put it in a Kettle and boil it with the Hairs sticking about it, and eat it not one quarter done." But like all other captives, he concedes that "Hunger will make a Man eat what he could not think on, and Necessity will force one to do any thing." When food was on hand, the English still complained. Instead of praising the practice of Indian sharing at great feasts, English captives scorned it as immoderate and wasteful. Elizabeth Hanson echoed the thoughts of many captives when she complained that "these kind of People, when they have Plenty, spend it as freely as they get it; spending in Gluttony and Drunkenness in two Days Time, as much, as with prudent Management might serve a Week." Cleverly, therefore, the English could criticize the Indians for both meanness and profligacy at the same time. "Thus do they live, for the most part, either in Excess of Gluttony and Drunkenness, or under great Straits for Want of Necessaries."[47]

Native communities did not suffer open expressions of disgust at their food or their manner of feasting, which they interpreted as an insult to their generosity. When they had food to eat, they shared it with their captives, and Indians customarily feasted until the food was gone. Some captives understood this central tenet of Indian etiquette, like Jemima Howe, who hoarded bread for a child of hers only to share it with all of the Indian children in the wigwam with him, "otherwise I should have given great offense." Other English captives did not learn this valuable lesson until they had suffered profoundly. Quinton Stockwell reported that in his captivity in the 1670s, he and his captors fled Deerfield, Massachusetts, for Canada in the dead of winter. At the end of a day's journey, they stopped at a lake where "[they] were again sadly put to it for Provision," and were "fain to eat Touchwood fried in Bears Greace." Happily, he writes, "[we found] a company of *Raccoons,* and then we made a Feast, and the manner was, that we must eat all." But Stockwell apparently rebelled at the Indian custom of eating until the feast was gone, perhaps wanting to save some for the difficult journey ahead. "I perceived there would be too much for one time, so one *Indian* that sat next to me, bid me slip away some to him under his Coat, and he would hide it for me till another time." But Stockwell was betrayed by his pretended ally: "this *Indian* as soon as he had got my Meat, stood up and made a Speech to the rest, and discovered me, so that the *Indians* were very angry, and cut me another piece, and gave me *Raccoon Grease* to drink, which made me sick and Vomit." Refusing to accede to Indian ways cost him more than just his meal that night. Amidst his sickness, he says "I told them I had enough; so that ever after that they would give me none; but still tell me, I had *Raccoon* enough: so I suffered much, and being frozen was full of Pain, and could sleep but a little, yet must do my work." When the Indians killed a moose "and staid there till they had eaten it all up," he does not say that he was invited to the feast. His situation grew graver still, when they were delayed in their journey for three weeks due to bad weather and "had no provision but *Raccoons,* so that the *Indians* themselves thought they should be starved." True to their threat at the last raccoon feast, Stockwell reports, "they gave me nothing, so that I was sundry dayes without any Provision." Only after Stockwell nearly dies of exposure and frostbite to his feet do the Indians begin to share food with him again.[48]

Beyond maintaining the stereotype of the poor Indian, complaining about their dinners (or lack of them) in captivity had other political uses, as Elizabeth Hanson's narrative makes clear. She connects the family's hunger to her master's failures as a man and uses it to make a broader critique of Indian household government. Because one of the great privileges of English headship was the legal ownership and economic control of all of the family's resources, one of the biggest responsibilities of a male head of household was to provide for its well-being. Husbands, fathers, and masters who failed to provide for their dependents were hardly worthy of the name of men, let alone the privileges of manhood.[49] Hanson reports that her Indian master did not live up to this most important test of an English man's worth, and what was worse, he took out his own failures on his dependents. Upon their return to the "*Indian* Fort" home to her Indian family, Hanson writes, "my Master went a hunting, and was absent about a Week." This was to be expected; Hanson and her family were captured in the late summer of 1724, so their return to the Indians' home base probably coincided with the beginning of the autumn hunt. Before he left for the hunt, Hanson writes that her Indian master ordered her "in his Absence to get in Wood, gather Nuts, &c. I was very diligent, cutting the Woods, and putting it in

Order, not having very far to carry it." Despite the fact that (as she tells it) Hanson performs as admirably as any Native woman at her work, "when he returned, having got no Prey, he was very much out of Humour, and the Disappointment was so great, that he could not forbear revenging it on us poor Captives." Although "he allowed me a little boyled Corn for self and Child," he "with a very angry Look threw a Stick or Corn-Cob at me, with such Violence as did bespeak he grudged our Eating." She grabbed her six-year-old son and ran out of the wigwam with him, but her master followed her, "tore my Blanket off my Back, and took my little Boy from me and struck him down as he went along before him." Such despotism was unmanly, as well as "unreasonable," a word Hanson uses repeatedly to describe her Indian master. She was at a loss to understand his anger at her and her son, especially since she believed that she had done as he had asked.[50]

When Hanson's master chased her out of his wigwam, his mother-in-law intervened on her behalf. Hanson reports, "[She] came and sat down by me, and told me, *I must sleep there that Night.* She then going from me a little Time, came back with a small Skin to cover my Feet withal, informing, that my Master intended now to kill us; and I being desirous to know the Reason, expostulated, that *in his Absence I had been diligent to do as I was ordered by him.* Thus, as well as I could, I made her sensible how unreasonable he was." As an English woman accustomed to the rules of household government, Hanson does not question his absolute right to beat her or her son—she complains about her ill treatment because she does not believe that she has given him any reason to be displeased with her (and implies that if she had been remiss in her duties, then she would understand his decision to punish her). Thus, he is not "unreasonable" for attacking her; he is unreasonable because, according to her lights, he does not have a good reason to use this form of household government. As he is unable to perform a man's duties in feeding his family, and "unreasonable" in his use of his power, Hanson calls into question the legitimacy of his rule.[51]

This incident was only the first of many in which Hanson was tormented because of her Abenaki master's inability to hunt successfully and feed his family, a problem that was exacerbated by the fact that war probably made them even more dependent on hunting and gathering rather than farming. "Not long after this, he got into the like ill Humour again, threatening to take away my Life. But I always observed when-ever he was in such a Temper, he wanted Food, and was pinched with Hunger." When his luck was better, and he brought home "either Bears, Beavers, Bucks or Fowls, on which he could fill his Belly, he was better humoured." Even with a full stomach, though, "he was naturally of a very hot and passionate Temper, throwing Sticks, Stones, or whatever lay in his Way, on every slight Occasion." Although Hanson clearly preferred a successful hunt to an unsuccessful hunt, she used this opportunity to criticize the household management practices of her Indian master and mistress. Once, "having shot some wild Duck; and now he appeared in a better Temper, ordering the Fowls to be dress'd with Speed." As Quinton Stockwell learned, much to his mortification, Indians ate when they had food and went hungry when they did not. This appeared to the English to be greedy, not to mention imprudent. Feast or famine, neither was the way of prudent English household government.[52]

While Hanson focuses her commentary on the inscrutable ill-temper of her "master," her own narrative gives some clues as to the distribution of power in the Abenaki family. When looked at from the Native perspective, the women in the family look much more in control of things than Hanson recognizes. In captivity she along with her infant daughter and her six-year-old son joined a family that consisted of her master, his wife, their daughter, and the aforementioned mother-in-law. Thus, there were at least two and possibly three adult women in the family, and they were the family members she spent most of her time with. When we revisit the anecdote of the master's attack on Hanson and her son, the women in this household seem to have not just influence but a small measure of power. When her master first strikes out by throwing "a Stick or Corn-Cob" at her, Hanson writes that "[a]t this his Squaw and Daughter broke out in a great Crying." In remembering this event, she casts them as victims of domestic violence like herself: "This made me fear Mischief was hatching against us." Perhaps they cried out not in fear, but to protest his cruelty, perhaps angrily demanding that he stop; the women were evidently not powerless, since the older woman stepped in at this point to separate Hanson from her master and to protect her through the night. After the mother-in-law settles her in a different dwelling, Hanson writes "She then going from me a little Time, came back with a small Skin to cover my Feet withal" and comforts her even though she brings bad news. The two women "reasoned as well as [they] could," Hanson writes, but how they did so is unclear since Hanson reports no familiarity with Abenaki and never suggests that the Indians spoke English. Nevertheless, she writes that the older woman told her, "my Master intended now to kill us; . . . advising me, by pointing up with her Fingers, in her Way, to pray to God, endeavouring by her Signs and Tears to instruct me in that which was most needful, *viz.* to prepare me for Death, which now threatened me." Once again, Hanson made sense of the mother-in-law's speech by putting it into a familiar context, explaining it by imposing upon it her Christian belief as well as an Englishwoman's belief in male mastery that she and the mother-in-law were powerless (except through prayer) to thwart her master's supposed plans. Hanson notes at one point that "the poor old Squaw, who was so very kind and tender," designed "what she could do to asswage her Son-in-law's Wrath." But note: instead of emphasizing the woman's agency, Hanson ascribes maternal virtues to her ("kind and tender") and writes that her efforts will be to "asswage" his wrath rather than to chastise him for it. Instead of portraying her as a confident matriarch, Hanson describes her as a "poor old Squaw," triply powerless by dint of poverty, age, and sex. Despite the older woman's active, successful intervention (her son-in-law "went to Rest, and forgot it"), Hanson does not credit the mother-in-law with taking control of the situation and demanding better behavior from her son-in-law but rather portrays her as a fellow victim, albeit a sympathetic one.[53]

In addition to their help in this dramatic confrontation, the women in this family regularly assisted and advised Hanson as she adjusted to life with them. While she notes in detail the valuable guidance the women gave her, in the end she portrays them not as powerful actors in family life but as agents of God's will, thereby crediting patriarchal and Christian power instead of recognizing Indian women's agency and authority over her. As noted earlier in this chapter, when her milk dries up and her infant daughter became "very poor and weak, just Skin and Bone; for [she] could perceive all its Joynts from one End of the Babe's Back to the other," the women taught her how to make a lifesaving pap of walnuts and corn meal. But, she says she was always confident that she and her children would survive not because of the Indian women looking after them, but because of the "over-ruling Power of him in whose Providence I put my Trust, both Day and Night." Although the mother-in-law eventually leaves the family, perhaps out of frustration with her son-in-law's violent behavior, Hanson's Indian mistress and daughter continue to advise her and to protect her son. But when Hanson reports that her master fell ill and thereafter promised to reform his ways, she credits not the Indian women of the family, or the medicine woman who consults with her master during his illness, but the great Master in heaven: "This I took as the Lord's Doing, and it was marvellous in my Eyes."[54] Because female headship or leadership in families was so difficult for English women to credit, Hanson blames her master for what she sees as the unruliness of his household, thereby denying Indian women's authority as well as undermining Indian men's authority. In the end, she gives the Indian family an appropriate male leader by making them subject to the will of God.

Like Hanson, Jemima Howe adapted successfully to her Indian family after a short while, as noted above, but also like Hanson she complains of the irrational despotism of the Western Abenaki man she deems the head of their household. Her Indian sister's husband, "having been out with a scouting party to some of the English settlements, had a drunken frolick at the fort, when he returned." Howe writes, "my sister . . . who never got drunk, but had often experienced the ill effects of her husband's intemperance, fearing what the consequence might prove, if he should come home in a morose and turbulent humour, to avoid his insolence, proposed we should both retire, and keep out of the reach of it, until the storm abated." Like Hanson, she casts the Western Abenaki woman as a fellow victim of male cruelty. They went away for a while, but Howe returned before her sister to find her adopted brother-in-law, as she tells it, "in a surly mood; and not being able to revenge upon his wife, because she was not at home, he laid hold of me," not to strike or abuse her, but "for a trifling consideration, [he] sold me to a French gentleman." She rejoices to be "beyond the reach of [the Indians'] insolent power," especially since her former brother-in-law eventually sobers up and gets angry that he sold her so cheaply to the French man. Because "his indignation rose so high, that he threatened to kill me if he should ever meet me alone, or if he could not revenge himself thus, that he would set fire to the fort."[55] Howe's narrative labors to show that her former brother-in-law, like all Indian men, was incapable of governing himself or his family.

Other stories of captivity emphasize the bloodthirsty irrationality that supposedly drove Indian men. Rebekah Taylor, taken in Queen Anne's War, was threatened with sudden and cruel death when "she was violently insulted by Sampson, her bloody master, who without any provocation was resolved to hang her; and for want of a rope, made use of his girdle . . . [and] attempted to hoist her up on the limb of a tree." However, "in hoisting her, the weight of her body broke it asunder, which so exasperated the cruel tyrant that he made a second attempt." After he failed again at that execution, he attempted to bludgeon her but was halted by another Indian man. Another woman taken in the same war, Hannah Parsons of Wells, Maine, allegedly was told by the Indians, "for want of food, [they] had determined to roast alive" her child. The babe's life was spared (according to the narrative's author) only when "a company of French Mohawks came down the river in a canoe with three dogs, which somewhat revived these hungry monsters, expecting to make a feast of one of them." The Mohawks rejected the offer of Parsons's child in exchange for the dogs, but they accepted a gun in return, "and by that means the child was preserved."[56] Elizabeth Hanson was similarly threatened by her "unreasonable" master that once her ailing child *was fat enough, it should be killed, and he would eat it.*" He even went so far as to order Hanson "to fetch him a Stick that he had prepared for a Spit, to roast the Baby upon." Then, he ordered her to "undress the Infant. When the Child was naked, he felt its Arms, Legs, and Thighs, and told me, *It was not fat enough yet.*" Could there have been any strategic reason for executing Taylor, or Parsons's and Hanson's babies? Presumably yes, if any one of them was lame, ill, or too big to carry and yet too small to walk quickly and quietly through the woods as their captors fled English capture. The suggestion that Indians would have eaten the babies can be rejected out of hand, as there is no evidence of Algonquian or Iroquois Indians eating human flesh as a desperate survival strategy. Perhaps the Indians were teasing them, or perhaps Parsons and her interlocutor were mistaken about Indian intentions entirely. (Hanson suggests that her master's ruse was merely a cruel joke: "Now tho' he thus acted, I could not perswade my self, that he intended to do as he pretended.")[57] But English authors of captivity narratives had no interest in making Indian men seem reasonable or rational.

While Hanson and Howe reveal the fact that their Indian mistresses and sisters were crucial to their comfort and survival, not all captive women saw their female captors as their allies. In fact, Mary Rowlandson greatly preferred her masters to her mistresses, and she was enormously resentful of the authority that other women had over her in captivity. She appears to suffer tremendously her loss of status as a middle-aged English wife and mother—someone who was the manager of a busy household and who was therefore at the height of her influence. Although Rowlandson recognizes Native women's authority more readily than Hanson, her narrative also works to challenge Indian sovereignty by portraying their families as disorderly. Whereas Hanson portrays her Abenaki family as disordered by the "unreasonable" tyranny of the Indian master, Rowlandson implicitly challenges Indian men's right to rule by dwelling on the power of the women and painting them as monstrous caricatures of "insolent squaws." From the perspective of the English, Indian masters were only diminished by their wives' and mothers' authority.

From the perspective of her Narragansett and Wampanoag captors, few captives were probably ever as annoying as Rowlandson. An elite English woman, Rowlandson's husband, Joseph, was a minister of some renown (despite his obscure western Massachusetts pulpit). She remained acutely sensitive not just to the loss of her roles as wife and mother in captivity but of the attendant loss in status she suffered in going from a minister's wife to a lowly servant of Quinnapin, a Narragansett sachem, and one of his wives, a ranking Wampanoag leader, Weetamoo. Earlier, we saw how she fought this loss of status by vigilantly defending her apron from the designs of a woman she deemed beneath her, to the point that she almost lost her life to preserve this remnant of her former life. Although scholars have convincingly argued that Increase Mather probably had a large role in its publication, and perhaps even in its authorship, Rowlandson's narrative was (and remains) popular in part because of the strong, clear voice of the narrator. Throughout the narrative this voice is one of utter and complete indignation.[58]

Rowlandson's narrative is different from Hanson's in two important respects: she reports that she continues to do traditional English women's work rather than Indian women's work, and she portrays the Indian women as powerful although she despises them for it. Indeed, Rowlandson blames the women in the fleeing band of King Philip's partisans for almost every hardship and insult that she endures. She carried meal for them along with her "knitting work," but when she asked to refresh herself with "one spoonful of the meal, [her mistress] would not give [her] a taste." Frequently she contrasts her hard work at providing the Indians with quality handmade English shirts and stockings with their base ingratitude and abuse of her. In her first week of captivity, Rowlandson writes that she "was at this time knitting a pair of white cotton stockings for my mistress." When Sunday came, she reports, "they bade me go to work; I told them it was the Sabbath day, and desired them to let me rest, and told them I would do as much more tomorrow; to which they answered me, they would break my face." One reason they probably threatened Rowlandson to keep working, and presumably to keep moving to safe territory, is that the English were in hot pursuit. She reports that the following day they burned their wigwams and fled, "on that very day came the English army after them to this river, . . . yet this river put a stop to them," so Rowlandson remained in captivity.[59]

By contrast, she portrays the men as nurturing and even kindly, perhaps because she more readily accepts their authority than that of their wives. When her captors join with Philip's group and trade news, she writes that she falls into conversation with a number of Indians. "One of them asked me, why I wept, I could hardly tell what to say: yet I answered, they would kill me: No, said he, none will hurt you. Then came one of them and gave me two spoonfuls of meal to comfort me, and another gave me half a pint of peas; which was more worth than many bushels at another time."[60] Since women controlled the food resources, especially food they had grown or gathered, it is likely that Indian women were the donors of these prizes, but Rowlandson portrays these Indian men as though they had the property rights of English men.

Unlike most other captives, Rowlandson parlays her skills in needle-work successfully, and a number of her captors ask her to make or repair a number of knit or cloth items for them. She makes a shirt and a cap for King Philip's son, and her master allows her to keep the money she made on the job. Earning her own money and food became a way for her to attempt to reclaim her status, as she relates an attempt to entertain her master, Quinnapin, and her mistress Weetamoo. After being paid with peas and some bear meat for making a shirt and stockings for some other Indians, "I boiled my peas and bear together, and invited my master and mistress to dinner, but the proud gossip, because I served them both in one dish, would eat nothing, except one bit that he gave her upon the point of his knife."[61] Weetamoo rejects Rowlandson's efforts to feed them and thus to reconstruct herself as their equal rather than their servant. Rowlandson bitterly resents this reminder of her powerlessness in captivity, chastising Weetamoo as a "proud gossip," an insult that suggests that it was Weetamoo and not Rowlandson who was the illegitimate mistress of the household.

Other narratives suggest that the English problem with authority in Native households was its divided nature—some captives identified not just one but several masters or mistresses. Instead of having one master to answer to, other men and women presumed to rule as well. Quinton Stockwell initially belonged to the man who captured him, but he was put into "great danger," when "A quarrel arose about me, whose Captive I was, for three took me. . . . They agreed to have all a share in me: and I had now three Masters." This hardly settled the dispute, certainly not from Stockwell's point of view, as he writes that his "chief Master" was the man "who laid hands on [me] first," but in this "was I fallen into the hands of the very worst of all the Company." According to Stockwell, it did not take long for this arrangement to break down. "Here I had a Shirt brought to me, to make, and one *Indian* said it should be made this way, a second another way, a third his way. I told them I would make it that way that my chief Master said." This displeased one of his other masters, "whereupon one *Indian* struck me on the face with his Fist. I suddenly rose up in anger ready to strike again, upon this hapned a great Hubbub, and the *Indians* and *English* came about me; I was fain to humble myself to my Master, so that matter was put up."[62]

Was the fury of Indian masters and mistresses so "unreasonable?" While captivity narratives focus almost exclusively on the pain, distress, and discomfort of English people trying to live as Indians, many of the narratives suggest that their presence in Native households was intrusive and annoying. Work seems to have been a focus of many of the conflicts between captives and their Native families, as families in wartime could not afford to support unproductive additional adults and children. As we have seen already, the work expected of captives was most likely not the kind of work they were accustomed to: Elizabeth Hanson came to blows with her master after she had been sent to gather firewood; Quinton Stockwell was put to English women's work rather than men's work; and Mary Rowlandson was resentful of any work compelled by mistresses rather than her Indian masters.

Susanna Johnson openly acknowledged the problems her presence might cause in the economic functioning of the Western Abenaki family she joined at the mission town of Odanak (also known as St. Francis) when she greeted them by saying that she was grateful "for being introduced to a house of high rank, and requested their patience while I should learn the customs of the nation." Johnson faced challenges even in the simplest tasks, like learning how to sit on the ground and eat from a common pot: "The squaws first fall upon their knees, and then sit back upon their heels. This was a posture that I could not imitate." She feared being thought "indelicate and unpolite" in her attempts to imitate this posture, but she recalls, "I advanced to my pudding with the best grace I could, not, however, escaping some of their funny remarks." More important, though, were the productive skills she lacked entirely: "I was a novice at making canoes, bunks, and tumplines, which was the only occupation of the squaws." Aside from this traditional labor, her new family evidently took advantage of the skills she possessed as an English woman, as she reports "the privilege of making shirts for my [Indian] brother" and that she was "allowed to milk the cows." Despite her clumsiness, her St. Francis family showed her a great deal of consideration, treating her "with the same attention that they did their natural kindred," and perhaps even granting her more leisure time

than other squaws, as she reports that she visited with other English captives in the village "daily, and spent our time in conjecturing our future
destiny." At one point, she was permitted to leave St. Francis for a week's
visit with a French family that was friendly with her Indian brother, and at
another time she was brought along on a fishing expedition by a number
of women. Still weak from her recent childbirth and the traumas of her
overland journey to St. Francis, Johnson says that these troubles "gave my
companions a poor opinion of me; but they shewed no other resentment,
than calling me 'no good squaw,' which was the only reproach my sister
ever gave, when I displeased her." Johnson's St. Francis family seems to
have tolerated her intermittent work habits with relative equanimity, perhaps because Johnson portrays herself as a captive who tried to avoid of-
fending them by adapting to Indian ways as best she could.[63]

Jemima Howe makes no mention of the work she did while at St.
Francis with another (presumably Western Abenaki) family, but she rejoices after being sold to a Monsieur "Saccappee" and installed in a French
home. "My service in the family to which I was now advanced, was perfect
freedom, in comparison of what it had been among the barbarous Indians."
Presumably she found working at European housewifery more attractive,
despite the fact that keeping house for Saccappee and his "warm and resolute son" turned into another kind of ordeal. Finding herself betwixt two
rivals for her affections, "I found myself in a very critical situation indeed,
and was greatly embarassed and perplexed, hardly knowing many times,
how to behave in such a manner as at once to secure my own virtue, and
the good esteem of the family in which I resided." These sorts of romantic
complications or intimations of sexual danger never appear in New England women's accounts of Indian captivity in this period.[64]

The ways in which former captives and other English writers portray
Indian families as deviant may have differed, although their effect was the
same: to undermine a central rationale for Native independence by portraying Indian families as ungoverned and out of control. Native men were
weak and unmanly on the one hand, and yet they were tyrants too. Their
wives were "insolent" and powerful, and yet they were subject to the unreasonable (or even abusive) demands of their husbands. Furthermore, Indian
children were allowed to run wild, whereas English captive children were
beaten or killed mercilessly. In suggesting that there was no logic to Indian
family life, English captivity narratives implicitly argued that there was no
sense in allowing Indians to govern themselves.

In colonial New England, however, captivity narratives largely served an Anglo-American reading public that liked to be reassured simultaneously of its virtue and of the savagery of Indians. After all, authors of captivity narratives were almost by definition people who had returned to New England and were eager to reaffirm its values. The stories of the captives who didn't come home—although largely unspoken and unwritten—were certainly more distressing than those who did.

Chapter 4
"A Jesuit will ruin you Body & Soul!"
Daughters of New England in Canada

> *When my Mother heard the talk of my being sold to a Jesuit, she said to me, Oh! my dear Child! If it were GOD's Will, I had rather follow you to your Grave! Or never see you more in this World, than you should be Sold to a Jesuit: for a Jesuit will ruin you Body & Soul!*
>
> —*John Gyles,* Memoirs of Odd Adventures *(1736)*

In the 1690s in the midst of the first war with New France, English depictions of frontier warfare and captivity shifted dramatically from identifying Indians as the primary danger to New England to portraying the French and their Catholicism as the chief threat to the New England way. While Indians were still formidable opponents in the battle, in New England they came to be feared more as agents of the French than as actors in their own right by the turn of the century. Even more threatening than cross-dressing Indians were European enemies who had studied the tactics of their Native allies so well. French Catholics proved more successful than Indians at encouraging English people to cross cultural borders and live among them for the rest of their lives. European Catholics were perhaps even more disturbing than Indian enemies because they were not all that different from English Protestants. They dressed the same, they did the same work, they ate the same food, they worshipped the same God—and thus they could be plotting and scheming just about anywhere and at any time. As we have seen previously, these similarities in an enemy were more frightening than readily identifiable differences.[1] Thus New Englanders began to worry less about Indian captivity and more about the vulnerability of captives in the hands of dedicated missionaries like the Jesuits, Ursulines, Sulpicians, and the Sisters of the Congregation of Notre Dame. Captivity narratives began to discuss the dedicated efforts that French priests and nuns made to convert their English prisoners of war, a theme that was entirely new in the 1690s and became a feature of the genre through the Seven Years' War (1756–63).

What was perhaps additionally disturbing about French successes in getting and keeping English captives is that the majority of the captives were New England's daughters, sisters, wives, and widows. While male captives always comprised the majority of New Englanders in captivity (mostly as prisoners of war, sometimes as adopted captives), female captives were vastly more likely to remain in Canada, convert to Catholicism, and marry.[2] This apparent danger to female captives jibed with long-standing puritan fears of women's greater vulnerability to spiritual corruption, as well as their specific susceptibility to the seductions of Catholicism. The sensually rich experiences of the Mass were believed to be powerfully attractive to unlearned, undisciplined women, as they had already proved to be to the Indians living in the French mission villages like Odanak (St. Francis), Kahnawake, La Montaigne, and Lorette.[3] Girls and women who remained in Canada became the focus of a great deal of familial and cultural anxiety in New England, as they lived lives that openly rejected the faith, language, and laws of their fathers. The following pages offer some explanations for their decisions to stay in Canada, choices that so baffled, wounded, and disturbed their families and communities in New England.

While for a time they were the subjects of intense diplomacy and worry on the part of their families and New England officials alike, these girls and women have been largely forgotten in the histories of the northeastern borderlands. This is partly because they did not write narratives about their experiences the way returned captives did, but it may also be due in part to their families' shame of daughters or sisters who stayed in Canada even when they were free to return to New England, and even in the face of parental and brotherly pleading and admonitions to come home. Because these women chose to remain in Canada, the sources for understanding their motivations and their lives in Canada are very thin.[4] Furthermore, once these girls and women decided to remain in Canada, their New England families apparently had very little to say about them. While some educated and well-connected families like the Williamses of Deerfield, the Wheelwrights of Wells, and the Storers of Wells and Boston corresponded with their daughters later in life in the hopes of convincing them to come home to New England, most New England families evidently disinherited and turned their backs on their disobedient daughters. (As we will see, the Wheelwrights and Storers disinherited their daughters, too.) Why is it that the usually prolific, expansive, and furious New England writers like Cotton Mather had so little to say about these girls and women who did not come home? Perhaps the shame and anger they felt both at being bested by the French, as well as because of their daughters' defiance, explains why these women's stories have been largely deleted from the family histories of New England.[5]

New England's paranoia about the designs of the French and their success- ful alliances with Indians emerged in local writings and publications as early as King Philip's War (1675–78). Reports on the war's progress on the Maine and western Massachusetts frontiers note the presence and influence of the French among the Indians. By the time of the first war with New France, the English came to see the French as their major—if not yet their only— rivals for the control of North America.[6] The clear success of the French in creating political and diplomatic alliances with Indians (particularly with the Eastern Abenaki and the mission Iroquois) made a formidable Euro- pean foe truly frightening to the English living in the northeastern border- lands at the end of the seventeenth century.

Fear and loathing of the French as enemies went hand-in-glove with the strong anti-Catholicism that was a foundational part of New England's sense of its historical and religious mission.[7] Because religion and national- ism were so intertwined for English Protestants in the early modern era, it is impossible to separate New Englanders' fears of French political and mili- tary victories and their fear of being compelled to embrace Catholicism. As we have seen, New England was founded by people who were especially zealous adherents to several versions of reformed Protestantism. They and their descendants believed that warfare and Indian captivity in the north- eastern borderlands were evidence, variously, of God's disfavor or his will- ingness to test their faith. New Englanders who saw Indian warfare as an opportunity to test and prove their faith were even more willing to see wars against Catholic New France as an extension of Christ's struggle against the Devil for worldwide domination. Furthermore, just as Indian warfare in North America was rich with gendered meanings, anti-Catholicism in Old and New England was also a strongly gendered phenomenon. Ever since the struggles between Elizabeth and Mary Queen of Scots for the English throne in the 1560s and 1570s, Protestant propagandists had effectively linked Catholicism with femininity and claimed that this feminization was both the cause and result of political and spiritual corruption. By the seven- teenth century, xenophobia and misogyny were knit into the fabric of trans-atlantic English nationalism. All English people were in theory united by their collective struggle against the "Scarlet Whore of Babylon," the foreign and feminized Roman church.[8]

With King William's War under way (1688–97), New England writers and publishers of the 1690s produced some of its first virulently anti-French and anti-Catholic books and pamphlets; unsurprisingly, Cotton Mather was one of the most enterprising purveyors of this propaganda. Mather connected French imperial ambitions to the ambitions of the Church of Rome and used specific historical examples to highlight the despotism of both the French crown and the Church. The chief threat to New England's security was a "French *Nero*," according to Mather, and he goes on to portray New England as Zion under the unforgiving sandal of Roman persecution. New Englanders' typological identification with the Israelites still resonated at the end of the seventeenth century; Mather's parishoners' and readers' grandparents and great-grandparents had fled persecution in England and understood their errand to New England as the Exodus, Israelites fleeing Egyptian slavery for the liberty of the Promised Land. Mather cites Isaiah, always a favorite of New England ministers in warfare because of its feminine imagery and references to doleful captivity: *"The Daughter of Zion . . . she being Desolate, shall sit upon the Ground."* Mather claims that this Old Testament prophecy foretold the Roman conquest of Judea: "there were Coins made in Commemoration of that Conquest, and on those Coins there was a Remarkable Exposition of this Prophesy. On the Reverse of those Medals, which are to be seen unto this Day, there is, *A Silent Woman sitting upon the Ground, and leaning against a Palm-tree, with this Inscription* IUDAEA CAPTA." He further explains the singularity of this kind of coin, as no "Conquered City or Countrey, before this of *Judea*, [was] ever thus drawn upon Medals, as, *A Woman sitting upon the Ground,*" and then suggests an appropriate commemorative token for his times: "if poor *New-England*, were to be shown upon her old Coin, we might show her *Leaning* against her Thunder-struck *Pine tree, Desolate, sitting upon the Ground.* Ah! *New England!* Upon how many Accounts, mayst thou say with her, in Ruth I 13. *The Hand of the Lord is gone out against me!*" Mather's books and other contemporary pamphlets show that both the Roman empire and the Church of Rome represented despotic power in the minds of New Englanders and stood only for the power to compel people of the true faith to worship false gods.[9]

For once, we cannot dismiss Mather's fears as mere paranoia, as the French had purposefully and determinedly sought to bring their religion to the Indians. Led chiefly by the energetic Catholic Reformation orders of the Jesuits and the Ursulines, religious men traveled down the St. Lawrence River to the Great Lakes, up to Hudson's Bay, and down the Mississippi to spread their faith, and they established successful Indian missions throughout New France and its borderlands from modern-day Maine and Nova Scotia westward to Ontario, Michigan, and the Mississippi River valley. Religious women established schools in Québec, Montreal, and Three Rivers that served as vital centers for the preservation and transmission of French language and culture as well as religion. The work of these French men and women stood in direct contrast to the distinctly underfunded efforts of the English to convert Indians and establish "praying towns." Only a minority of English ministers and settlers expended any efforts whatsoever on preaching to and converting Native Americans, efforts that would by the eighteenth century mark a preacher who spent any time at all with Indians as a distinctly marginal character. An English advocate for Protestant missionaries in western Massachusetts in the mid-eighteenth century observed tellingly that candidates for such work "must be strongly actuated by self Denying Princepalls as well as Zeal for Religion." There were certainly no other rewards for the work.[10]

Cotton Mather agreed with other frontier observers that New England had failed grievously in its neglect of the souls of the Indians, and he argued that King William's War was in part God's punishment of New England for failing their duty to spread the gospel as energetically as French priests had brought their religion to the New World: *"This is the Vengeance of God upon you, because you did no more, for the Conversion of those Miserable Heathen."* But Mather's concern about Protestant missionary work was not simply for fear of the Lord's judgment; he also saw how French missionary work had paid off in their strong military alliances with the Eastern and Western Abenaki in particular. "Had we done, but half so much as the *French Papists* have done, to Proselyte the *Indians* of our East, unto the *Christian Faith,* instead of being, *Snares and Traps* unto us, *and Scourges in our Sides, and Thorns in our Eyes* they would have been, *A wall unto us, both by Night and Day."* Mather supports this observation with the claim that English captives of the Indians had been told by their captors that *"had the English been as careful to Instruct us, as the French, we had been of your Religion!"* While at other times in the same book Mather scorns the close association between the French and the Indians, disdaining the *"Frenchified Indians"* and *"Indianized French"* that were the result of such New World alliances, in the end he recognizes the advantage of their cooperation and blames New England

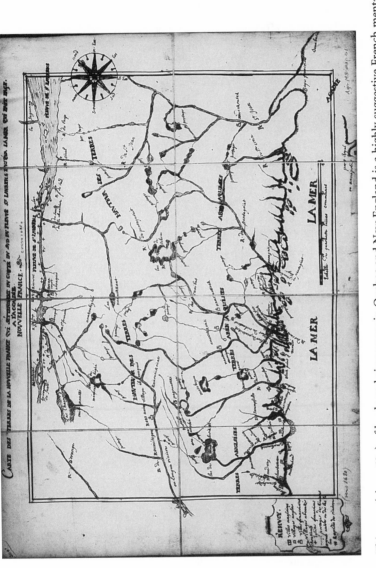

Figure 11. This map (circa 1680) of lands and rivers now in Quebec and New England is a highly suggestive French mental map of the northeastern borderlands at the outset of the imperial wars. French settlements are grouped at the top of the map, with thick development suggested by dozens of crosses along the St. Lawrence River. Additionally, French influence and interest is signaled by the four missions spread throughout the "Terres Abenaquises" toward the bottom of the map. According to the key at the bottom left of the map, the same symbol—a square topped with a cross—is used for both "Villes Francoises" and "Villages Abenakis." English settlement ("Terres Angloises") is acknowledged only in the far lower left of the map and along the coast. Moreover, English towns and villages are marked by plain squares, significantly not topped by crosses—an indication of French disdain for Protestant Christianity. Courtesy of the Newberry Library.

for not reaching out to the Indians. "[I]f the Salvages had been Enlightened with *The Christian Faith,* from us, the *French Papists* could never have instill'd into them those *French Poisons.*"[11]

Perhaps it was therefore natural that Mather played a key role in introducing explicitly anti-Catholic themes to captivity narratives with the publication of Hannah Swarton's story in 1697. Even amidst her difficult removes with the Indians after her capture from Casco in 1690, she reports, "yet I dreaded going to *Canada,* to the *French,* for fear lest I should be overcome by them, to yield to their Religion; which I had *Vowed* unto God, *That I would not do.* But the Extremity of my Sufferings were such, that at length I was willing to go, to preserve my Life." Like many New England captives who were brought to Canada, she was relieved to receive the hospitality of the French and gloried in eating familiar foods and dressing in European clothing once again. But this was the danger of consorting with the French—their way of life was so comfortable to English captives, especially after months or even years with the Indians, that it made captives all the more susceptible to seduction by "popery." After being taken to Québec and so "kindly Entertained" and "courteously provided for . . . so that I wanted nothing for my Bodily Comfort, which they could help me unto," she was inevitably cast into a conflict that caused her intense spiritual discomfort. (Many readers might have assumed that as a woman, she was naturally more easily seduced by creature comforts that appealed to her carnal nature.) But Swarton, as we hear her through Mather's pen, was all too aware of the dangers that faced her: "Here was a great and comfortable Change, as to my *Outward man,* in my *Freedom* from my former Hardships, and Hard hearted Oppressors. But here began a greater Snare and Trouble to my Soul and Danger to my *Inward man.*" Her mistress in Québec, and several priests and nuns "set upon me . . . to perswade me to Turn *Papist.*" Swarton, through Mather's narrative, claims that they sometimes used scriptural arguments, "which they pressed with very much Zeal, Love, Intreaties, and *Promises,*" and sometimes "Hard Usages," even threatening to send her "to *France,* and there I should be *Burned,* because I would not Turn to them." This kind of rhetoric served two purposes: it would stir up the emotions of the New England reading public to hear of the allegedly barbarous methods of French proselytizers, but it also gave Swarton and Mather the opportunity to demonstrate the steadfastness of her faith and prove herself a worthy model for other New Englanders to emulate.

Mather's presence as an author is very evident as he strives to portray her as both a warrior for her faith and as a dutifully submissive English woman. Through Mather's pen, Swarton becomes quite a proficient de-claimer of the truth of Christ, writing that through her ordeal she was com-forted by Psalm 118:17–18, "*I shall not Dy but live, and Declare the works of the Lord.*" She confessed that "I had very often, a secret perswasion, That I should *Live to Declare the Works of the Lord.*" Lest her declarations leave her open to charges that she presumed to preach, she and Mather reassure the reading audience that despite her apparent recall of several lengthy passages of scripture, she could not always remember what arguments and reasons she gave in defense of her faith during the long conversations with her Catholic interlocutors. "Its bootless for *me* a poor Woman, to acquaint the World, with what Arguments I used, if I could now Remember them; and many of them are slipt out of my memory." Although many women's nar-ratives were written with the assistance of a local minister, only Mather's works so hard to undermine his subject's authority, in the end making it unnecessary for Swarton to defy her Catholic masters directly. For example, after resolving "never to come unto" their "*Idolatrous worship*" again dur-ing her captivity, Swarton describes the sleepless night she spent worrying about "what I should say to them, when they urged me to go again, and what I should Do." But her prayers were answered the next morning, when a French woman told her that "if I would not be of *Their* Religion, *I* did but *mock* at it, to go to their Worship, and therefore bid me, That . . . I should go no more."[12] Swarton thus escapes Catholic worship without en-gaging in an aggressive or unfeminine confrontation with male authorities. The power of prayer solved everyone's problems—Swarton's problems as a Christian woman and Mather's problems as a narrator of her story.

Joseph Bartlett's narrative of his 1708 captivity from Haverhill, Massa-chusetts, presents an interesting contrast to Swarton's narrative, as he proudly displays a callous and self-confident resistance to Catholicism throughout. Although he is a young man of ordinary background and edu-cation, he routinely scoffs at the advice of Catholics and discusses in detail his religious disputations with lay Catholics and priests. Bartlett's narrative is also significant because he reports being approached by one of the most determined and successful French proselytizers, the Sulpician priest Father Henri-Antoine de Meriel. Meriel's name appears frequently in the notarial records of New France as the priest of record baptizing and marrying En-glish captives. Meriel was an obscure figure until the early 1690s, when he became the chaplain at the Hôtel-Dieu (hospital) in Montreal. As an En-glish speaker, Meriel had the opportunity of working with large numbers of English captives taken in the late seventeenth and early eighteenth centuries. Because of his extensive work with English captives and their Native captors as well as his language skills, English authorities knew of him and consulted him in their efforts to return high-profile captives like Eunice Williams, daughter of Deerfield minister John Williams.[13]

After Bartlett agrees to attend Meriel's "meeting," as he calls it, he mocks the Catholics for their Latin Mass and for their belief in transubstantiation. Describing their elaborate equipment and ritual of the Eucharist, he writes derisively that "they worship [the host] as much as if Christ came bodily among them." It was important for Bartlett to note in his narrative that he did not observe the expected rituals of the Mass, but that nonetheless the French were "very civil to me, not compelling me to kneel." In contrast with Swarton, Bartlett presents himself as someone willing to get into theological disputation with the priest despite his lack of formal training. "After a short time, the priest came again to visit me, and asked me how I liked their manner of worship. I told him it seemed strange to me." He decided to accept Meriel's offer to prove that all Catholic doctrine was biblically based. After quizzing the priest on purgatory and confession, "I told him I understood that they prayed to angels and saints, and asked him what scripture authority they had for that. He said nature and reason would teach us to do so; for, said he, had you any great business with the king, you would get some great man to speak for you." Not satisfied, Bartlett offered proof of his own: "I said the cases were not similar, for we are invited to come to Christ. Hebrews iv.16—Let us therefore come boldly to the throne of grace, that we may obtain mercy and find grace to help in time of need. We are forbidden to pray to saints and angels, or to give divine worship to any creature. In Rev. xxii.2 and 9, John was forbidden to fall down and worship before the feet of the angels. It is said of Cornelius, Acts x.2, He prayed to God always; and if he prayed to God always, he did not pray to saints."[14] New England religious conventions that encouraged spiritual leadership in men and absolute silence in the meetinghouse from women were reflected in captivity narratives. Thus Swarton's fretting and prayer was cast as an appropriate way for her to resist Catholicism as a woman, whereas even young men like Joseph Bartlett were permitted to be more openly confrontational with their Catholic masters.

But the tension in portraying Swarton as possessed of both womanly submission and Christian fortitude was not Mather's biggest problem in crafting her captivity narrative. The gaping hole in Swarton's narrative of triumph over French priestly designs is the fact that Swarton's own daughter Mary remained in Montreal after she herself returned to New England.

She and Mather end her narrative with an earnest request for the "prayers of my Christian Friends, that the Lord will deliver" her. Captured with her mother when she was fourteen, at the age of twenty-two Mary married an Irish fellow convert, John Lahey (more often rendered in the French records as Jean LaHaye) in 1697, the same year Mather published her mother's narrative. They presented eleven children for baptism over the next twenty years, three of whom had New England-born godmothers, Christine Otis, Freedom French, and Mary Silver. As eloquent as Mather and Swarton are about her heroic efforts to resist conversion, they are silent about the decision her daughter made to become a French *bonne femme* instead of an English goodwife.[15]

As Swarton's narrative and personal experiences with captivity suggest, children (and especially daughters) were more vulnerable to the various cultural and religious conversions that might be required of them in captivity. Elizabeth Hanson was grateful when she was purchased by the French in 1725, whom she reports "were civil beyond what I could either desire or expect." "But," she reports with some alarm, "the next Day after I was redeemed, the *Romish* Priests took my Babe from me, and according to their custom, they baptized it." The priests explained that "if it died before [baptism], it would be damned, like some of our modern pretended reformed Priests." Hanson, a Quaker, worked in an insult aimed at other Protestants in her discussion of priestly intervention. Significantly, Hanson also reports that the priests gave her daughter a new Catholic name: "Mary Ann Frossways" (actually *Françoise*, or French).[16] The captivity narrative of John Gyles, published in 1736, nearly fifty years after his boyhood capture and captivity among the Maliseet (Eastern Abenaki) in 1689, illustrates how completely French Catholics had replaced Indians as the enemies of New England and highlights particular fears of the vulnerability of children to conversion. After his initial capture, his Indian "master" shows him to a Jesuit missionary, who Gyles says "had a great mind to buy me. . . . I saw the Jesuit shew him Pieces of Gold, and understood afterward, that he tendered them for me." The politics of the mid-eighteenth century surely shaped his memories of 1689, as he reports a great deal of anxiety about conversion. "The Jesuit gave me a Bisket, which I put into my Pocket, and dare not eat; but buried it under a Log, fearing that he had put something in it, to make me Love him: for I was very Young, and had heard much of the Papists torturing the Protestants &c. so that I hated the sight of a Jesuit."[17]

Fear of being made to "love" a priest may also reflect other dangers

Catholic clergy represented in the minds of English people: their sexual am-
biguity, and the possibility that they may replace English mothers and
fathers, as Indian men and women had for many captives. Just as Catholicism itself was suspect because of its allegedly feminized nature and its
greater appeal to women, so priests were often held in suspicion by Protestants as "unnatural" or feminized men. Men who lived intimately together
and shunned marriage were suspect in a culture that elevated heterosexual-
ity to a near-sacrament and regularly depicted Catholicism as a shield for
all manner of sexual improprieties.[18] Additionally, New Englanders may
have feared that French priests (or nuns) might offer their captive children
another alternative family, just as Indian families successfully adopted
and converted English children. After all, they were called "Father" and
"Mother," "Sister" and "Brother," and like the Indians, they renamed their
converts and even re-dressed those entering monastic life.

A poignant moment in Gyles's narrative suggests that priests might
represent both of these kinds of danger, sexual and familial, at the same
time. The last time Gyles saw his mother alive, he told her that he might be
sold to a Jesuit, and he reports that she reacted with great alarm: "Oh! my
dear Child! If it were GOD's Will, I had rather follow you to your Grave!
Or never see you more in this World, than you should be Sold to a Jesuit:
for a Jesuit will ruin you Body & Soul!"[19] This remarkable speech surely
reflects the fact that it was composed in the 1730s rather than the 1690s.
Seventeenth-century captivity narratives never suggest that a mother of this
period would have been more concerned about her children going off with
a French missionaries rather than a band of Indians. Nevertheless, Gyles's
story about his mother gives us some insight into English rhetoric about
Catholicism. By the time he wrote his narrative in the mid-eighteenth century, Gyles would choose to prove his mother's love and piety in retrospect
as a preference for his death rather than conversion. Perhaps death would
have saved him from bodily and spiritual corruption, as well as prevented
him from being incorporated into any other family. This speech also reflects the history of the previous fifty years, in which numerous English
people taken initially by the Indians were redeemed by the French and remained in Canada, becoming French Catholics and blending into *habitant*
society—something Gyles's mother could not have anticipated in 1689.

By the beginning of the eighteenth century, New England captivity
narratives clearly reflected a fear of two enemies, both Indians and the
French. They even suggest that New Englanders' fear of the French was
greater because of their clearer similarities to the English in material culture

and religion. Captivity narratives composed from the turn of the eighteenth century on suggest that a culture that could offer clothing, beer, bread, butter, soft beds, and bibles was more ideologically formidable than one that offered only straw mats and meager fare. Furthermore, the French had proved their success at gaining Indian converts and allies in the northeastern borderlands. Based on the numbers of English captives who remained in Canada, New England's fears of their Euro-American enemy were neither idle nor paranoid.

Authors of captivity narratives were necessarily those who returned to New England rather than stayed with their Indian or French families, and we have almost no direct testimony from captives who remained in Canada. What little evidence we have of these people, their lives in Canada, and their reasons for remaining there comes from their slight communications with their New England families and their chance encounters with other captives who returned to New England to author narratives of their captivity among the Indians and the French.[20] The numbers and demography of those who remained in Canada speak powerfully to the notion that their fates were not accidental. While they were always in the minority of those taken during the border wars (approximately 392 of 1,579 total captives, or less than a quarter of the captive population), girls and women were much likelier to remain in Canada, convert to Catholicism, marry French men, and (presumably) fill Canada's need for European housewifery. Of ninety-five captives taken between 1689 and 1755 who can be reliably traced through the Canadian notarial records, sixty-five (nearly 70 percent) were girls and women. While overall only about one captive in twenty stayed in Canada, female captives were nearly seven times as likely to stay in Canada as their male peers. This discrepancy between the representation of females in the overall captive population and their likelihood to remain in Canada is too great to dismiss as an accident. Furthermore, while a bare majority of the female captives who remain in Canada were abducted as children, almost a third of them were adolescents or adults—a few women were even married mothers or widows in their thirties and forties when they undertook this dramatic crossing of enemy lines.[21]

What made these (mostly) girls and young women remain in Canada? More than half of them (thirty-four out of sixty-five) were taken into captivity before their thirteenth birthday, many of them as very young children. These captives, who frequently lost all memories of their English families and mother tongue, were the most easily assimilated into Canadian life.

William Pote tells the sad story of Rachael Quackenbush, whom he saw while in prison in Québec during King George's War (1744–48). "This Child had been with ye French Ever since she was Taken with her Parents which is about 18 months. There was her Father & mother, Grandfather and Grandmother In this prison. They Endeavour'd to make her speak with ym, But she would not Speak a word Neither in Dutch nor English."[22] Even for those captive girls who remembered their families and their native language, after spending several years in Canada, learning French, converting to Catholicism, and marrying a French man, it may have been simply unimaginable to return to a home a family they no longer knew nor remembered well. However, twenty of these captives were adolescents or adults when taken into captivity, young women who were almost fully grown and fully acculturated as English-speaking Protestants, and who would have been unlikely candidates to forget their native language and homeland. The choices of these twenty women are difficult to untangle, although given their age, it is appropriate to call their remaining in Canada a choice. Many of these older captives—especially the older teenagers—had probably adapted to life in Canada and perhaps had already converted to Catholicism. Many may have met a French man they fancied by the time they were free to return to New England. Some of them may have resented or disliked their natal families; surviving court records indicate that at least one of them was eager to escape an abusive home in New England, as we will see.[23]

Historians who have considered the question of New England captives remaining in Canada have emphasized marriage as the major factor in their decision to stay.[24] While it is probably true that French husbands served to bind their English wives to Canada ever more closely, marriage was only one of the many ties these women would have had to Canada. One thing we must consider is the fact that Canada offered several economic advantages to women that New England did not. Furthermore, New England was more forgiving of sons who crossed these borders, and considerable public funds as well as family money were offered to them if they returned to New England. New France, on the other hand, needed all the Euro-American women it could find. Perhaps it is no wonder, then, that New England was more successful at luring its captive men back home, and Canada found more success at keeping New England women.

There are some broad economic and legal facts that might have made New France a more attractive place for women. In stark contrast to the English common law tradition, French Canadian laws governing the "communauté de biens," or the "marriage community" of husband and wife, followed the Custom of Paris, which said that except for wealth in land owned by either partner prior to marriage, husbands and wives owned marital property equally. Although husbands were designated "masters of the community," neither husbands nor their wives could sell, mortgage, or alienate their joint property without the written consent of the other. Furthermore, French men had little power to use inheritance law to control family affairs from beyond the grave, as inheritance laws dictated the disposition of their estates. Upon the death of either spouse, the widow or widower inherited half of all real and personal property, as well as half the debts; the other half of the property and debts went to the children.[25] Thus, women in French Canada were not economically disenfranchised in marriage as were their sisters in the English colonies. We will never know the extent to which French marital laws were major factors in these women's decisions to turn their backs on New England. However, these property laws may be indicative of a culture that was generally more welcoming and tolerant of women as economic producers and decision makers.[26] This autonomy might have been especially attractive to former captives, as many of them would have spent significant time among Indians before they were purchased by French masters, and they may have come to expect the authority over family resources exercised by their Indian mothers.

Beyond this legal framework, it is clear that New France had very good reasons to want to recruit and retain New England girls and women in the late seventeenth and early eighteenth centuries. French agricultural settlements in the St. Lawrence River valley had long suffered from an imbalanced sex ratio and they were desperate for women trained in European housewifery skills like dairying, baking, and working with textiles (spinning, knitting, weaving, and sewing). Censuses of seventeenth-century New France are unreliable and vary greatly, but they indicate that the scarcity of women was a problem in colonial New France. One historian has put the overall percentage of women among French immigrants to Canada at 12.3 percent for the seventeenth century. A pair of 1685 and 1686 censuses suggest that the numbers of adult men and women and of small children were evening out, but that the numbers of *grands garcons* and *grandes filles*—adolescents and young adults, the usual age group of servant migrants—was still unbalanced, with more than three young men for every two young women.[27] Women skilled in European housewifery would have made the lives of male *habitants* more comfortable, to be sure, but these skills were also central to European identity in a place that was dominated by other people and other cultural ways. Indians in the colonial northeastern borderlands did not keep cows or consume dairy products; they did not bake European bread; and they did not produce their own thread or cloth.[28] Furthermore, in the later seventeenth century, French officials came to see that the more obvious fruits of marriage might be important to the colony's political future. Observing the rapidly increasing English population along the Atlantic seaboard and in the Connecticut and Hudson River valleys, Canadian officials concluded that recruiting and retaining women with strong bodies and European skills was not just a personal convenience for male *habitants*; it was a political necessity if the French were going to best their rivals for the control of North America.[29]

Officials in New France spent considerable money and energy recruiting French women for Canadian settlement or, alternatively, training Indian girls to become like French wives and mothers, and religious women played a key role in these efforts in the 1670s and 1680s. Teaching not just French girls but English captives and Indian girls and women in their convent schools, the nuns instructed them in academic subjects, religion, and women's domestic skills that were in such scarce supply in early New France. This dedication to girls' education resulted in a literacy rate higher among French women than men before the British conquest, although in the end few Indian girls and women crossed over to become French housewives—the majority of Native women trained in French schools assumed Indian ways when they returned to their villages and married there.[30] Church and secular officials complained too about the quality and virtue of the French women who agreed to come to Canada. Most modern historians reject the judgment of the seventeenth century on these unfortunate women, but nearly every French official and ecclesiastic involved in this recruitment effort claimed to be disappointed with their female immigrants. In 1684, the intendant of Canada reported to government ministers that "towards La Rochelle we picked up six wretched servant girls who were found out on the streets whom we would have very much liked to send back to France because they were not of good repute." He also claimed that the nuns and priests who met them in Canada wanted the women removed "for fear that they would corrupt their entire community and also the Native girls" in their tutelage. There was danger in bringing women like this to Canada, he warned: women were so scarce that "the girls will not fail to find someone to marry in the country; for these sorts of projects we need decent, mature, and skilled women, and these girls are young, vicious, and very ignorant." Just eighteen months later, the governor general himself warned, "we have in the country a certain number of rogues and particularly women of ill repute who live wretchedly. In truth, monseigneur, this spells the ruin of the entire youth of the land; these people are of no help there, but are able to destroy everything and spoil everything and even are involved in many divorces." Like the intendant, he recommended quarantine for this contagion in Canadian society. "If we were able to shut them up here and feed them, it would be the best thing we could do. If you would permit me to get them picked up and authorize them being put on a boat it would be a great benefit."[31]

Because of their failures in recruiting French and Native women to housewifery in Canada, it is not surprising that French officials would want to entice English captive girls and women to remain in Canada. A look at the evidence we have on the New Englanders who stayed in Canada confirms the timing of this particular effort: While captives were taken by the Indians and purchased by the French throughout the near-century of warfare between England and France in North America, over ninety percent of English captives who stayed in Canada were captured during King William's War or during Queen Anne's War (1702–13)—not coincidentally the very years following New France's aggressive efforts to remediate its sex ratio with Indian and immigrant French women.[32]

Perhaps civil and Church officials were inspired to augment their numbers by their Indian allies, who had traditionally used enemy captives to replace dead or missing family members. Perhaps the fact that their allies had captives to sell, by way of sustaining a substitute wartime economy, also inspired them. In any case, without the example and assistance of their Native allies, Canada would not have been able to convince so many New Englanders to cross the border and stay in Canada. We therefore might see French policy toward English captives in particular as a borrowing of Indian strategies of adoption and acculturation of the enemy. After all, the French also stripped and redressed the captives when they joined their households, and like the Indians, they looked after the education and marriage prospects of their new family members. Indian and French practices look strikingly similar when compared to the fitful and halfhearted efforts of the English to bring either Indian or French captives into their culture.[33]

One of the most striking things about the treatment of English female captives in Canada was the attention and personal involvement of the colony's highest officials.[34] Governor of Montreal (1698–1703) and then governor general of New France from 1703 to his death in 1725, Philippe de Rigaud, Marquis de Vaudreuil, was a powerful central player in the politics and diplomacy of the first two intercolonial wars. Thus it is revealing that

Figure 12. This map depicting Sir William Phips's attempt to take the city of Québec in 1690 shows it to be a well-defended city surrounded by stone walls and a prosperous countryside. By the 1690s, most English captives taken by Algonquian and Iroquois allies of the French were only temporary visitors in Indian families and were usually traded to the French in Québec or Montreal at the earliest convenience. Robert de Villeneuve, "Québec & Ses Environs en la Nouvelle France, Assiegé par les Anglois le 16e d'octobre 1690," Composite Atlas 1690. This item is reproduced by permission of the Huntington Library, San Marino, California.

he took a personal interest in several female captives during his governorship, even bringing some of them into his household and looking after their educations. He was the godfather of Mary Silver when she was baptized in 1710 among the Sisters of the Congregation of Notre Dame in Ville-Marie (near Montreal), and he placed Mary Scammon among the Ursulines in Three Rivers in 1725. Also at the direction of Vaudreuil beginning in 1709, Esther Wheelwright spent time among the Ursulines in Three Rivers and with other nuns in Montreal before beginning her novitiate with the Ursulines of Québec in 1712, where she remained for the rest of her life. Furthermore, Vaudreuil took a personal interest in the plight of the Williams family, providing hospitality to the Reverend John Williams after his redemption from Indian captivity and laboring to secure the release of Eunice, who nevertheless married into a Kahnawake family and remained there for the rest of her life. Vaudreuil claimed to be as disappointed as any of her English family that she married François-Xavier Arosen before his diplomacy could run its course. Significantly, the girls and women that Vaudreuil took such a personal interest in were high-status captives. In order to preserve diplomatic relations, he would have had a strong interest in ensuring these young women's health and happiness as much as possible, given their circumstances. However, the measures he took—putting them into convent schools and witnessing their baptisms and marriages—doubtlessly served to bind them closer to their adopted home. Other officials of New France also served as godfathers and witnesses at the marriages of English captives, as the notarial records are full of references to "Intendants" performing these duties. In contrast, no New England governors ever expended equal funds or political capital to get these young women back.[35]

Vaudreuil's son Pierre de Rigaud, Marquis de Vaudreuil-Cavagnal, who was governor of Three Rivers and then Louisiana before he became governor general of New France in 1755, carried on his father's tradition of looking after English captives, especially the girls. He witnessed their baptisms, put them into convent schools, and took them into his home. He placed Jemima Howe's daughters Mary and Submit Phipps in the Ursuline convent school in Québec during the Seven Years' War with the instructions that "they should both of them together, be well looked after, and carefully educated, as his adopted children." When he brought Mary Phipps to France with him after the French capitulation in 1760, her mother reports that she was married there "to a French gentleman, whose name is Cron Lewis." Submit became so enthusiastic about her new faith that she refused to leave her convent. "[S]he absolutely refused," wrote her frustrated mother, "and all the persuasions and arguments I could use with her, were to no effect." Only because the younger Vaudreuil himself insisted that she be returned to her mother did Submit finally live up to her name, but she returned to her mother quite unwillingly.[36] This very personal touch was doubtlessly influential in the lives of the young women taken in by the Vaudreuil family over a half-century, but perhaps more significantly, it suggests how important these girls and women were to their new country.

Beyond this personal and official encouragement of English captives, the French crown also directly assisted their assimilation into Canadian society by offering naturalization and even cash payments to male and female captives alike. In 1702, Canadian officials secured two thousand livres of crown support for thirty-eight Catholicized English captives (twenty-one women and seventeen men). In May of 1710, Louis XIV naturalized twenty-eight male and thirty-eight female war captives, and again in 1713 he naturalized another thirty-four men and four women. (The heavy representation of men in this last group is due to the fact that many were captured soldiers from the last war). After 1714, the efforts to Catholicize and naturalize New Englanders dropped off for a few interrelated reasons. With the end of Queen Anne's War in 1713, peace officially held between Britain and France for more than thirty years. Perhaps more importantly, by 1713 the sex ratio had stabilized in New France, so that the government there had less incentive to try to keep English captives. Furthermore, English captives of the mid-eighteenth century wars were overwhelmingly soldiers who would have only added to any demographic imbalance that remained. In fact, the *conseil supérieur* seems to have actively discouraged naturalization in 1722 with its requirement of a hundred-livre fee for each application for naturalization.[37]

The interest of government officials in the fates of these captive girls and women was important, but they relied heavily on Church officials to bring the young women over to French language, culture, and religion. While priests alone had the power to administer the sacraments of baptism and marriage that were so important to bringing ex-captives into Canadian society, much of the daily hard work of these multiple conversions was done by the nuns of Québec, Montreal, and Three Rivers through their convent schools. As we have seen, these female-run institutions were central to seventeenth-century efforts to bring Native girls and women into French society, so adding English girls to their lists of pupils required little adjustment on the part of the sisters who gloried in their evangelical work.[38]

We know that all of the captives who stayed to make lives in Canada were persuaded by this evangelism—or, at least that they accepted the necessity of converting to Catholicism in order to be naturalized. There is too little evidence on the religious opinions of former captives in Canada for us to generalize about their religious experiences. Renouncing Protestantism and converting to Catholicism was an enormous ideological leap, as religion and nationalism were so tightly bound to each other in New England. Even English families on the far borderlands of New England had a strong sense of the moral and intellectual superiority of English Protestantism versus their perceptions of the so-called despotism and corruption of French Catholicism, although they may not have appreciated the finer points of doctrinal difference. Nevertheless, many former captives may have become earnestly devout Catholics. For those who came from frontier communities that may not have been served regularly by a minister, attending Mass in Canada might have been their first regular experience of organized religion and the beauty of its ritual. For those who had spent months or years among Indian families who were not living in mission towns, they may have felt a welcome familiarity upon seeing a cross, hearing European music sung, or taking communion again. Some might have come to Catholicism through the practice of Indian families who adopted them. Other New England female captives might have been put off by the foreignness of the experience of Catholic ritual, as the captivity narratives described earlier demonstrate. We know that four of the sixty-five known female captives became nuns—surely a sign that they at least were spiritually moved to embrace Catholicism.[39] It is likely that many of their secular sisters in Canada were also moved to Catholic devotion, although none of them have left any evidence of their religious opinions.[40]

While officials of both the church and the state clearly played an important role in acculturating English captives, the girls and women themselves established bonds with one another that appear to have eased their adoption into Canadian society. The fact that English captives created and maintained their own networks that lasted decades is further evidence that remaining in New France was a choice, not a fate, for most of them. Canadian notarial records show that ex-captives witnessed one another's baptisms, weddings, and children's baptisms; this spare information suggests that these women were friends and neighbors who continued to support one another through their lives.[41] Expatriate New Englanders who had already established thriving homes and families in Canada might have made compelling examples for convincing other English women to stay. As perhaps the only English-speaking people the captives would have had regular contact with, their reasoning (and possibly, their persuasions) might have been decisive.

We get only a haphazard picture of these networks through the captivity narratives of returned New Englanders, as authors of the narratives frequently mention meeting English people who began their stay in Canada in captivity, sometimes decades earlier. In John Norton's narrative of his experiences in a Montreal prison during King George's War in 1747–48, he describes his meetings with several ex-captives who chose to stay in Canada. He writes of a "considerable Discourse" he had with Aaron Littlefield, "taken a Lad from Piscataqua, and so continued with the French and lived, having a Family at *Champlain.*" He also met with a woman he calls "*Hannah Rie.* She had been married to a Frenchman, by whom she had four Children," and another ex-captive taken from Maine whose name he could not recall. During his stay in Montreal, he meets "the Major of the Town," who tells Norton that "he married an Englishwoman whose name was *Storer.*" This was Jean Baptiste Dagueil (sometimes called L'Equille or Leguil), who had married Priscilla Storer. Priscilla (now Marie Priscille) lived in Montreal near her cousin Mary Storer (now Mary St. Germaine, the wife of Jean St. Germaine), who had been taken into captivity at the same time. This "Mrs. *St. La Germaine,* one of his Wife's Cousins, who was also taken with her, came with the Major," and Norton informs us that she served as the translator for the men's conversation as she "was able to discourse in the English Tongue." She was no mere cipher for her French cousin, however, as she used the meeting with Norton to let her know who she was and of her New England connections. "She told me that the Rev. Mr. *Storer* of *Watertown* was her Brother, and that she wanted to hear from her Friends; but I was not acquainted with any of them." More than forty years after being taken from her parents' home, Mary St. Germaine still spoke English, was closely associated with her cousin and her cousin's family in Montreal, and was interested in communicating with other New Englanders. This was no new interest of an old woman, as reports of Mary St. Germaine had circulated years earlier, suggesting that she and her cousin Marie Priscille Dagueil were at the center of a lively community of English visitors, captives, and ex-captives. An English emissary on a journey to retrieve English captives had visited her, her cousin, and Dagueil in Montreal in 1725 and reported that she lived "grandly" there.[42]

Similarly, Susanna Johnson reports being approached by two ex-captives turned Ursuline nuns when Johnson and her sister as captives went to the Ursuline convent in Québec to visit Jemimah Howe's daughters, Mary and Submit Phipps. "We here found two aged English ladies, who had been taken in former wars." One of them was Esther Wheelwright (now La Mère Marie-Joseph de l'Enfant Jésus), and the other perhaps Sarah Davis, who took the name Marie-Anne Davis de Saint-Benoit. Mother Esther (as she called herself) was taken in the same 1703 raid on Wells, Maine, along with the Storer cousins Mary and Priscilla, including Priscilla's sister Rachael who also married a French man but settled in Québec rather than Montreal. Mother Esther too expressed interest in the English visitors to her convent, and she told Johnson that she had "a brother in Boston, on whom she requested me to call, if ever I went to that place." After she was redeemed and returned to New England, Johnson followed up on the connection. "I complied with her request afterwards, and received many civilities from her brother."[43] Mother Esther, Mary St. Germaine, and other captives clearly had the connections to go home if they wanted to. They were interested in and affectionate toward their New England friends and families, but they had made their home in Canada.

Saying that these girls and women had made a choice to remain in Canada may be stretching the meaning of the word, although "choice" had a severely qualified meaning throughout colonial North America. However, there is no evidence that the French put these children or women into servitude or slavery, or that their marriages were arranged or forced.[44] In other words, French captive adoption appears to have been modeled along the lines of Indian customs, which forbade sexual coercion or assault. If sexual danger were even hinted at by returned captives, New England's enthusiastic anti-Catholic presses would surely have broadcast the news far and wide. Instead, most captivity narratives that acknowledge the existence of these girls and women are tight-lipped about the circumstances that led the ex-captives to stay behind—either they ignore the question altogether or suggest that some mild (though never criminal) duplicity on the part of French Canadians was to blame. All in all, there is precious little published commentary about the captives who remained in Canada, aside from some ideological boilerplate in New England sermons and political works trying to galvanize anti-French sentiment. This relative silence on such a weighty topic suggests that these women had indeed made a choice to remain with their new homes and families in Canada, and their choice was so painful and even shameful to their families and communities that they chose to forget them.

Hannah Swarton was hardly alone as a devout, ideologically correct returned captive who nevertheless lost a daughter to Canada. Many other ex-captives had teenaged or young adult daughters who refused to return to New England with them. Elizabeth Hanson's captivity narrative reveals the difficulties New England families faced when a daughter refused to return home with them after captivity among the Indians and the French. It also suggests that captive girls and women retained some control over their eventual fates. Hanson and her family were taken from their home in Dover, New Hampshire, in 1724, a party of captives that included sixteen-year-old Sarah, fourteen-year-old Elizabeth, a young servant girl, a six-year-old son, and her newborn daughter (the child baptized "Mary Ann Frossways" mentioned above). After a few days on the run, Hanson's daughters and the servant were given to other Indians, while she, her six-year-old son, and her infant daughter remained together for the year of their captivity with French-allied Eastern Abenaki and then the French in Montreal. Her husband John Hanson successfully retrieved their youngest daughter from captivity, but Sarah proved more difficult to deal with. She had been settled with a family at Lac des deux Montaignes (Lake of Two Mountains, now Oka, Québec), a mission town on the Ottawa River populated for the most part with Iroquois Indians as well as a few Hurons and Algonquins. In her captivity narrative, Hanson first suggests that Sarah's Indian family at Lake of Two Mountains refused to part with her, explaining "for the Squaw, to whom she was given, had a Son which she intended my Daughter should in Time be prevailed with to marry." It was probably easier psychologically and politically to think of unredeemed captive teenagers as victims who had no control over their own destinies. However, in reassuring her reading audience that Sarah was not in any danger of rape or defilement, Elizabeth Hanson suggests the possibility that Sarah's preferences mattered to her Indian family: "the *Indians* being very civil toward their captive Women, not offering any Incivility by any indecent Carriage (unless they be much overgone in Liquor, which is commendable in them so far)." If Sarah was not free to leave her new family, neither was she being utterly manhandled. After several "Attempts and Endeavours" to retrieve Sarah, Elizabeth and John Hanson turned regretfully homeward, as the Indians' "Affections . . . for [their] Daughter, made them refuse all Offers and Terms of Ransom." Further evidence of her Indian family's affections, and of their intention to keep her as an adoptee, is indicated by the fact that she was given an Iroquois name for her Catholic baptism: "Catherine Kijitekak8e."[45]

Sarah's English family did not give up, and in the spring of 1726 John Hanson undertook another journey to Canada to retrieve her, along with another family member and his wife who were after their own captive children as well. Sarah's rejection of the New England way might have been especially difficult for her father to bear, since disorderly households and disobedient children reflected most poorly on their fathers. Also, as a Quaker, John Hanson's manhood and patriotism had been questioned by his puritan neighbors. Quakers were always under suspicion in early New England, and they were especially disparaged for their pacifism in wartime. Although puritan families always made up the vast majority of victims of Indian attacks and captivity on the New England frontier, disapproving observers blamed John Hanson's faith for his family's ordeal. Samuel Penhallow wrote condescendingly that Hanson, "being a stiff quaker, full of enthusiasm, and ridiculing the military power, would on no account be influenced to come into garrison; by which means his whole family (then at home) being eight in number, were all killed and taken." Perhaps Elizabeth Hanson wrote to avenge this portrait of her husband as a foolish and heedless man, when she wrote, "my dear Husband, poor Man! could not enjoy himself in Quiet with us, for want of his dear Daughter Sarah." The Lake of Two Mountains mission was an arduous journey from coastal New Hampshire at any time of year. But, "not willing to omit any thing for her redemption which lay in his Power, he could not be easy without making a second Attempt." The trip proved too much for John Hanson, who died in his kinsman's arms along the way.[46]

Although their relative continued his mission to try to bring Sarah home, not even the tragic death of her father could induce her to come away. Once again, Elizabeth Hanson suggests that her daughter did not make this decision herself. The "old Squaw," Sarah's mistress, "intended to marry her in time to her Son, using what persuading she could to effect her end, sometimes by fair Means, and sometimes by severe." Hanson never suggests what these "severe" means were for coercing Sarah to marry, but in a surprising twist, she reveals that "in the mean time a Frenchman interposed and they, by persuasion enticed my Child to marry [the Frenchman], in order to obtain her Freedom, by reason that those Captives married by the French, are by that Marriage made free among them." Having renamed Sarah and adopted her, however, her Indian mistress more likely treated her like a daughter and allowed her to marry the man of her choice. Hanson insists that Sarah married only to gain her freedom from the Indians, but her convoluted explanation nevertheless reveals that Sarah's preference in the end wins the day with her Indian mistress, "and she was accordingly married to the Frenchman." Hanson makes no further comment on her daughter's fate and, very much like Hannah Swarton, ends her narrative rather abruptly after this strange explanation for her daughter's failure to return home. Although she said nothing further about Sarah in her captivity narrative, Hanson may have carried on her husband's quest to bring their daughter home, this time with Sarah's French husband. In the summer of 1728, the Dover Men's Monthly Meeting considered offering Sarah's husband, Jean Baptiste Sabourin, "a Sum of money to get him in a way to Live in This Country," if he "returns from Canada with his wife the next spring to settle and take up his abode here." In the end, they refused to offer him a set price, but they allowed people to contribute to a fund for that purpose if they so chose. Instead, Sarah and Jean Baptiste married at the Lake of Two Mountains mission and raised a family of six in Canada.[47]

Mary Swarton and Sarah Hanson seem to have married men of their choosing, a decision that bound them to Canada more closely. However, at least one of the women who stayed in Canada fled some of the more dramatic consequences of New England patriarchy. Abigail Willey (or Willy) stands out as an "unredeemed captive" because of her age and her marital status: taken in 1689 from Oyster River, New Hampshire, she was a married woman of 32 with two daughters who were about thirteen and eight. Her young daughters were prime candidates to stay in Canada, but why would someone of such a relatively advanced age, and with a husband and other children remaining in New Hampshire, choose baptism and (eventually) remarriage in New France? In a 1683 statement to the New Hampshire colony court, Abigail Willey outlines the harsh reality of her life as an English goodwife. She complained of her husband's chronic violence against her and her isolation as an abused woman: "I have for several years past lived and spent, without making my addresses to any in authority, with Stephen Willy, my husband, often suffering much by sore and heavy blows received from his hand, too much for any weak woman to bear." She also relates his frequent threats "to take away my life by the evil disposition of his own mind, seeing that neither his own relations, neither my own natural brothers, dare countenance in any way of natural friendship [with Stephen]." Abigail Willey describes herself, in short, as "the suffering subject of his insatial jealousy." Her claims in this petition are supported by an accompanying deposition by a neighbor, Joseph Hill, who one night heard Stephen Willey yell, "I will kill her or whore." (Perhaps Hill meant to indicate that Willey said either, "I will kill her," or "I will kill the whore.") He apparently went into the Willey home to intervene in the violent affair, and found

"John Willy, his brother, standing between the said Stephen and his wife, to prevent them from danger."

She had not brought her situation to the attention of local officials and instead suffered for years in silence, perhaps because she believed herself to be the victim of the English courts as well as of her husband. An earlier experience before the bar was grievously humiliating: when Stephen Willey brought her before Judge Edgerly, Willey reports that her husband "at his own request procured of said judge the shameful sentence of ten strips, to be laid upon me at a post." The judge later reversed himself and cancelled the whipping, accepting a twenty-shilling fine instead. But then, when Willey went to visit her sister in Kittery, she reports "said judge sent after me as a runaway, to be procured; the second time to be dealt with according to law." This latest judgment was apparently the reason Willey was compelled finally to make her case to the colony's highest court. Clearly, she saw this English magistrate and English law as operating at the whim of her disreputable and abusive husband. Perhaps she chose to remain in Canada because she saw an opportunity to escape not just a despotic husband but a legal system that did not operate in her interest.[48]

Colonial Anglo-American women's historians have shown how difficult it was for women to procure a divorce on any grounds other than desertion or sexual insufficiency on the part of the husband. Catholic Canada was hardly a libertine's playground—in fact, divorce was nonexistent—but French Canadian women could claim greater economic self-sufficiency when their marriages broke down, and for a wider variety of reasons. There were two types of legal separation available to aggrieved couples: division of the marital property without physical separation, or a separation of bed and board in addition to the division of all assets. Of 149 petitions for separation in the seventeenth- and eighteenth-century St. Lawrence Valley, most were filed by wives, and most focused on the profligacy of the husband and his inability to manage domestic affairs, situations that were frequently linked to drunkenness and domestic violence. Magistrates resisted granting bed and board separations—in fact, only 20 percent of the sample cited above requested physical separation from their spouses—but domestic violence such as that described by Abigail Willey would perhaps have gained her physical and economic autonomy had she pursued her case in Québec rather than New Hampshire. New France, like New England, tolerated wife-beating, but evidence from separation petitions suggests that repeated spousal abuse, death threats, insanity, and venereal infection could gain wives a bed and board separation from men like Stephen Willey. The differences between the New France and New England legal systems are telling, with Canada offering women more flexibility and control in both happy and unhappy marriages. New France's legal tradition offered abused wives more economic rights and autonomy in marital separations than the Common Law tradition in New England.[49]

We know comparatively little of Willey's life in Canada and can glean only a few details from the notarial records that note her transformation from English wife and mother, to French servant, and eventually to wife of a Montreal *habitant*. Willey was baptized as a Catholic in 1693, took the name Marie Louise Pilman (presumably a transcription error, after her maiden name Pitman), and was described as a servant to Hector de Callières, a Montreal official; apparently even servitude was preferable to her life as an abused New England wife. Her husband Stephen's 1696 will made no mention of her name or her existence whatsoever; neither did he recognize or remember his two daughters in Canada. He died sometime in or before 1700; Mary Louise Pilman married Edouard de Flecheur in 1710 and was naturalized the same year, at the age of fifty-three. Her two daughters had preceded her in marriage to French men. After working for the Sisters of St. Joseph as a receptionist at their hospital in Ville-Marie, the eldest married in 1698 in Québec when she was probably about twenty-two. The younger Willey daughter married four years later in Québec, when she was about twenty-one. Widowed at the age of twenty-three, she remarried and lived the rest of her life in Canada like her mother and sister.[50] We can only speculate as to the effects their mother's abuse at the hands of their father and New England law had on the daughters' decisions to stay in Canada. However, given the different ways in which the colonial French and English legal systems responded to marital breakdown, we cannot dismiss the possibility that because of their mother's experience, the Willey girls preferred the advantages of marriage (and if necessary, separation) in New France.

The experience of Abigail Willey as an abused wife may have been unusual, but the fact that she and her daughters were disinherited by Stephen Willey's will was not. English families used inheritances and inheritance law to compel their captive children and siblings to return to New England, although this tactic was used differently depending on the sex of the captive. Based on the fragmentary evidence available in wills and probate records, it appears that daughters' inheritances were more likely to be contingent upon their return to New England, while New England's captive sons were twice as likely to receive their inheritances without returning to New England.[51] Of course, it is very difficult to argue that probate records—wills and inventories—can give us uncomplicated insights into the emotional life of families. They are legal documents, full of formulaic language and ruled by their own generic conventions. Furthermore, these documents were written under certain legal restrictions and requirements, thus the fact that female captives in Canada fared worse than their male counterparts when it came to their inheritances may be unsurprising, given the patriarchal nature of inheritance law in general: eldest sons reaped great privileges that eldest daughters did not. Furthermore, property ownership was itself a gendered phenomenon, because the law of coverture meant that Anglo-American women might easily spend the majority of their lives as *femes couverts*, and thus not as property owners. But even beyond this, evidence indicates that parents of children who remained in Canada of their own choice used the power of inheritance to communicate disapproval of their children's decisions, or to compel a return to New England, especially when it came to their daughters. Finally, although the actions of individuals were powerfully shaped by the conventions of the law, we should remember that the legal structures of Anglo-American society communicated very clearly whose work was valued and whose was not; and whose interests were directly represented and whose were not. We will never know to what extent the concepts of coverture versus the marriage community (in New France) influenced the thinking of captive girls and women, but it was a difference that they were likely aware of, especially those daughters who were threatened with disinheritance.

The way in which William and Mary Moore's parents' estate was settled in 1694 reveals a clear double standard of male and female captives' inheritance. Whereas brother William could receive his portion of the estate "provided said William be alive & demand it," sister Mary could receive hers only if she returned to New England: "if Mary More doo not return from captivity, then her redemption money and her portion to be equally devided among the rest of her brethren and sisters." More often than not, other captive daughters received the same kind of treatment in their parents' wills. Dorothy Milberry was disinherited by her father, Henry, in his 1695 will: "Unto my Deer Daughter in Captivity with the Indians Dorothy Millbury I will and give the summ of five pounds. In Case she return by Gods good Providence from Captivity but if [partly erased] not till then to be paid; which Legacy I intend not payable by my son at all if she never return." The language parents used could be very specific: daughters could not simply come home to claim their inheritance (like William Moore would have been permitted to); they had to renounce French law, language, and religion, and come home to stay. Joseph Storer wrote in his 1721 will: "I Give & Bequeath to my beloved Daughter Mary St. Germain Fifty pounds in good Contrey pay upon Condition that She return from under the French Government & Settle in New England." Mary Storer's fellow captive Esther Wheelwright was similarly disinherited by her mother's 1750 will, unless she "by the Wonder working Providence of God be returned to her Native Land and tarry & dwell in it."[52]

Captive sons fared much better, retaining inheritance rights twice as often as not. Stephen and Nathaniel Otis, taken from Dover, New Hampshire, in 1689, both decided to remain in Canada and took on Frenchified names after their baptism: Stephen became Joseph-Marie Autes, and Nathaniel took the name of Paul Otis (or Hottesse). They did not receive their inheritance, but only because they specifically renounced all claims to it and generously bestowed it upon their brother-in-law. Another captive, Charles Trafton, was taken from York, Maine, in 1693 at age twelve, and baptized in Québec the following year. When his father's estate was settled in 1707, he was granted the rights to his father's fulling mill. Trafton eventually returned to claim his inheritance, but not until after his father's death. Even such high apostasy from the New England way as conversion to Catholicism couldn't cheat Aaron Littlefield out of his inheritance. Littlefield was captured by the Abenaki in a raid on Wells, Maine, in 1703, along with Mary Storer and Esther Wheelwright, and like them he chose to remain in Canada. His mother died intestate in 1726, and he returned to Maine to sue for his inheritance only in 1738. The jury issued a conditional verdict: "if a Papist is by Law Debarr'd from maintaining an action for a Real Estate then Cost for ye Def[endan]ts but if not the Jury find for the Pl[ain]t[iff] ye Land Sued for & Cost." The trial judge ruled that Littlefield, as a "Papist," had no standing to bring suit and thus decided for the defendants, but this decision was overturned on appeal and Littlefield was granted his inheritance.[53] Three children were taken from the same town, and all three decided to remain in Canada. While Littlefield's claim on his mother's estate was controversial, in the end he prevailed, whereas the two female captives did not.

Even when their claims on inheritance were disputed, returned male captives had good luck in court, especially with the help of a mother's testimony. William Hutchins, taken from Kittery, Maine, in 1705 when he was nine, was apparently presumed dead when the state ordered the division of his late father's estate in 1721, as he was left entirely out of the proceedings. When he returned to Maine in 1733 to claim his inheritance, he became a kind of Martin Guerre of New England captivity tales. His brothers denied his identity, so he decided to sue them for his inheritance. Many neighbors testified that he was in fact the real William Hutchins, but in the end his mother's judgment that "he is the first born of my Body" prevailed. Hutchins not only received an inheritance, he won the double portion due him as the eldest brother. Conveniently settled, he married a New England woman in 1734 and remained for some time in Kittery.[54] Clearly, English male captives who remained in French Canada were still seen as legitimate heirs, by their families and by the courts, even decades after they had left New England. Their sisters were not so lucky.

Families and local communities were not the only ones to extend forgiveness to men who crossed borders, and to see value in the skills and connections they might bring. In some cases, the return (or possible return) of male captives was greeted as a political and diplomatic opportunity by New England officials, one that they were willing to pay dearly for. As we saw earlier, the active intervention of French officials seems to have encouraged English female captives to remain in Canada. Here too the intervention of local or colonial government seems to have worked to induce male captives to return to New England. Thus while the parents of longtime captive sons could hope for assistance from their governments, parents of daughters were most often forced to rely on their own wits and resources to try to get their daughters back.

Elisha Searls, taken from what is now Easthampton, Massachusetts, at the age of nine in 1704, was baptized Catholic in 1705 and remained with his Indian captors until 1722. Not surprisingly, he had forgotten how to speak English, but he returned anyway, allegedly to claim his inheritance. He never apparently received any, but in consideration for his remaining in the colony and serving in a garrison, the House of Representatives voted to give him ten pounds. (Local officials allegedly exerted some force to separate Searls from the Indian friends who had accompanied him on his return to New England.) A man with Searls's language skills and knowledge of French-allied Indians would have been an important asset, especially on the western Massachusetts frontier at Deerfield or Northfield, where colony officials intended to station him. In the end, Searls took the colony's offer and the following year earned the praise of one of his officers as a "discreet and careful man" whose services were being requested at Fort Dummer. An even more elaborate package of incentives and benefits was offered to John and Zecheriah Tarbell, who had been taken from Groton, Massachusetts, with their sister Sarah in 1707. The brothers ended up marrying Indian women and settling in the mission village of Kahnawake. Thirty-two years later, the Tarbell brothers traveled to Groton at the expense of their English brothers remaining in New England. The exact reason for their 1739 journey is unknown—perhaps they returned to Massachusetts to claim their inheritances. Their return home was subsidized not just by their brothers but by the governor and council of the colony, who offered the Catholic Indian Tarbell brothers forty pounds cash for themselves, for their wives, and to cover their traveling expenses. Why did their return to Massachusetts attract such attention from the colony's leaders? Perhaps belatedly and half-heartedly, New England officials were awakening to the value of loyal Indian allies in their contest against the French. The English-born Tarbells might have seemed a surer bet than any other Indians because of their family connections, and because one of them apparently rose to a leadership position in Kahnawake. Governor Jonathan Belcher suggested that this generosity might "release them from the Errors and Delusions of the Romish Faith." More importantly, he argued, "their living among us might, in Time to come, be of great Advantage to the Province." Beyond the immediate cash incentives, the brothers were offered land and salaries for the mere consideration of "behaving themselves peaceably and Orderly Among us."[55]

The publicly subsidized resettlement plans offered Searls and the Tarbell brothers stand in stark contrast to the treatment received by Eunice Williams (renamed A'ongote) and her husband, Francois-Xavier Arosen. In John Demos's telling of the Williams family's ordeal, he convincingly shows how much her family hoped desperately for her return, and that her defection from such a high-profile family was a matter of public concern. Eunice Williams was not disinherited—her father died intestate in 1729, which was very strange for a man worth more than 2,300 pounds. She was entitled to her portion as a surviving child, but she apparently would have had to return to New England to claim it. Rumors reached the Williams family that A'ongote had come as far as Albany the month after her father's death, and that she planned to return again soon; Demos suggests that this inheritance was perhaps the reason she might have ventured into English territory. When she and her Kahnawake family finally visited Massachusetts in 1740, however, officials never apparently tendered any offers of cash or support for their resettlement in New England despite their generous offer to the Tarbell brothers just the previous year.

A'ongote, as the daughter of a famous puritan minister and the sister of another, certainly would have had the fame and the connections to make her an attractive candidate for resettlement at the colony's expense. She was arguably an even higher profile celebrity captive than the Tarbells or Searls; after all, her father wrote a best-selling captivity narrative about his family's experiences, which went into six editions in the eighteenth century alone. Her return was a celebrated local event in Longmeadow, where her brother served as the town pastor, but all A'ongote and François-Xavier Arosen apparently received for their trouble was a week's hospitality with her English family and some heavy-handed advice from her brother Stephen to stay in New England. A'ongote's and Arosen's experience with Longmeadow was similar to the offer that the Dover, New Hampshire Quakers considered making to Jean Baptiste Sabourin, rather than to his wife, Sarah Hanson. Demos discovered some evidence that A'ongote and Arosen were offered a little cash in 1743 and an annual allowance from the Massachusetts General Court if they resettled in Massachusetts, but this offering never induced them to abandon Kahnawake. (Predictably, A'ongote and Arosen were offered much less money than the Tarbells—nearly thirteen pounds cash up front, and then just under an eight-pound annuity, as opposed to the Tarbells' princely forty pounds.)[56] Just as Canada valued its female captives and induced English girls and women to remain there, so New England valued its male returnees and enticed them to come home with offers of cash, land, and prestigious jobs. It is no wonder, then, that Canada was more successful at retaining women, and New England at retaining men.[57]

Some might argue that this disinheritance of daughters (in contrast to the more liberal claims retained by male captives) was not a judgment of their decision to remain in Canada; perhaps New England parents wanted to preserve a nest egg for their children should they choose to come home again. Perhaps these parents were uninterested in letting French or Indian sons-in-law take their daughters' inheritance back to Canada. But there are some wills that indicate more rage than practicality at work in these decisions, because a few fathers chose to leave paltry sums to their children to register their discontent. For example, John Stebbins, who had lost two sons and two daughters to Indian captivity and then to life in French Canada, promised them each an "eighth part of my lands provided they come and live in New England." It might make good economic sense (as well as practical sense) to withhold an inheritance until a son or daughter returned home to claim it, especially if it were in land and not in cash or moveables. After all, returning captives would need some kind of maintenance while they went about the business of recreating a life for themselves and any French or Indian family they might bring home with them. However, many parents were like John Stebbins, who went a step further to make sure that no one mistook the nature of his wrath. He vowed that "those that will not live in New England shall have five shillings apiece and no more." Five shillings—the pettiest sum, and being awarded that kind of inheritance was worse than being ignored or completely disinherited. A few shillings let children know exactly how little their parents thought of them and of their choices. Stebbins was not the only parent to leave such a poignant sum to his children in Canada. Not surprisingly, it was the father of a runaway daughter who bestowed a similarly damning petty inheritance. Joseph Storer, father of Mary Storer, decreed that if she didn't "return from under the French Government & Settle in New England," she would receive merely "the Sum of Tenn Shillings in Contrey pay to be paid by my Executor." Mary Storer's mother and brother let Joseph's judgment stand, and they also refused to release her inheritance if she did not accede to their wishes and return to New England. The resentment that festered between Mary and her family in Boston eventually ended Mary's correspondence with them permanently.[58]

The case of Mary Storer and her contested relationship with her English family bears closer examination, both for what it suggests about the female captives who remained in Canada and for one family's reaction to this exercise of daughterly will and determination. The surviving correspondence of Mary Storer St. Germaine consists of nine letters to her eldest brother, Ebenezer, one letter each to her mother and another brother, five letters from her husband, Jean St. Germaine, to Ebenezer, and two letters from Ebenezer, one addressed to Mary, the other to her husband, a total of eighteen letters that span nearly thirty years, from 1725 to 1754. Read together, these letters offer valuable glimpses into family relationships in colonial New England. More importantly, they are almost the only direct words we have from a female captive who remained in Canada, and thus offer us some insight into the mind of one captive as she attempts to reconcile the English and the French sides of her family and her own identity.[59] Mary's brother Ebenezer seems to have functioned as the go-between for his sister and the rest of their family in these letters, performing as the executor of not only his father's will but also his family's wishes regarding Mary in general.

The correspondence begins twenty-two years after Mary was taken by the Indians, when both she and Ebenezer were middle-aged parents. Mary Storer was taken in the 1703 Abenaki raid on Wells, Maine, when she and her cousins Rachael and Priscilla Storer were taken in the same attack as Aaron Littlefield and Esther Wheelwright. Unlike Littlefield and Wheelwright, who were both young children when they were taken from their natal families, the Storer girls were teenagers: Mary was eighteen, Priscilla nineteen, and Rachael about sixteen. All three Storers were therefore young women at the time of their captivity, not children, which may have contributed to greater resentment among the Storer family of their daughters' choices. All three married French men and remained in Canada—Mary and Priscilla (the latter baptized by Father Meriel as "Marie Priscille") lived near each other in Montreal the rest of their lives, and Rachael (baptized "Marie Françoise") settled in Québec with her husband, Jean Berger.[60]

The occasion for what seems to have been a new or renewed epistolary relationship with Mary's brother Ebenezer was a visit she made to Boston in the late spring and summer of 1725, as the first letters she writes are posted from Newport, Rhode Island, where she was awaiting the ship that would return her to Montreal. These first letters, all but one addressed to Ebenezer, communicate her distress at having been so long separated from her birth family and indicate that like the Williams family, her family wanted to return her and her children to New England and thus to the Protestant faith. In her own handwriting and crude spelling, she assures brother Ebenezer, "my harte is alwais full of sorey and my eyes full of ters to think that I have toke sech a grate jorney to come to se my deare father and mother and had no coumforte to staye longe with them." In another letter she repeats the same sentiments in similar language: "[While] I am not with you my harte and tender love is alwaise with you I shall never for git what every good peple has sead to me becaus I know that is for my good and I pray to god onley that it maie be so an if I can sende one of my childrine I will."[61] Another letter, which was probably intended for her brother Seth, a congregational minister in Watertown, Massachusetts, also gives thanks for some good counsel she received during her visit: "I had but a litel time with you who I thought woulde show and teach me more then aney bodey [sir?] but what you have saide to me I will not forgett it and I hope god will in able me in all my aflections and that it may be for the best and good of my soule deare brother."[62] Clearly, Mary's natal family had urged her to the Protestant fold, as well as tried to convince her to return to New England. Her notation to Ebenezer that "if I can sende one of my childrine I will" seems to indicate that the Storers were interested in taking in and evangelizing her Catholic children as well.

Mary's family was not content to convince her to return to New England with loving words alone. Her father used words, backed up by inheritance law, to compel her return. Joseph Storer's will spelled out his resentment of his daughter's choice to remain in Canada with her French husband, requiring her to "return from under the French Government & Settle in New England" if she were to have her fifty-pound inheritance, a portion equal to her siblings. As we have already seen, this was by no means an extraordinary gesture.[63]

Although Mary wrote that she understood that the Storer family's counsel to return to New England and to puritanism was "for the goode of my soule and bodey," she had no intentions of remaining with them. Her continuing correspondence with Ebenezer suggests that she was adept at shifting between identifying with her natal family in Boston and with her husband and children in Montreal. Continuing to address herself to Ebenezer before her return home, she writes, "Dear brother it grievs me to thinke of my father and mother that I had soe litel time to staye with theme but I finde the time very longe with strangers and longe to be with my famelie." Thus by calling her natal family "strangers," as opposed to her "famelie" in Montreal, she makes it clear that her family of first allegiance was in Montreal, not in Boston. And while she implies that her Boston family are "strangers" to her, her emotional attachment to them was quite powerful immediately after her 1725 visit. "Deare brother I remember what you have saide to me I thanke you and all that has spoke for my goode." Then again using formulaic language, she writes, "I desier your prayers for me who is youre sister til death with a harte full of sorey and my eyes full of tears fearewell my deare brother and sister I remaine your loving and sorrowful sister," and signs herself, as she did through most of their correspondence, "Mary St. Germaine, Mary Storer," as though to signify her awareness of her two families and her two identities. With only a few notable exceptions, however, her married name was written above her maiden name.[64]

Unhappily, the Mary Storer papers do not include all of the replies Ebenezer must have sent to his sister over the years, but we may assume they carried on a correspondence, based on the letters of hers that survive. Two years after she returned from her Boston trip, she remembers her promise to see if she might send one of her children down to Boston, but, she writes, "my Son is not willing to goe frome us my deare brother I thank you with all my hart for your good will my Children remembers respects to you."[65] For eight years after her visit to Boston, Mary and Ebenezer continued to exchange letters every year or two, updating each other on family news and sending along formulaic but apparently warm good wishes.[66] When Ebenezer sent news of their father's death, Mary once again affirmed her connection to her Boston family. In her reply, she tells Ebenezer that she felt "a grate grief to me the death of my deare father my hart is alwaies a sighing and my ies full of tears." She seems at pains to establish her credentials in her brother's eyes as a mourner for her father. Although she lived apart from her family her entire adult life, she wants Ebenezer to know she shares equally in the grief of her brothers and sisters: "I pray to god to comforte us all wee are father les children [while] I am hear [in Montreal], you may beleive my harte love is with you all we are al the same blode you can not denie it."[67]

Mary Storer St. Germaine was in touch not only to express her grief but to announce her interest in her rightful portion of her father's estate. Once again, with the hope of an inheritance, she demonstrates her ability to shift allegiances between her English and French families. She also uses different strategies in her attempt to convince her family to release her inheritance, alternately demanding her rightful share, complaining that politics prevented her from traveling to New England, and professing dutiful submission. In a letter to her mother, she writes that Ebenezer told her, "my deare father maide his will that I [might?] be equal to my sisters you may believe my dear mother [while] I am far of[f] from you and my deare familei I belave that is not cappable to kep it frome me in conseonc that is for me who is youre [own] child." Regarding her father's command that she remove herself from "French government" in order to receive her inheritance, Mary then claims it is impossible for her even to visit Boston: "wee have a governer & he will nat give any permission to goe in [New] Ingland to our contre[y]," she writes, and names the merchant in Boston whom she had designated to receive and convey her inheritance. Whereas she had earlier described her Montreal family as her family, and her natal family as "strangers," now she claims them as her "dear familei" again. While she is firm about remaining in Montreal, she calls New England "our contre[y]." Furthermore, she signs her letter, "your dutifull daughter," a departure from her usual practice, and a maneuver that suggests an effort to recast herself as a properly obedient and submissive daughter.[68]

There exists no letter of reply from Mary's mother, but brother Ebenezer's reply underscores the differences her New England family drew between Mary and her siblings. It also underscores his role in these family negotiations, as no direct reply from her mother appears in the collection. In response to her request, Ebenezer does not promise her inheritance, but he writes that he will remind their mother of her request, and assures Mary, "I know she will do any thing yt is proper & it be not against ye will of our

Father deceas'd."[69] The problem was that what Mary was requesting was clearly against her father's will. Joseph Storer had decreed that "if She doth not returne [to New England] Then I Give & bequeath to her the Sum of Tenn Shillings in Countrey pay."[70] This paltry remembrance stood as a rebuke to Mary's resistance of her father's will, and her mother and brother were apparently willing to let the rebuke stand. Legally they could not have directly sent Mary St. Germaine her portion directly from her father's estate, but they could have chosen to give her her portion out of their own fortunes.

Perhaps not surprisingly, there is no record of Mary St. Germaine ever receiving her inheritance, and the surviving correspondence between her and her brother ceases for several years. Only in the autumn of 1739, nearly six and a half years since her last surviving letter to Ebenezer, Mary wrote to him, and the tone of that letter suggests that she is still annoyed with him and his role in her non-inheritance. Whereas before she had always written him in English in her own hand, this letter appears to have been written by an amanuensis; it is also, significantly, written in French. She opens this letter with a standard, if cooler, salutation to Ebenezer, and then quickly announces the purpose of her letter: "I desire the favour to Let me hear from you & your family for as I have not heard any knews of mother I dont know whether she is on the Land of the Living which obliges me to adress my self to you to lett me hear from her." Notice how her language has changed since her fervent correspondence around the time of her father's death: "You and your family"—not my "dear fameli"; "Which obliges me to adress my self to you"—a phrase that lets Ebenezer know that she writes him only to hear news of their mother, from whom she has also been estranged. "If you still have any Love for me I hope you will not refuse me that Comfort," she adds, in further confirmation of her alienation from her natal family. She passes on news of her family, briefly reporting her children's marriages and sadly noting the death of her youngest son the previous year.[71] We do not know if she ever received a reply from her brother or from anyone in her natal family.

This may well have been the last letter Mary St. Germaine wrote to her brother Ebenezer, for the next letter in the collection is by her husband, Jean, dated eight and a half years after Mary's last letter. Like Mary's last letter, it too is written in French. Seven months after the fact, he wrote the man he addressed as his "very dear brother" to let Ebenezer know of his sister's death. "She died with all possible resignation to the will of God, that is to say as a perfect Christian, and as she had been here 39 years that we were together we had a blessed union and we never had a single difficulty. You know well my dear brother that her death is a great affliction to me, but I must submit to the will of our Creator, as it was he who gave me one of the best women in the world." After passing on some brief family news, he signs the letter, "your very humble and obedient servant and brother, Saint Germaine."[72]

St. Germaine received no reply to this letter, whose emotional language makes it stand out in this family correspondence as a touching tribute to his love for his wife and as his honoring of her memory. Neither did he receive a reply to his next letter a year later. Did Ebenezer fear that St. Germaine would press the issue of his wife's inheritance? It is a tempting theory, but in fact St. Germaine never brought up the issue of the fifty pounds in the surviving correspondence, never even hinted at financial matters, and seems to have desired merely a recognition of his loss and perhaps a renewed connection with the Storers.[73] When Ebenezer Storer finally replied to St. Germaine after a third letter, he did so rather dismissively, "Your kind Letter of ye [1]7th April last I recd. wherein you complain of my long Silence tho I have wrote by every opportunity. I am pleased with your assuring me, yt notwithstanding my Indifference, as you are pleas'd to call it, I shall yet have ye Pleasure of hearing from you," and said that he had indeed already replied regarding his sister's death. This letter does not reiterate any sympathy for St. Germaine or good wishes for his sister's soul that might have been included in that first response.[74] Perhaps Ebenezer was happy to forget his sister, her French husband, and their Catholic children in Montreal.

Stories like that of Mary Storer St. Germaine show the effects that choices like hers had on the workings of patriarchal power within New England families. The Storer family was typical of other New England families, like the Hansons, the Williamses, the Wheelwrights, and the Howes, who also went to great lengths to recover their daughters and save them from the twin evils of French government and Catholicism, or to punish them for their rejection of New England government and Protestantism, or both. Any captives who turned their backs on New England by converting to Catholicism and remaining in Canada represented a painful and shameful failure of the New England way, boys and men as well as girls and women. But New England communities and colonial governments actively courted the return of male ex-captives by offering them cash and jobs, whereas former female captives were offered little if any incentive to return. Instead, it was the government of New France that went out of its way to retain female captives from New England, especially in the years 1689–1713. Mary Storer St. Germaine's story demonstrates that New England families interpreted their daughters' conversion to Catholicism and marriage to French men and Indians as a rejection of New England patriarchal authority. Instead of dutiful obedience and submission to their fathers' (or brothers') household government, women like Mary Storer St. Germaine set themselves against New England's prescribed gender roles when they refused to come home and return to puritanism. While their own decisions to abandon New England is no doubt part of the reason they have been written out of New England history, perhaps their families' shame and desire to forget these daughters are also responsible for the fact that so many of them have disappeared from the New England record.

"Who will be Masters of America The French or the English?" Manhood and Imperial Warfare in the Eighteenth Century

> Who will be Masters of America The French or the English; and grief if it is not desided by a united vigorous blow at the Root. The French will run away with what the English call theirs, if the French have a No. of years to plan & Contrive & Effect, having got the Indians they without a spirit of prophesey will Effect their ambitious designs.
>
> —William Williams to Israel Williams (1756)

As we have seen, English and Indian men saw war and politics as important fields for proving manhood and establishing mastery over the enemy. Similarly, when the imperial struggle between Britain and France moved to the center of wars in the northeastern borderlands, English and French men experienced their struggle in part as a contest of masculinities. After decades of losing English captives to French Catholic Canada, New Englanders were especially eager for a decisive victory over the French. With the outbreak of the last two imperial wars in the 1740s and 1750s, which raged almost without interruption in North America, English and New England soldiers, war captives, and intellectuals wrote with more hostility about their French captors and foes than ever before. Because New England's focus turned away from their former Algonquian enemies to fix almost exclusively on the French, religion came to the fore in conceptualizations of the enemy. These imperial wars gave new force and vitality to the rivalry among Canadian Catholics and New England Protestants, inspiring a particularly fierce New England anti-Catholicism. Drawing on both the political and religious hostilities that had marked Anglo-French relations for hundreds of years, New England's private letters and journals as well as its print culture portrayed King George's War (1744–48) and the Seven Years' War (1756–63), also known in North America as the French and Indian War, as an apocalyptic confrontation between English Protestant virtue and liberty on the one hand, and French Catholic depravity and despotism on the other. The French Canadian viewpoint is more difficult to discern, as Canada had no native presses, nor was literacy as widespread as it was in New England.[1] However, the correspondence and papers of French colonial officials, and chance encounters between French and English men, give some insight into the French perspective on these last two imperial wars. In French eyes, New Englanders found themselves cast in the very same role they themselves had cast the Indians: Canadian officials complained frequently of the near-anarchy of New England and its hodgepodge of polities who asserted their own sovereignty, much like Indian tribes. French colonial officials saw English liberty therefore as libertinage, founded on Protestant "errors" established by an adulterous king.

Yet again, New England and English men evoked ideals of manhood to illustrate the political conflicts and religious differences between England and France, and by extension between New England and Canada. As in earlier Anglo-Indian conflict, ideas about gender and gendered language were used to describe the imperial wars in both English and New England print culture and private letters and diaries. Although the landscape and peoples of the northeastern borderlands had changed dramatically in the previous century, the ways in which New Englanders understood warfare did not, and to a remarkable degree New England civil and religious leaders used the same sacred language and ideas about gender to call its men to war once again.[2] Despite these similarities, these wars changed not just the political and cultural landscape of the northeastern borderlands but also the ideals of manhood that originally motivated New England men to fight Indians in the seventeenth century and both Indians and French men in the eighteenth century. What had once been a masculinity based on household headship, Christian piety, and the duty to protect both family and faith by force of arms became a masculinity built around the more abstract notions of Anglo-American nationalism, anti-Catholicism, and soldiering for the empire. By examining English and New England men's diaries, letters, and published works during the last two imperial wars, we will explore the emergence of this new masculinity and its close connections to eighteenth-century Anglo-American nationalism and anti-Catholicism.

While the mid-eighteenth century imperial wars were in fact different from the border wars of the seventeenth and early eighteenth centuries, the great-grandchildren of veterans of the earlier wars used remarkably similar words and ideas to explain and justify their wars. The same language that English people and New Englanders used to express their anxieties about Indian power and sovereignty in the seventeenth and early eighteenth centuries was applied with few changes to explain their fears of the possibility of French Catholic dominion in North America. Because of the close alliances the French cultivated with Native Americans, perhaps it is not surprising to see that the language used to anticipate and describe warfare between English and French men is strikingly similar to the vocabulary and ideas expressed concerning earlier Anglo-Indian wars. As we have seen, French and Indian allies cooperated in the taking of English captives, and the French proved themselves such faithful students of their allies that they were even more successful at adopting the English and keeping them permanently. So in the mid-eighteenth century with the revival of wars with France, once again New England religious rhetoric became charged with reference to the need for "Christian Soldiers" and the insistence that the Lord is above all "a Man of War" (Exodus 15:3). New England men were called to battle French Catholic foes, not just because doing so served the state's interests, but because (according to the state's magistrates and ministers) it was a central duty of manhood.[3] The two-hundred year Protestant association of Catholicism with femininity and corruption (as opposed to manly Protestant restraint and virtue) appears again in eighteenth-century artillery sermons.[4] And as in the seventeenth century, combatants on both sides accepted this duty and delighted in taunting their enemy about their shortcomings in battle and thus their inferior masculinity.

Artillery sermons of the mid-eighteenth century used the same bible lessons, language, and rhetoric as their seventeenth- and early eighteenth-century counterparts to compel New England men to become warriors for Christ.[5] But in the process, they invented a new and uniquely North American style of anti-Catholicism. Sermons of the 1730s to the 1760s use the same biblical texts to call men to battle as their forefathers heard in the 1620s, 1670s, and 1690s. For example, John Davenport urged his radical puritan flock to arm and train themselves in a 1629 sermon based on 2 Samuel 1:18, before their emigration to New England—"*Also hee bade them teach the children of* Judah *the use of the Bow.*" More than a hundred years later, in 1732 and 1737 respectively, Oliver Peabody and Thomas Ruggles used the same bible verse and the same reasoning to urge their men to prepare for war with the French.[6] Samuel Nowell, whose 1678 sermon *Abraham in Arms* lends its name to the title of this book, himself borrowed the notion of basing his sermon on Genesis 14:14: "And when Abram heard that his brother was taken captive, he armed his trained servants, born in his own house, and pursued them unto Dan." Nowell's sermon was then perhaps used as inspiration by eighteenth-century New England ministers who used the same bible verse, Peabody and Ruggles again among them. Not surprisingly, the themes of attack on one's household, the necessity to prepare for such an attack, and the taking of captives by enemies were themes that still resonated with many New Englanders.[7]

Eighteenth-century New England writers borrowed rhetoric from the Indian wars and grafted it onto the conflicts surrounding the imperial wars. One phrase in particular, evoking enemies "whose tender mercies are cruelties," wends its way through New England political and religious discourse from the late seventeenth century to the mid-eighteenth century. This phrase adopted from Proverbs 12:10, "a righteous man regardeth the life of his beast: but the tender mercies of the wicked are cruel," was usefully applied to a changing cast of enemies in the northeastern borderlands. Cotton Mather applied it to Hannah Duston's Abenaki captors in 1697, as did an artillery sermon forty years later that used New England's turbulent history to remind the congregation that "under GOD, our Lives, our Religion, our Liberties are owing to the Valiant & Martial Atchievements of those of our Fore-fathers, who were mighty in Battle. Else to all Humane probability, they would have been swallowed up at once, as it were, by the Vast Numbers of Indian Enemies, *whose tender mercies are Cruelty.*" The Protestant rebuttal offered in *A Letter from a Romish Priest in Canada* adopts this phrase and applies it to Catholics in 1729, suggesting that the horror of the Inquisition "is the manner of those *whose mercies are cruel,* according to *Solomon,* Prov. xii. 10." Similarly, Jonathan Todd's 1747 sermon also extended this phrase to include the French Catholics, who "have sent upon us the Barbarians of the Wilderness, whose *tender mercies are cruel,* and stir'd up their Savage Minds to Cruelty & Bloodshed."[8]

Aside from recycling bible verses and phrases, these eighteenth-century writers also borrowed the same gendered language used earlier to urge men to war. War was not just a duty to the state but a manly duty that would be the measure of them. Over and over again, New England men were told "how much it is a Duty for men to become Expert and Valiant Souldiers: that they may be able to answer that noble Exhortation of Joab to the Souldiers of Judah, 2 Sam X 12, *That they be of good Courage, and play the men for their People and for the Cities of their God.*" Thomas Ruggles goes on to explain what should have been self-evident to New England men by the 1730s. "There is so much true Manliness and Grandure in Military Exercise: It inspires the Mind with such Just, Honourable and Exalted Notions and dispositions: it so much tends to banish Littleness and meanness, and fill men with Greatness of spirit. . . . I say, were it upon these Considerations only, Every person who has any Relish for what is Just, Manly and Honourable, would labour to maintain it for the good of Mankind." In an aside, he notes the consequences for neglecting a martial spirit among New England men: "Its observable of the old *Romans,* as a martial spirit Decay'd among them, in proportion Luxury prevail'd; and consequently Effeminacy and a Train of Vices overspread them." Oliver Peabody, striking a familiar chord, urges military men to attend their training exercises faithfully and seriously, to "make a Business of them in their Season; and endeavour to make yourselves Masters of the *Art of War.* And O keep your selves from *Effeminacy* and Intemperance, which has been the ruin of so many Soldiers." Although New England's enemy had changed, Indians were still instructive models of manhood to avoid: "this honourable *Artillery Company* are not taught the Manner of fighting used by the *Salvages in the Wilderness,* so much as the more noble and manly Exercises of the more polished and civilized Nations." Ebenezer Gay echoes these concerns, reminding New England men that "Playing the Fool unfits you to *play the Men* for your People, and the Cities of God."[9]

Sermons of thanksgiving preached after New England's victories in the imperial wars suggest that it was not just a generic ideal of manhood that New England soldiers lived up to; they argued that it was New England's particular focus on independent land ownership, household headship, and piety that suited its men particularly well "to *play the Men*" at war. Nathaniel Walter found it a badge of honor at Louisbourg, Nova Scotia in 1745 "to see so many *likely Men,* and I conclude the most of them Owners of Lands and Houses, or Heirs of the same, and many Religious, in all our Towns, readily listing even as private-Soldiers." This description of valiant New England manhood was so felicitous as to be used verbatim two years later by Thomas Prince, in a sermon published by the same house as the Walter sermon. Protestant piety and responsible headship together were at the center of New England manhood—qualities they believed distinguished them not just from their Indian and French enemies but from English regulars as well. Ebenezer Bridge also focused on the piety and household orientation of New England manhood and its connections to his military duties. In a

1752 artillery sermon, he discusses the character of Cornelius, a Roman cen-
turion and early convert to Christianity: "He *appears to have been a pious
Head of a Family, a devout Man, and one that feared God with all his House,*
says the Text—Tho', in an elevated Station of Life, and used to manly Exercises Abroad." It was this combination of attention to both domestic and
religious duties that explained his success: "having his Heart possessed of
the Fear of God, he is desirous that his House or Family should be well
instructed and religiously educated—He was careful to exhibit a good Example to his Household, and to instruct them, and train them up in the
Knowledge and Service of the true God." Manhood was not expressed
through soldiering alone, but soldiering well was an extension of a man's
domestic duties.[10]

Walter elaborates on his thesis in a 1746 artillery sermon that it was
New England's "manly Piety and their *English* Bravery" that won Louisbourg, "Piety and Bravery which you, *Gentlemen,* will copy after, whenever
GOD shall call you to play the Men in the Cause of Liberty and Virtue." He
evokes New England history to explain the peculiar nature of New England
masculinity, handed down through seventeenth-century bloodlines: "In
You is deposited, as it were in a direct Line, that Divine Ardour, and that
Godlike Zeal for the Maintenance of the Rights of Truth and Justice, which
our Fore-fathers were animated with: Men whose Character shines with
endless Glory, especially in their martial Exploits against an innumerable
savage Foe." The question that every generation of New England men must
ask, then, is: "shall we their Sons ever prove a degenerate Race? Shall we
tremble when Cannons roar, when Bullets fly, and when all the glittering
Instruments of Destruction stand apparent before us? No, never shall it be
said, that the Troops of NEW-ENGLAND were backward to rush upon the
Sword, or afraid to face the Mouths of Cannon, at the Call of the LORD OF
HOSTS."[11]

New England soldiers of the 1740s and 1750s did not need to be reminded so strenuously of their heritage; they already saw their contemporary struggle against the French as a conflict with deep roots in the English
and New England puritan tradition. Interestingly, the memory of Oliver
Cromwell—not just a military man, but a puritan warrior—was on the
minds of common soldiers and cultural elites alike. Cromwell makes an appearance in *A Letter from Québeck,* a pamphlet purporting to be intercepted
French intelligence published in Boston in 1754 that was undoubtedly a
forgery designed to serve as hawkish Anglo-American propaganda. The author of the pamphlet evokes the memory of Cromwell to suggest that he is

an ancestor of particular relevance to New England men. *A Letter from Qué-beck,* supposedly written by an Irish Jesuit, Father "M'Laish," reports that New Englanders are poor soldiers who will be easily defeated, "except those *Oliverian Heretics* who took our *Cape-Breton*; these cast a Damp on our Undertakings." In case anyone might miss the point, "M'Laish" uses clearly gendered language to evoke the glories of manhood in war, as he goes on to explain: "they have the same Governor *Shirley,* who is an enterprizing, resolute Man; and when he, and the Puritan Ministers, say to the Inhabi-tants, *Go, fight for your Religion and Country,* they rush like Lions, and had rather die in Battle, than submit to the Dictates of our Holy Fathers, Jesuits, Friers, and Monks, and become Members of our Mother Church." Above all, New England men "retain the most martial Spirit of any in *North America,* and have a Tincture of *Oliver Cromwell's* Blood remaining." The history and memory of Cromwell must have been in the air in the 1750s, as it appears also in the private diary of a soldier from Framingham, Massa-chusetts, in 1758. On an expedition to Ticonderoga, Joseph Nichols records the misery of camp life as well as the excitement of the Battle of Ticonder-oga, July 6–8. While he writes that "in the Late Actions our men Behav'd Bravely not the Least Daunted when Order'd to Battle" despite their even-tual defeat, the poor rations and camp diseases are what he (quite rightly) fears the most. "The spirits of men seam to [Fail] I Doubt we are Loosing our oliverean Courage That in years past we had the Credit of . . . I make no Doubt if in Case our Natures was Refreshd with Diet Agreeable to what we are us'd to our Strength & Courage would Come to us Like an Armed man." Nichols's handwriting in this quarto volume is delicate and his spell-ing regular. He seems to have been a thoughtful and pious man, though probably not a formally educated one, thus his evocation of "oliverian Courage" indicates that the memory of the Lord Protector was still very much alive in New England nearly a century after his death and the end of puritan rule in England.[12]

Further evidence that New England men were called to revive a partic-ular puritan warrior tradition is evident in the strain of anti-Quakerism that was revived in the mid-eighteenth century. Quaker men, as members of a peace church, refused to bear arms and therefore were reviled in the New England press as weak men whose flawed understanding of the Bible en-dangered all of colonial British America. The lawfulness and righteousness of bearing arms was a recurring theme in eighteenth-century artillery ser-mons, which argued (after Cotton Mather himself) that "to *Learn War,* or to use the *Sword* and the *Spear,* is not only a *Lawful,* but also a *Needful,* yes, and a very *Nobile* Thing." Mather also specifically argues against the Society of Friends, calling them "a Sect of men at this Day in the World, who Succeed the old *Marichees,* as well as other old *Hereticks,* in declaiming against all *Military Discipline,*" writing that "this is not the only thing wherein they shew themselves no less *unscriptured* than *Irrational.*" The fictional *Letter from Québeck* of 1754 has Father *"M'Laish"* saying that "the Inhabitants of *Pennsylvania,*" a colony founded by Quakers, "are a meek peaceable People, who will neither furnish Money, Arms, nor Ammunition, that if you take their Coat, they will give you their Cloak also." So as to make sure that New England was spared these kindnesses, local officials during King George's War and the Seven Years' War punished Quaker men who shirked militia duty and coerced Quaker towns to meet their quotas for military service.[13]

While Cromwell might have been a more appropriate role model for the descendants of New England puritan men, the religious aspect of the wars with the French seems to have stirred some widespread nostalgia for the puritan dictator in England as well. An engraving published in London in 1755 suggesting the beginning of another English siege to recover Louisbourg is a riot of phallic imagery. In the lower right corner, a British soldier and sailor are shown behind a cannon captioned "Cromwell's device" (see figs. 13–14). Both young and fit, they stand in clear contrast to the elderly and weak French man helpless at the mouth of the cannon. The obviously phallic cannon is just the beginning; in case anyone missed the contrast of potent English masculinity versus French effeminacy or impotence, two flowers grow beneath the cannon's barrel and are helpfully labeled "the English Rose erect, the French Lilly drooping." In an even more aggressive suggestion of the connections between sexual and military violence, the British sailor seated behind the cannon is shown with a rooster in his lap, both his hands around its neck, and as he chokes the "Gallic Cock" in a pantomime of masturbation, it disgorges the names of "French usurpations in America."[14] It is difficult to imagine a scene of greater sexual hostility and violence than this one, published before the official declaration of war in Europe.

New England in particular felt the brunt of "French usurpations" in the 1740s and 1750s. While King George's War officially ended in 1748 and the next war was not recognized by Europe until 1756, New England's northern and eastern frontiers suffered almost continuous attacks and raids for captives at the hands of French-allied Eastern and Western Abenaki—or as those in New Hampshire and Maine had come to call them, the "Canada Indians."[15] Reports of this continued borderlands violence make a striking

Figure 13. L. Boitard, *British Resentment or the French Fairly Coopt at Louisbourg* (London, 1755), celebrates the renewed siege of the key Canadian city of Louisbourg, Cape Breton, Nova Scotia, in 1755. This engraving illustrates English mastery and French submission with a number of stock images and allegories, including a sun and moon in the upper left corner captioned "The British Arms eclipsing those of France," a lion described as "The British Lion keeping his dominions under his paw, safe from invaders" in the lower left, and, between them, "Britannia attending the complaints of her injur'd Americans, receives them into her protection." Notably, the French men imprisoned in the chicken coop on the right are called "Starving French" in the caption at the bottom (number 9), and they appear to be looking in the grain troughs before them and begging for food. The political uses of the notion of French Canadian poverty and its connections to a compromised masculinity are clearly apparent here. Courtesy of the John Carter Brown Library at Brown University.

contrast to the aggressively martial rhetoric about New England manhood, as what is striking about these dispatches is the vulnerability and even help-lessness of men on the New England frontier. As early as 1750, desperate stories of English homes pillaged and burned and families rent by captivity were recorded in petitions to the Massachusetts governor and his Council, the petitioners begging for temporary relief as well as ransom money to help them purchase their families back. James Whidden, of Merrymeeting Bay, Maine, reports that of an extended family of thirteen, only "your Memorialist with his Wife saved themselves by getting down the cellar, which they had but time to do without putting on their Cloaths to Cover their

Figure 14. Detail of *British Resentment or the French Fairly Coopt at Louisbourg.* The riot of unsubtle phallic images and puns here play on the animal used to represent France in allegories, the "coq," or Rooster. The title of the engraving shows the "French fairly Coopt" in a chicken coop labeled "Louisbourg 1755." Additionally, in the lower right a caption describes the scene as "An English Saylor encouraged by a Soldier, Squeezes the Gallic Cock by the throat & makes him disgorge the French usurpations in America." Next to the sailor stands a cannon captioned "Cromwell's device," and underneath the barrel of the cannon stands "the English Rose erect, the French Lilly drooping." Courtesy of the John Carter Brown Library at Brown University.

Nakedness." Their eleven children and grandchildren were taken to Canada in September of 1750. This image of a poorly clad grandfather shivering in a cellar, pathetically bereft of almost his entire family as well as his clothing, illustrates the gap between the expectations of English men and the reality for many of them in the northeastern borderlands. In a related attack the same month, Samuel Webb's son was taken into captivity and held for three hundred livres' ransom. Webb's petition to the governor and Council reveals the depths of his desperation. He recognized that there were many in "Like Surconstances," though he writes, "I believe none so deploreable dificalt as mine by reason of extreme poverty and my wife has bin sick ever since my Son was tacken." Other family illnesses and "extreme dificaulties" made him fear that he was "not able to redeme him if he should be made a slave by another nation all his dayes." But perhaps no family of survivors was as haplessly caught in and between the wars as the Ross family of Sheepscot, Maine. Family patriarch William Ross "was taken at Sheepscoat where he had his house and Subsistance burned by the indians the last warr," and then in September of 1750 "what they had obtained by their industry was again burnt in a Garrison by the Ennymy," and Ross and his eldest son were taken captive. The neighbors who petitioned on behalf of Mrs. Ross reported that "said Ross is a lame man and has left this woman and three small children not able to help her in poor Circumstances."[16]

Petition after petition confirms the sufferings of civilians on the frontiers of New England, and their almost complete inability to prevent attacks on them and their children. The following summer of 1751, Samuel Whitney of Brunswick, Maine, was mowing hay with his son and five other men when they were "Surrounded and Surprized by nineteen Indians & one Frenchman who were all armed." When one of the men attempted to escape, he was "Killed in a barbarous Manner & Scalped," and after that the Indians laid waste to twenty or thirty head of cattle. Family members of these men begged consideration of the governor and Council, that their menfolk might "be Delivered out of a land of Darkness and State of Captivity that they may be Brought to Injoy not only civiel but Sacred Priviledge in this their Native Land." The women petitioners in particular "beg your Honours would think on the troubles of your Honours Hand-maids who have had our Husbands Carried and kept from us and we Left in the wilderness without a [illegible] or any to Provide for us or our Childering."[17]

These apparent breaches of the Peace of Aix-la-Chappelle vexed New England officials. Writing to Governor-General Pierre-Jacques de Taffanel, Marquis de la Jonquière, in 1750, Governor William Shirley of Massachusetts declared that these continued attacks on frontier non-combatants "would not be reckoned a very generous manly way of annoying an Enemy after a Declaration of War; how much to be condemned then in a Time of Peace?" While they carried on diplomatic relations and continued to exchange both English and Abenaki captives taken during King George's War, New England officials protested vainly about these disruptions of the peace.[18] Because so many New England families continued to be weak and vulnerable, the manly rhetoric of war was perhaps a necessary comfort as well as a useful tool for inspiring would-be soldiers and papering over the devastating realities of war. Men in the northeastern borderlands perhaps already understood that the next war would not be forestalled for very long.

While New England ministers looked to the past for models of New England manhood to fight the eighteenth century's wars, New England men were beginning to define themselves in more abstract terms as men who enjoyed liberal English civil and religious liberties, unlike the French Canadian men they fought. But like their clerics, New Englanders used old templates to frame contemporary concerns as they mapped their prejudices about gender and family life onto the French when the French became, in the words of New England writers, "the inveterate enemy." This process was under way already by the end of the seventeenth century, but it intensified with the renewed outbreak of hostilities in the northeastern borderlands in the 1740s and 1750s. New England men still saw their French foes as unmanly, as they had tried to paint their Indian foes, but with some important differences: New England combatants and writers of the earlier colonial period presumed that Indians were unmanly because their families and communities were too loosely governed; ineffective male leadership, they believed, explained proudly ungovernable women and children (or alternatively, irrational male despotism over their "squaw drudges" and fearful children). While mid-century English and New England observers saw Indians and French men as equally compromised men, the causes of their emasculation were different. French men were portrayed as weak and unmanly in English-language publications in the 1740s and 1750s not because they were dominated by women and children, but because they submitted willingly to the twin despotisms of Paris and Rome: their masters from Paris took the form of appointed French governors and intendants, and from Rome, the form of Jesuit, Recollect, and Sulpician priests and missionaries who owed their allegiance to the Pope. Additionally, the relative scarcity of French women and the fact that many men in the St. Lawrence valley remained unmarried may also have contributed to the perception of New Englanders that French Canadian men were not true masters of independent households—a key component of colonial masculinity—and so were more boys than men.

As "disorderly" Indian men and their "licentious" wives and "undisciplined" children had served as excellent foils for New England men who were true masters of their households, so English and New England observers crafted a mid-eighteenth-century stereotype of French Canadian men as illiterate *habitants* who were happily servile to the arbitrary authority of civil and religious despots. The means were different, but the ends the same: French men, like Indians, were essentially feminized or infantilized by their political impotence and thus not fit for self-sovereignty, let alone mastery over New England men. This construction of French men as servile also suited changing notions of New England manhood in the mid-eighteenth century, which focused less on men's roles as husbands and fathers and more on the civil and religious liberties that were central to emerging notions of English and Anglo-American nationalism in the eighteenth century.

Captain William Pote was captured by the French and Indian enemy (or "spawn of hell," as he called them) while running a supply schooner up to Port Royal, Nova Scotia in 1745. The tone of his captivity narrative reflects some of the hostility and contempt New Englanders held for the French by the 1740s. When French soldiers told the English captives "we should have ye Pleasure of seeing Canady," Pote comments acidly, "they supposed [it] to be one of ye most famouse Places in ye whole Universe." Pote reports derisively that his Indian captors also bragged about "what Sumtious Living I might Expect when we arrived to Canedy and Boasted Verey much of their Libertyes and previledges above any other Nation, and told me they was In Subjection to no king nor prince In ye Universe."[19] Whereas English captives from the late seventeenth century through the 1720s had described their great joy at being sold to French masters, who would feed them bread and butter and give them European-style clothing, prisoners of the 1740s and 1750s extended few such compliments to their French captors. This was doubtlessly because captured English men in these later decades were treated like the prisoners of war they were rather than like individual captives purchased from the Indians. They were held in prisons rather than housed with families, and so they suffered the indignities and hazards of eighteenth-century institutionalization—disease, discomfort, bad food, and boredom.[20] Whether it was Indians or the French boasting of the glories of Canada, English and New England prisoners, soldiers, and writers mocked such talk in their writing. In a published letter (purportedly) from an English officer in Canada, the anonymous author lays out Anglo-American stereotypes of Canadian misery and servility while at the same time warning how objectionable it would be to imagine the English in such a servile condition. Canadians, he says, are slavish men, as "the Governor of *Canada* has not even a Shew of Parliaments as his Master has in *France*, his Will is Law, and no one dare controul him." Deprived of a franchise, Canadian men were thus subject to despotic taxation and draconian measures like hanging or imprisonment for life for neglecting militia duty. William Bolan, in a volume written shortly after the English victory at Louisbourg in 1745, asks rhetorically, "Can it be supposed that a People so utterly detesting Popery, Slavery, and Arbitrary Power, would subject themselves to a Government, under which they can expect, and are sensible, would find nothing but the Loss of their Religion, Liberty, and Property?"[21] English and Anglo-American men kept as prisoners were doubtlessly quite sensitive to their own deprivation of religion, liberty, and property.

The anonymous English officer suggests that this slavery permeates all of Canada when he complains of the large number of English war captives bought and sold in Canada "like Negroes" and then shamelessly urges the English to fight back by adopting the same policy of hiring Indian allies to kidnap French settlers. He recognizes how controversial such a policy recommendation would sound "as inconsistent with the municipal law of civiliz'd Nations, especially the *English,* whose Pride and Boast is Freedom," although of course English people were always much more concerned about their own liberties than those of French people, Indians, or Africans. But this drastic measure was the only relief he saw for desperate New Englanders, who "are themselves actually enslaved in *America,* by a Handful of *Canadians,* the very Indignity hereby offer'd to us, by a People who stile themselves the politest in the World." This humiliation, he argues, "should awaken that Spirit of Bravery and Resentment, so peculiar to our Ancestors." Being enslaved might be good enough for "Negroes," but to be the slave of a slave was utterly intolerable for a New Englander, or any other Anglo-American or English man. The author relates some anecdotes that illustrate Canadian disregard for the rank and rightful privileges of their English captives. He indignantly reports that Captain Grant, captured at Crown Point, "instead of being used like an Officer and Prisoner of War, was obliged to perform the most servile of Offices." But, he suggests that sometimes English love for liberty is irrepressible, as in the case of "a young Lad, of good Family," taken with Grant at Crown Point by Indians, given as a gift from his Indian master to the governor of Québec, "who immediately set him about Offices of Servility in his House; the Boy, who had Spirit, refused to comply with his Orders, and was determin'd his Master should not get any Good of him, which Monsieur perceiving, applied to Colonel *Schuyler* to buy him." Schuyler bought the proud boy for two hundred livres, according to the author.[22] In addition to showing English love for liberty, this anecdote also suggests that French men—even colonial governors—were harldly a match for mere English boys, let alone English men.

Why would working for a French Canadian man be such a humiliating proposition? According to New England observers, French men in Canada were like Indians or slaves not just because of their form of government, but because they were not landowners. While this was technically true, New Englanders did not understand that being a *habitant* was quite different from being a European peasant. French settlers could have all the land they could profitably use, with a secure title and the payment of nominal seigneurial dues. Because running one's own farm in Canada did not require the investment of capital in land, access to land and household headship was arguably more democratic in Canada than it was in the English colonies. Furthermore, since the seigneurial land-tenure system prevented land speculation, the great differences in wealth and poverty that characterized colonial Anglo-America by the middle of the eighteenth century did not emerge in Canada. Therefore it is likely that *habitants* enjoyed a more egalitarian society than that of proto-Republican New England.[23]

Besides looking askance at the different conventions of land ownership, English people and New Englanders also suggested that Canadian farms were rude and that the people there lived in poverty. As we have seen, allegations of poverty could serve as a kind of political attack and a subtle means of questioning French sovereignty. We have seen how stereotypes of "poor Indians" with inferior quality and quantities of food were used as oblique arguments against Indian sovereignty in captivity narratives, so it is perhaps unsurprising to see the same stereotypes refreshed and fitted for French Canadians at a time of intense Anglo-French conflict. William Pote's captivity narrative echoes this suggestion of Canadian poverty when he complains that his French captors show little if any hospitality. He received no blankets, food, or drink, but he says the French "Complemented us with their Usuel Complement to prisionners, Courage my Friends, fortune of war." Like most captives he found himself underdressed, and asks for a shirt, "which I was in Great Need of at ye time, having but one Corse shirt & yt began to be Considerably Inhabitted with french Vermin which our straw was full of at yt time." Note his particular disdain for being infested with "french Vermin," presumably more noxious pests than English or New England vermin. Only once does Pote appreciate the hospitality offered to him by the French, on an occasion where he notes significantly that there were "so many Genteel Courteous, Gentlemen and Ladys Round me." He was given food and drink—including beer—and "treated with a Great Deal of Civility, and Good Usage." Was it the beer or the company, both of which better suited his notions of his status, that finally allowed him to show some gratitude for his Canadian captors?[24]

Stereotypes of poverty and filth in New France abounded in some de-

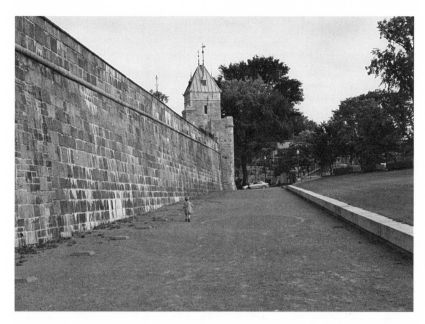

Figure 15. Even today, Québec's city walls and stone buildings make it look and feel like no other city in North America. Photo by author.

scriptions of Canadian dwellings and towns. New England soldiers and sailors were generally impressed with the stone buildings and walls of cities like Montreal, Québec, and Louisbourg, which contrasted favorably with the wooden palisades and wood-shingled houses that characterized colonial New England architecture. However, English observers, who were somewhat better traveled and more cosmopolitan in their outlook, were especially disdainful of Canadian towns and people. One anonymous account of the second siege of Louisbourg describes it as a town of "several narrow, paltry, stinking *Lanes* they call *Streets*. There is hardly a tolerable *House* in it, besides those of the *Governor* and *Intendant,* that are built of Stone and Brick without any Elegance." He writes,"the best of all its Buildings are, the *Hospital, Nunnery,* and the *Magazines,"* but he insults the houses of the common people as no more "than a better Sort of *boarded Cottages* a Story high." To underscore his point about Canadian poverty, he heaps contempt upon the enemy by writing that "one could not help observing many Marks of the *shewy Beggary* of their late Inhabitants—to say nothing of the *Dirt* and *Slovenliness* of that *nasty fine* People whom the *English* ape with so

much Fondness, and so little Taste." Another English soldier reports that
Québec's grander buildings were "tolerably well build," but most of them
"indifferent," and all in all he deems Québec "a very filthy disagreeable
Place." The main reason for his impressions revolves around what he describes as their "dependence." "Their entire Dependence is on the Furr
Trade, every Thing they want is sent them from *France*, they have not one
single Thing manufactured among them." According to this soldier, dependence on the Indian trade made them economically vulnerable, because
their Indian allies require French goods to continue the trade, and because
"now they have got so many more People to feed than they us'd to have,
their Country being insufficient to supply them without Assistantce; nor
could they ever do it in peaceable Times, which may easily be prov'd by the
New-England-Men, who supply them with a great quantity of all sorts of
Food."[25] Here the portrayal of New England men as farmers—an image
that served so well as a foil against unmanly Indian men who did not cultivate the ground—is revived to highlight New England productivity and independence, in contrast to Canadian men's profligacy and dependence.
What further proof was needed to show how weak Canadian men were, if
New England men had to feed them and their families?

French officials in Canada essentially agreed with New England's analysis of the differences between their societies. They put a significantly different spin on them, however. Instead of New England's vaunted "liberty,"
French officials saw anarchy. They complained of the bureaucratic confusion brought on by the pretense of sovereignty of individual colonies—
there were too many "governors" of equal rank to deal with rather than
one governor of New England. (Ironically, this judgment of anarchy was
exactly the one that English people and New Englanders applied to Indians,
as even a century and more after living beside Native peoples, they still
judged the complexities of Indian decentralized government harshly.)[26]
French religious men and women too saw great danger not just in the usual
errors of Protestantism but in the decentralized nature of congregationalist
self-government, without an episcopal hierarchy to guide them. One priest,
writing to a former convert who returned to New England and abjured Catholicism, pleaded with her to return from "where there is nothing but
Darkness and Irreligion, Schisms, Divisons and Confusions. . . . else fear
and be perswaded, that your Death will be unhappy, and attended with
madness and despair." What else would result from such a religion,
founded as it was upon the desires of a venal ex-priest and his nun wife
and spread by the brute force of an English king desperate to legitimize his

scandalous sex life? According to French officials and priests, New England's religion was just as anarchic and flawed as its patchwork of a government.[27]

New Englanders returned this suspicion of their religion in kind, perhaps to an even greater degree. Just as the French saw New England's civil and religious errors as linked by their anarchy, so New Englanders saw French civil despotism compounded by the corrupt and authoritarian rule of the Church of Rome. As we have seen, religion was a large part of French and English mutual resentment in the eighteenth century, as it had been since the sixteenth century. This is not to suggest that we can trace a static anti-Catholicism in New England, but rather to suggest that anti-Catholicism was a familiar old garment in which to cloak particular New England fears and resentments in the mid-eighteenth century.[28] The wars of the 1740s and 1750s revived New England anti-Catholicism to a murderous pitch, however. In New England, Catholics were to be hated and feared not just because they were successful at converting both Indians and English captives—they were to be reviled because their faith was despotic and the Church of Rome had dreams of world domination. In the minds of many New Englanders, the battles in this chilly patch of North America were part of a larger war with worldwide and otherworldly implications. Because of the vibrant print culture of New England, the remnants of its anti-Catholicism far eclipse evidence of rigid anti-Protestantism in the minds of French Canadians.

Whether this is merely a problem of evidence, or whether it accurately suggests a disproportionate religious prejudice on the part of New Englanders, is difficult to say. Protestants were officially forbidden to settle in New France, but a colony so desperate for laborers was not in a position to worry too much about the confession of their migrants. Protestants were prominent among the seventeenth-century charter companies that maintained the colony for the Crown, although they were not allowed to practice their religion, hold office, or to acquire land—the same restrictions put on Catholics in New England through the colonial period. By the end of the century, French soldiers garrisoned in Canada also included a substantial minority of Protestants. When Huguenots arrived (the vast majority of them men, like most Canadian sojourners), those who stayed most often made their abjuration and joined the faith of their neighbors—a requirement for anyone who wanted to marry in Canada. Thus perhaps some Protestant men, after King Henri IV, decided that a wife was well worth a Mass after all.[29] In the 1750s and 1760s, English and New England observers reported that Protestant corpses either were refused burial inside the walls of Canadian cities, or were dug up and thrown into rivers by outraged Catholic priests. Even if some of the more lurid accounts of abuse of corpses were true, living Protestant visitors appear to have been received courteously before the British conquest.[30]

Artillery sermons and sermons preached to commemorate English victories in the mid-eighteenth century steeped New England's soldiers in this revived anti-Catholicism. In Thomas Ruggles's artillery election sermon preached in Guilford, Connecticut, in May of 1736, the shift in the identity of New England's true enemy is made very clear. "The French . . . are the most Inveterate & Dangerous Enemies to the English Nation. These are that that nearly Border upon; yea, in some sense Compass us round about. Who both by Interest, and more especially the Prejudices of their Religion, are set against us; so that perhaps, no People are more Envied, and hated by their Neighbours. And should Wars break forth among the Nations, which may be sooner than our Expectations, we can expect no other but there would be those who would Endeavour and use all their Power to swallow us up." While many preachers still recognized the important role of Indians in warfare with the French—condemning the "fatal Rage and Fury of *French* and *Indian* Demoniacks," for example—New England's ministers drew on their fear and loathing of Catholicism to identify the French as the major threat to New England's security. By the 1730s, enemy Indians in New England writings and publications were reduced to the role of handmaidens of French governors and priests, as in this 1747 sermon by Jonathan Todd: "[The French] have sent upon us the Barbarians of the Wilderness, whose *tender mercies are cruel,* and stir'd up their Savage Minds to Cruelty & Bloodshed. . . . They have laid many of our Towns waste, and carried many of the Children of our People into Captivity: Where they have been Slaves to Barbarians, or been teazed with Jesuits, and the superstitious Devoters of Rome." In English and New England rhetoric, Indians no longer had a politics or foreign policy of their own; by the 1750s most New England observers assumed that Indians existed only as possible allies of the French or of the English, not as people who might wage war or make peace for their own reasons or on their own terms. With the capture of Québec in 1759 and Montreal in 1760, New England ministers interpreted the English victory as the result of the apocalyptic struggle between good and evil described in the book of Revelations, and saw clearly the hand of God in these events. "This Part of the Globe, for Ages unknown, has had nothing be Heathenism in the grossest Degree: And now, when a Popish Prince settled *Canada* with a

People which bare the Image of the Beast, how visible is the Truth and Justice of the divine Proceedings in pouring this Vial of his Wrath upon them!"[31]

As we saw earlier, the literature of New England anti-Catholicism in the late seventeenth and the early eighteenth centuries frequently fixated on priests as devious foreign agents. Priests were equally fascinating to anti-Catholic writers of the mid-eighteenth century. While New England's ministers regularly advised and assisted soldiers before and during battle, evidence of French priests' involvement in war was always described as utterly insidious by English-language writers, who saw it as further proof of the deviousness of French designs. When sighted on or near the battlefield, priests were noted in New England journals and letters with disgust and foreboding. Although Protestant soldiers and officers supposedly rejected the notion that Catholic priests possessed greater access to spiritual power than other men, at some level they must have believed that priests had access to some kind of supernatural powers—divine or diabolical—as their presence in battle was always noted. For example, an anonymous English journal of the 1745 siege of Louisbourg suggested that a French official schemed to retake the fortress, although he "denied he knew anything of the Matter but it now appears that he and his Brother in law were in the Plot and probably a French Priest too." The presence of a priest serving as a French officer was perhaps used to justify the brutal slaughter of enemy prisoners in a shocking tale from 1759. In a published account of the siege of Québec, the English author reports that a detachment of marines surprised "a party of Canadians, headed by a priest." Those not killed in the skirmish were captured, but they were not taken prisoner according to the rules of war: "in return for many acts of cruelty," which the author does not specify, "the priest and the rest of the prisoners were put to death, and scalp'd by our rangers." Scalping was a practice decried as "savage" when practiced against one's own dead, especially by New England and English observers. Perhaps the presence of a priest in this Canadian war party justified (in the minds of their English attackers) their summary execution and scalping.[32]

When real priests could not be found scheming or in battle, New Englanders invented them, like "*M'Laish,* an *Irish* Jesuit, of the Order of St. Patrick,* a politic ingenious Man" in the aforementioned *A Letter from Québeck.* New Englanders, he says, "are sensible, that when once we become their Masters, Fire and Gibbet will be their Portion, if they do not fall down and worship the Images we shall set up." This pamphlet is almost certainly a fake, as it too perfectly reflects New England fears and menaces its readers with an over-the-top portrait of French and Catholic cunning. Nevertheless, it highlights the central role in such nefarious schemes that most English and New England readers assigned to priests. The successes of French priests only made them more fearsome, as their Protestant enemies recognized the crucial role they played in advancing French political, economic, and military goals.[33]

Priests may have inspired especially murderous bouts of violence on the part of English and New England Protestants in battle, as the tale of Father Ralé suggests. No priest was hated or feared more in New England in the early eighteenth century than Father Sebastien Ralé, or Ralle, the enormously successful and long-lived missionary at Norridgewock, on the Kennebec River in Maine. New Englanders believed this Jesuit in the marchlands possessed diabolical powers, as nothing else could explain his extraordinary success in converting generations of Eastern Abenakis and securing their alliance nor his ability to evade capture by New England troops more than once. After having served in the Illinois country as a missionary, Ralé along with Father Vincent Bigot founded a mission at Norridgewock in 1695, where his work would nettle New Englanders for nearly thirty years as they struggled to lay claim to the beaver-rich rivers and open fields of coastal Maine. In a 1705 attack on a temporarily deserted Norridgewock, New Englanders burnt the village and church but missed a confrontation with the Jesuit. The end of Queen Anne's War in 1713 brought a few years of peace to the region, but by the early 1720s, English authorities in Boston had decided that Ralé was a threat to English commercial interests as well as a formidable political and military foe whose allegedly near-demonic influence on his Abenaki converts posed a continuing threat to English designs on settlements at the Eastward. The colony had finally decided to fight Ralé on his own terms by installing the Reverend Joseph Baxter at a rival Protestant mission near Norridgewock in 1718. Baxter spoke no Indian languages and made no converts, as he spent most of his time at Fort St. George at the mouth of the Kennebec River speculating in land and trading with the Indians. Clearly, he was no peer of Ralé's as a missionary or as a linguist—his Abenaki syllabary listed just three phrases with which to enthrall his prospective Indian converts: "How do you do," "I do not care," and "I forgot." Nevertheless Ralé and his Indian allies were irritated by this incursion into the Kennebec. Ralé warned his converts not to truck with the English, and although he attempted to engage Baxter as an intellectual and theologian, he found Baxter sadly wanting.[34]

As New England's dealings with Ralé illustrate, English and New England anti-Catholicism was more than just a cultural attitude that served to link English speakers through their shared Protestantism; it was in fact a passionate prejudice that drove much of New England's policy and use of its military force in the eighteenth century. While Ralé fought with his pen in correspondence with Baxter and Boston officials, the English were betting on the sword to end this controversy. Colonel Johnson Harmor and Captain Joseph Heath were sent on a mission to capture Ralé in January 1722, but as they were slowed down by poor moccasins and snow shoes, Ralé's Indian allies had time to warn him of the English approach. When the scouting party of fifty men got to Norridgewock, they were dismayed to learn that Ralé had departed not long before, as they found that "tho the weather was Exceeding cold & [his] study had no fire place in it, yet neither his Ink in his Standish or Drink in his pot were froze——." Despite the spartan chill of his unheated chamber, Harmor and Heath manage to confirm English stereotypes about the luxury and effeminacy of Catholic priests, as they describe his room as "well provided with good things for housekeeping," including "a considerable quantity of furs," both to keep him warm and enrich him. In the fall of 1722, the English made another attempt to capture Ralé, this time with a small army of 230 men, but once again his Abenaki friends tipped him off and helped him escape.[35]

Ralé and his mission Abenaki were not so lucky on August 23, 1724, when the English landed another army in the Kennebec River for a final reckoning with the mission and its devoted father. According to a letter from Fr. Pierre Joseph de la Chasse, superior-general of the missions in New France, the Abenaki were badly outnumbered, having only about fifty warriors at the mission. Nevertheless, "at the first noise of the muskets, they tumultuously seized their weapons, and went out of their cabins to oppose the enemy." But the English and their Mohawk allies were not as interested in the Abenaki as they were Ralé, and both French and English accounts of his death portray it as a bloody rout. According to la Chasse, "As soon as they perceived the Missionary, a general shout was raised which was followed by a storm of musket-shots that was poured upon him." Heroically, not to mention picturesquely, Ralé met the musketry like a man and then "dropped dead at the foot of a large cross that he had erected in the midst of the Village." Samuel Penhallow, a New England chronicler of the early imperial wars, writes, "some say that quarter was offered him, which he refused, and would neither give nor take any," agreeing with French accounts that portray Ralé as embracing his death. Ralé's corpse was then mutilated by his conquerors, with his head split open, his legs broken, and his whole body trampled. La Chasse states that it was the Mohawks, not the English, who were the leaders of this treatment of Ralé's body, in what seems like a hurried enactment of the Indian ritual torture and execution of a live captive. Perhaps it was the New Englanders, then, who turned to defiling the mission church, where they "rifled the altar, profaned the adorable host and the sacred vessels, and consummated what every civilized man must term, their atrocities, by firing the church." Then again, perhaps the New Englanders participated in some of the gorier violence after all. Penhallow claims, "the number of the dead which we scalped, were twenty-six, besides Monsieur Ralle the Jesuit," implying that it was New England soldiers who did the scalping, in an account that makes no mention of Mohawk involvement in the action whatsoever. Perhaps the New England soldiers thought it was a fittingly savage end for Ralé, who had been so happy to give his life over to Indian ways. He was in their eyes, after all, "a bloody incendiary, and instrumental to most of the mischiefs that were done us, by preaching up the doctrine of meriting salvation by the destruction of hereticks."[36]

This rather lopsided attack on the Norridgewock mission was celebrated as the central English victory of Dummer's War (1723–27), a series of borderlands struggles between the English and Abenaki (also known as Grey Lock's War among the Western Abenaki.)[37] Penhallow called it "the greatest victory we have obtained in the three or four last wars: and it may be as notable an exploit (all things considered) as ever happened in the time of King Philip."[38] In a broadside quickly published in Boston in 1724 to commemorate the English triumph, Ralé is portrayed as a murderous villain rather than as a man of God. In this English account, Ralé put up considerably more violent resistance than in French and Catholic accounts of his death (or martyrdom). New England readers were invited to revel in the bloody father's bloody end:

> But I must not pass over
>   old Fryar *Rallee's* Fate,
> Who staid it out most firmly,
>   and fought with cruel Hate.
> A Lad that was his Prisoner
>   he shot and wounded sore,
> Likewise Lieutenant *Dimmick,*
>   and also one Man more.
> They entred then his dwelling
>   and shot him in the thigh;

Figure 16. "The Rebels Reward: or, *English* Courage Display'd, being a full and true Account of the Victory obtain'd over the Indians at *Norrigiwock*" (Boston: J. Franklin, 1724) was a broadside celebrating the slaughter of Father Sebastien Ralé and dozens of Abenaki at the mission at Norridgewock during Dummer's War. The song and woodcut together constitute an almost pornographic celebration of the violent deaths of the priest and his allies. Contrary to both French and English reports that stated that Ralé met his fate manfully, the woodcut on this broadside depicts the fair-skinned priest cowering in the fort while his naked, dark-skinned converts attempt vainly to defend him. "Old Rallee's flag" is depicted as a standard composed of French crosses and Indian bows and arrows, suggesting the hybrid identities forged by Ralé and his Abenaki allies. This item is reproduced by permission of the Huntington Library, San Marino, California.

> Yet he refused Quarter
> and for his Gun did try.
> But still he cry'd, I'm ruin'd,
> alas I'm ruin'd;
> At which an English Soldier
> did shoot him thro' the Head.

A marvelously primitive woodcut dominates the top third of the page (see Fig. 16), depicting clothed New Englanders firing on naked Indians, whose complexion is rendered darker by crude lines drawn on them. Father Ralé is shown inside the French mission on the left, awaiting his fate rather than standing manfully prepared for battle (which contradicts even English accounts of his conduct). Flying above it is "Rallee's Flag," a standard with French crosses and bows and arrows on it, symbolizing the union of French and Indian political and religious interests.[39]

The people of Boston may have been pleased to put an end to the story of Father Ralé and wrap it all up with a bloody broadside, but communities on the Maine frontier continued to be roiled by the violent controversy, as trader John Minot reports in a 1732 letter to his father. That summer an English woman in Brunswick who sold rum to the Indians told them that one Richard Jacquish was Father Ralé's killer. After Jacquish left the Brunswick fort, Minot reports that, "twenty Indians way layd him as he came along with another man one Mackness where they Started out uppon him, and told him he was the man that kild the Jesuite. held him down by his hair & beat and bruisd him very much, notwithstanding all he could say to them to passifye them. [He] told them it was peace now, and that they ought not to doe so." Jacquish did not deny that he had delivered the fatal blow to Ralé, but he pleaded rather that "it was warr wen he did it, and that he [Ralé] would not taike quarter." Interestingly, Jacquish had been warned by another Indian that trouble would come his way if he left the fort, but "the answer he made him [was] that he was about his business and would not turne aside for none of them." During the attack, the two English men returned the blows with clubs and "very likely brook one of ye Indians skulls that dyed a few dayes agone." Minot worries about "what will be the Consiquence of this fray"—for his business, not for Anglo-Indian relations. In fact, he shares Jacquish's belligerent attitude, telling his father, "I think if he had kild them all he had done them justice for they abusd him Shamefully & beat him that his sides were all black & blue." He concludes indignantly that "if men can [tear in paper] roade about their bussiness for a percell of Drunken Indians there will be no Living here," and urges that the trading post "be shutt up and Satisfacktion demanded of them for this abuse."[40]

The death of Father Ralé appears to have inspired Indian outrage at the English for decades. A report of an aforementioned attack on Brunswick, Maine, nearly thirty years later suggests that by ridding themselves of Father Ralé, New Englanders had only purchased the lasting enmity of the Indians at the Norridgewock mission. Samuel Whitney reports that of the nineteen Indians that attacked Brunswick in the summer of 1751, "nine of them [were] of Norridgewock Tribe, one of whom was well known, the other were Canada Indians." Tellingly, Whitney also says "that the Norridgewock Indians appeared more forward for Killing all the Captives, but were persuaded by the other Indians" to take their prisoners to Canada.[41]

Like the producers of the broadside celebrating the English victory at Norridgewock, New England writers and printers from the late 1730s to the 1760s worked together to create a print culture that surely represents a high-water mark of virulent anti-Catholicism in America. Boston printers self-consciously drew on the roots of English anti-Catholicism by producing cheap duodecimo pamphlets like *Martyrology, or, A brief Account of the Lives, Sufferings, and Deaths of those two holy Martyrs, viz. Mr. John Rogers and Mr. John Bradford* in 1736, recounting a tale of two Protestant martyrs that was then nearly two hundred years old. This "martyrology" was useful invective for creating provocative pamphlet titles, as the author of *The Cruel Massacre of the Protestants in North America; shewing how the French and Indians join together to scalp the English, and the manner of their Scalping* (London, 1760) discovered, even if religious conflict was not the primary interest of the author. This title is long on scalping but short on the religious nature of the conflicts it describes. Even Quaker Philadelphia got in on the act when a printer there produced *The French Convert: Being a true Relation of the Happy Conversion of a Noble French Lady from the Errors and Superstitions of Popery to the Reformed Religion, by Means of a Protestant Gardiner, her Servant*, in 1758. The title of this tale suggests not just a conversion of religion but also an inversion of class: Protestant servants had more authority in religious matters than French Catholic noblewomen.[42]

Perhaps because of the renewed circulation of anti-Catholic sermons, pamphlets, and broadsides, the prejudices held by ministers and elites in London and Boston seem to have been widely accepted and shared by everyday New Englanders. An anonymous correspondent of Colonel Israel Williams, a supply officer from western Massachusetts during the last imperial wars, used language reminiscent of the most charged anti-Catholic screeds upon the news of the "Bloody Morning Scout" at the Battle of Lake George on September 8, 1755. French troops and their Indian allies had set a trap that claimed the lives of fifty New England troops as well as Mohawk Sachem Hendrik and Williams's cousin Colonel Ephraim Williams. Although in the end the English were victorious in the Battle of Lake George, New Englanders were gravely concerned about the course of the war: two months earlier, the English suffered the shameful destruction of Major General Edward Braddock's army in western Pennsylvania, which (along with 450 provincial soldiers from Virginia) had been destroyed by a combined force of French, Canadian, and Indian soldiers half its size. In his letter to Israel Williams about the "Bloody Morning Scout," the correspondent describes the horror of "Deaths upon Deaths, striking & awfull; Cruel, barbarous, & Inhumane actions . . . too surprizing & shocking for humane & civilized Nature to Stand the Test even of a bare Rehersal." He goes on to predict that this skirmish might be "a preliminary & foretaste of the Dreadfull things that are to overtake us, from the Powers of Hell by the hands of the Men of Rome. . . . A new and glaring Instance, carrying the highest Evidence of the Devil as their Dictator & Lawgiver."[43]

Everyday New Englanders also expressed anti-Catholic views even in relatively peaceful encounters with French Canadians. An anonymous manuscript journal of the siege of Louisbourg in 1745 documents the disdain of the common soldier or officer of the lower ranks for the rites and rituals of Catholicism. The author, probably a member of the 4th Massachusetts Regiment, commanded by Colonel Samuel Willard, and the Third Company, led by Major Seth Pomeroy and Captain Ebenezer Alexander, writes that shortly after the French surrender, "I went into the Hospital to See the French People Say Mass. I Cou'd'ent help Wondring to see Gent_men who were men of Learning (I suppos'd, & Doubtless of good Natural parts also) So Led aside as to worship Images. to Bow Down to a Cross of Wood. & to See So many of all Ranks seemingly Devout. when we've Reason to think they never had any Communion with GOD Through the Course of their Lives. Being Ever so Strict in the Practice of their Religion." Like captives in previous decades, this man was drawn to witness the Catholic rite himself out of what seems to be a mixture of fascination, dismay, and pity for the deluded faithful. After being taught for years about the shocking rite of the Mass, many New England men were probably drawn to witness it themselves as part of the horror and the wonder of war. (Because Catholics were forbidden to enlist with New England's forces in the Seven Years' War, New England's soldiers were assuredly Protestant.)[44]

This was a kind of field trip that was probably common among New England soldiers occupying Canadian cities—one that the priests and sisters doubtlessly encouraged, whatever the motives of the curiosity-seekers. William Pote was brought to Mass by his Catholicized Huron captors in 1745, "but they was not pleased with my Behaviour." Instead of following the rite, Pote reports that he stood firm in his Protestant principles, which his Indian masters may have interpreted as mockery or simply bloody-mindedness on his part: "Viz I made no use of ye holy water in Entring ye Church, and Likwise Refused to accept of ye Consecrated bread when it was offered me, and did not Cross my self as they did. Therefore I was Intirely Excommunicated, and they would not suffer me to Enter their Church afterward."[45]

The late imperial wars—King George's War and the Seven Years' War—introduced changes in weaponry and tactics that made the fighting in these wars somewhat different from the small-scale border wars of the previous century in New England and New France. In many ways, however, warfare in the northeastern borderlands remained the same: attacks on villages and small fortifications continued, so fire continued to be one of the most important weapons of war. But in addition to the violence visited upon English and Indian settlements, French farms and towns were attacked and destroyed for the first time, particularly in Nova Scotia with the removal of the Acadians.[46] There were no innovations in small arms, just a shift in tactics: musketry remained notably inaccurate, except that a European enemy meant that more engagements resembled classic confrontations between massed formations of large armies. Artillery was deployed on a large scale for the first time in the 1740s, for two reasons: for the first time British and French armed forces were sent to North America, with all of their manpower, wealth, and engines of war. Second, because of the resources and leadership of the British Army and the Royal Navy, English forces could and did attempt sieges of well-fortified cities like Louisbourg, Québec, and Montreal. Their successful siege and occupation of these key cities, moving upriver from the mouth of the St. Lawrence River and through its valley, allowed the English to declare victory over the French in North America.[47]

Narratives of the experience of warfare in the northeastern borderlands in the 1740s and 1750s suggest that New England soldiers did not just hear sermons passively, gaze at engravings and broadsides, and march silently off to war. Instead, there is good evidence that like Joseph Nichols, they imbibed these lessons in manhood, tried to live up to them, and sometimes gloried in the ways in which their enemy did not measure up to the same standards. Earlier, we saw the importance of verbal jousting on and off the battlefield as English and Indian men sized up their opponents and attempted to establish themselves as the real men who fought proper wars. Similarly, in the eighteenth century we see Anglo-Americans and English men trying to puff themselves up with rhetoric, and French men seem to have engaged in the same rhetorical battles, although this is documented to a lesser extent. Published journals and war stories tend to be richer in ideological material than the unpublished diaries and letters written by soldiers and officers. However, the language and ideas found in both kinds of sources is strikingly similar: eighteenth-century men still saw war as a contest of masculinities and used gendered language to describe what they did and what they witnessed in the wars. This discussion of warfare and manhood is not a comprehensive military history of King George's War or of the Seven Years' War. Instead, it focuses on some key encounters in which New England soldiers played a large role: the capture of Louisbourg by the British in 1745, their victory in the Battle of Lake George in 1755, and the surrender of Fort Oswego to the French in 1756.

As the artillery sermons taught, manhood in battle was proved by a display of courage in the face of possible or even certain death. Men who lived up to this ideal of soldierly behavior were described in words that emphasized both their bravery and their masculinity, as these ideas were intertwined. Very often, tales of heroism issue from surprise attacks in which British and New England men were seriously outnumbered by the enemy. For example, in an ambush on the western frontiers of New England in King George's War, three soldiers escorting a small family from a local garrison were attacked by Indians, killing and scalping the head of the family and wounding his wife and daughter. However, "one Soldier play'd the Man, fir'd several Times—defended and bro't off the Woman and her Daughter to the *Fort*, who are recovered of their Wounds." A few years later, forty New England men on a scout from Fort Number Four (Charlestown, New Hampshire) to Fort Shirley were pursued by 150 of the enemy. Allegedly, "there immediately began a very hot Fight: The Enemy rushed on very violently, but our Men stood their Ground and gave them a warm Reception," despite being outnumbered nearly four to one. After three hours, the New Englanders drove off the enemy after having lost only three of their men. "The Enemy doubtless lost many; they went off without Shouting, and when some Captives saw them about a Week after, they looked very sorrowful." In short, "this was a very manly Fight; and all will

grant our Men quitted themselves like Men, who Need not be ashamed"
—as opposed to the dejected Indian men whose disappointment was allegedly obvious even to their captives.[48]

Quite often, in both private journals and published accounts of battles,
English and New England writers use boilerplate language to describe their
encounters in battle, always emphasizing the manly vigor with which they
met the fight. The same words and phrases appear over and over in these
records, giving their stories of battles a kind of order and predictability that
was probably very elusive in the heat of war: battles were joined "smartly,"
and soldiers marched or fired "briskly," or "smartly." Sometimes English
and New England writers allowed that the enemy as well as their own men
"fought bravely." The only indication of disorder is the use of the phrase
"Hilter Scilter," usually in reference to an attack by Indians on the flanks of
an orderly English column, or in reference to a speedy retreat. But showing
"undaunted courage" and the "utmost fury Imaginable," English and New
England soldiers acquitted themselves admirably, for the most part, even if
they lost the battle in the end. Strikingly, these same phrases appear repeatedly in English-language accounts of the late imperial wars, even when English or New England men were performing an action that was less than
entirely heroic.[49] For example, Seth Pomeroy describes "a very hansom retreet they made" at the Battle of Lake George in 1755 "by Continuing there
fire & then retreeting a little & then rise and give them a brisk Fire." After
all, as Charles Chauncey argues concerning the same retreat, the retreat was
not cowardly but rather a superior kind of bravery: "A good retreat is the
next glory to a victory. . . . Had our men been upon equal terms [numeri-
cally] with the enemy, I should have tho't they had acted unworthy of the
Name of *New-England* men, if they had given way upon any consideration
whatever." But as they lived to fight out the afternoon, the retreat was also
valorous.[50] For their part, French men boasted too, of course. One French
soldier, describing a daring approach to a battle, writes, "[t]his they did
with great courage and spirit, displaying the true impetuosity of the
French." Even though the French ultimately lost this battle—the Battle of
Québec in 1759—the French man suggests that the English conquest wasn't
accomplished with the defeat of Montcalm's army and the surrender of the
city. The English "would, however, find it necessary to actually conquer
[the countryside], for the French were determined to dispute every foot of
ground, giving up only when forced to do so."[51]

Another recurring conceit in these accounts is a story of French acknowledgment of English or New England bravery and superiority in battle,

and vice versa. Genuine or not, these stories demonstrate the fact that the compliments of a worthy foe were valued by all sides in these wars. One example of enemy compliments comes from King George's War, when New England's first victory over Louisbourg in 1745 was seen as a miracle against great odds. The journal of one English soldier, who described himself as a "Gentleman Voluntier," claims that an old French veteran of Queen Anne's War said that "in all the Histories he had ever read, he never met with an Instance of so bold and presumptuous an Attempt" as New England's late successful siege. "'[T]was almost impracticable, as any one would think, for only 3 or 4000 raw, undisciplin'd Men, to lay Siege to such a strong, well fortified City, such Garrisons, Batteries, &c. for should any one have ask'd me, said he, what Number of Men would have been sufficient to have carried on that very Enterprize, he should have answer'd no less than thirty Thousand. To this he subjoin'd, that he never heard of, or ever saw such Courage and Intrepidity in such a Handful of Men, who regarded [heeded] neither Shot nor Bombs." The author gratefully accepts the compliments of the old man, adding as a kind of benediction, "May Courage, Resolution, Life and Vigour, be forever conspicuous in all our *English* Officers and Soldiers!" Another diarist suggests that the 1745 victory at Louisbourg had changed French men's minds as to the courage of New England men. As a camp chaplain in occupied Louisbourg, former Indian captive Stephen Williams overheard Morepang, the Port Captain of Louisbourg under the French, "that he thot the n England men were Cowards—but now he thot that if they had a pick ax and Spade—they would dig their way to Hell and Storm it which they had done." French opinions, so disparaged by most New Englanders, were greedily seized and recorded if they offered even grudging respect of New England's military resolve.[52]

The same interest in complimenting vigorous enemy resistance continued in the Seven Years' War. One French soldier said that Lord Jeffrey Amherst, the victor at Fort Lévis in 1760, was nevertheless impressed by French fortitude even though they lost the siege. He was rather "astonished that such a small force held out so long and prevented their attempt to land. The enemy general [Amherst] could not keep from praising the French, with the remark that he was surprised that more men had not been killed, since he had partially destroyed the fort." For their part, French officers and generals reportedly returned the compliments, especially in defeat. In a letter to Colonel Israel Williams after the Battle of Lake George in 1755, Seth Pomeroy writes that "the Enemy Fau't with undanted Courage & the gratest Part of ye English with Heroick Bravery. . . . The French General

Saith that our People made such a regular Retreet & gave them such Close shots yt Dampen'd his Indians & Canadians." All in all, Pomeroy judges that his victorious men performed "with undanted Bravary & well answer'd ye Caractter of Englishmen." The French general apparently agreed, as Pomeroy reports that he said "[i]f we give them one more such a Dressing Crown Point & all there Country will be ours."[53]

Of course, not all encounters between French and English men were so mutually complimentary. One New England prisoner of war and his captor continued a verbal joust with one another long after their battle had ended. While being marched from Fort Massachusetts to Québec after his 1747 capture, the Reverend John Norton fell into conversation with one M. Dumuy, who gloried in telling Norton of the French victory at Brest. According to Norton's description of this taunting, Dumuy said that the French king was sending on new men and vast stores of supplies to achieve a similar triumph in North America: "their King was very angry with *New England* for their taking *Cape Breton* [Louisbourg]; and it was probable he would bring them into Subjection." Dumuy also brought news of the Jacobite Rebellion, promising that "the Pretender's youngest Son, was in the *North of England,* and had a powerful Army . . . and it was probable he would prevail to dethrone King George." This news, if true, would have been sorely provoking for a Protestant minister to hear, as it suggested the possibility of Catholic domination of the British throne. After hearing this news from Dumuy, French soldiers joined in taunting Norton: "several of the young Men came laughing to me, and by Signs endeavored to inform me what the News was." Unfortunately, Norton neglected to describe the variety of hand gestures and signals they might have employed, so they are lost to history. Days later, Dumuy approached Norton to gloat about news of another French victory, this one much closer to home, "viz, 'that one of their Men of War had taken an English Man of War near *Louisbourg,* after a whole Day's Engagement; that the Blood was midleg deep upon the Englishmen's deck when he surrendered.'" Here, Norton reports that they get into a conversation about the nature of heroism in war. "I told him they fought courageously. He said, 'True, but they were taken notwithstanding.'" While Norton's side lost the ship, he reports with pleasure that Dumuy's estimate of 320 prisoners was surely inflated, as the so-called Man of War "was nothing but the *Albany* Sloop, one of the Men of War's tenders, which Governor *Knowles* sent with a packet from *Louisbourg* for *Boston.* There were but seventy Men in her."[54]

Norton battles Dumuy's taunting and the soldiers' teasing in the pages of his narrative, after consulting other sources of information. This kind of resistance to French provocation was undoubtedly a safer course while he remained within the walls of the prison in Québec, and it was strikingly effective. By publishing the story of his captivity in Québec, Norton could make sure he had the last word with Dumuy although their conversation was long since over. Similarly, William Pote insults his French captors in his captivity narrative when he reports his observations of a French *habitant* military training day. When a fire swept through the prison in Québec, Pote writes that they were marched to a temporary encampment by a local militia. "I must Confess these militia appeared much more Ignorant in ye military Discipline, then our New England men, yt had never been train'd, for they took some Considerable time for Consideration, whether it was proper to Carrey ye armes of a Soldier, on their Right Shoulder or their Left."[55]

While the English and French focused on one another as the "inveterate enemy" in this period and saw Indians simply as allies to their causes rather than people with a political agenda of their own, both European foes recognized the importance of courting and retaining the loyalty of the people they called "our Indians." Not surprisingly, one of the ways English and French men competed for favor among the Indians was by demonstrating their superior manhood, and by extension, their strength, power, and access to the desired European trade goods. Nowhere was this rivalry more intense than in New York, for the allegiance of the Six Nations of the Iroquois. Both the English and the French had cultivated allies among different tribes and factions of the Iroquois—the Mohawks were traditional British allies, and the Catholicized mission Indians to the north were allies of the French. In 1755 William Clarke warned New England to heed the consequences of their "feeble Resistance against these violent [French] Encroachments," which he said would "give [the Indians] a mean, contemptible Opinion of them: They will look upon the English as dastardly Cowards; upon the French as brave Men; upon the one as fit to be relied upon for Protection; on the other as unworthy of the least Confidence, & rather wanting Assistance & Protection from them, than capable of affording them any." He dramatized this with a story from a recent conference between the Six Nations and British commissioners at Albany, where an Iroquois sachem said, "You talk, said he of your Strength, were do we see it? The French build Forts, and keep them when they have done; the English do not hinder them." In short, said the sachem, "the French behave like Men, the English like Women." Clarke found this loss of status with the Six Nations particularly troubling, as he believed they were worthy men themselves, the "bravest Warriors of all the Indians." Seth Pomeroy, an officer in both of the late imperial wars, was more optimistic in his estimation that same year that "the Indians with ye Franch army dayly leaving of them; the Franch Tremble for fear" of losing their trusted allies.[56]

The easy surrender of the British Fort Oswego to the Marquis de Montcalm in August of 1756 proved Clarke's warnings prescient, as this French victory appears to have cemented their alliances with Indians. Oswego was isolated by hundreds of miles from British settlement on the shores of Lake Ontario, at the far end of an insecure supply line, and the British had had difficulties in previous years making sure that it had the men and supplies it required. After just a morning's cannonade—wherein the fort's commanding officer was dramatically beheaded by a cannon ball—the British surrendered Fort Oswego. The Marquis de Montcalm judged that the next in command, Lieutenant Colonel John Littlehales, did not defend the fort manfully, and he withheld from him the honors of war. This meant that the entire garrison was taken prisoner rather than being allowed to retreat with their personal belongings. Montcalm's Indian allies compounded this humiliation by taking their spoils of war: aside from looting personal property and supplies and taking many captives from among the families of the soldiers and traders, they killed the sick and dying British soldiers—anywhere from thirty to a hundred men in all.[57] This practice made sense to the Indians if they were faced with the prospect of taking the entire garrison into captivity, but it was judged cruel and mortifying by Montcalm, who was embarrassed by what he and other European observers saw as a loss of control over his Indian allies. But in the end, men on all sides of this conflict understood that the greatest humiliation was to the British, one that not only gave French men an opportunity to glory in their defeat, but also gave their Indian allies reason to reconsider their alliance. "[Y]e french officers much Ridicule our officers for Giving up Oswago So Soon," wrote Colonel Ebenezer Hinsdale. "[Y]e Indians were very backward [reluctant] in going out to Warr before they took Osswago but are now one and all Engaged with ye French." Another officer from western Massachusetts, William Williams, summed up the Indian perspective: "they had been waiting two Seasons to see what great Feats we were capable of Doing; and found we were incapable of doing any thing." Worse, "the French were quite otherwise that they told What they designed open & Boldly, and when they had so Done they Effected it." In another letter Williams claimed that "Such a Shocking an Affair [the surrender of Oswego] has never come within the English annals—nor I hope ever will be matchd.

To give up such an important place; so many people and such Treasure, without any resistance and the loss of but 7 Lives—What Shall I call It name it yourself—The loss is beyond Acct.—but the dishonour done his Majestys army—is infinitely greater."[58]

However dismissive the Europeans and Euro-Americans were of Indian politics and sovereignty, it is clear that Indian men valued and performed the same rituals of manhood in war that they had in the seventeenth century. An anonymous journal kept by a French soldier serving in Ohio and Pennsylvania during the 1750s suggests that the ritual torture and execution of a captured warrior was a way of honoring his valor, and a means by which the prisoner could continue to display his manly courage. The author describes the roasting of a Mohawk warrior by a party of Illinois Indians, claiming, "the Mohawk began to sing, daring his tormentors to do their worst." He was merely delivering the expected performance, singing something like "'I am brave and fearless; I do not fear death. Those who fear it are cowards. They are less than women. Life and death are nothing to the man who has courage. . . . I have done so many brave deeds. I have killed so many men! All my enemies are dogs! If I find them in the land of spirits, I will make war on them. Now I lament my body; I am coming to death like a brave." As in nearly identical scenes in the seventeenth century, the French soldier explains that "a savage going to his death would not be considered brave if he displayed any feeling under his tortures. This would be a sign of weakness, for which they would scorn him." As in European and Euro-American cultures in the eighteenth century, weakness and dependence was a childlike or womanlike state, not to be borne by men of honor. Misogyny strikes the French soldier as particularly strong among the Indians, suggesting that "perhaps no nation in the world scorns women more than these savages usually do. The bitterest insult that can be offered a savage is to call him a woman."[59]

Establishing oneself as a man was more complex than showing bravery in battle and resolution in politics, and avoiding being weak or fearful "like a woman." Manhood also meant establishing one's humanity—that is, one's identity as a human being rather than as an animal.[60] For in addition to being disparaged as women or children, enemies could be reduced further to an even more servile and dependent state: that of dogs. We saw above the example of the Mohawk's "victim's song," in which he shouted, "All my enemies are dogs!" French and English men understood the meaning of this insult very well and used it against their enemies, too. One boastful New Englander serving under Colonel Samuel Waldo in the 1745 siege of Louisbourg described the inhabitants of that city scornfully: "These Scoundellus french Dogs they Dare not Stay to fite—But Set there houses on fire and So Ran into the Sitty by the Light." Instead of fighting like real men, this diarist suggests, the enemy fouled its own nest (as even animals know not to do) and danced about like savages. Another anonymous diarist of the same siege told a story of how one Captain "Donnahoo" (Donahue) had captured four French-allied Indians by tricking them into thinking he was a French man. The Indians, wary of a man aboard an English vessel, were mollified when "[h]e told 'em he had taken it from the English. & had aboard 25 good fat English Doggs all his Prisoners, & so Persuaded them aboard. N:B: He Could speak French well."[61] French, English, and Indian men alike knew what it meant to be called a dog.

Just as being called a woman, child, or dog was an insult meant to undermine one's manhood, "master" continued to signify quite the opposite quality, that of mastery. As in the previous century in New England, "master" appears as a very gendered and politicized term in the wars of the eighteenth century. Describing an attack on Haverhill, Massachusetts, in 1704 from the vantage of the 1720s, Samuel Penhallow writes that the town was "unhappily surpriz'd" by the Indians, "who skulking at a distance, and seeing the gates open and none on the sentry, rushed in and became masters thereof." In 1715, some nervous denizens of the Maine frontier wrote Massachusetts asking for five hundred pounds and fifteen soldiers to repair and man a fort, "in case it should be assaulted by the French as well as Indians." They were convinced—quite rightly as it happens—that "if a War should arise It may be expected they will leave no Means untryed, to become masters of [the fort], towards which the Remoteness from Succour will give them great Advantage."[62] As we have seen, the English had good reason to fear that they might be mastered by the French, given the experience of so many of their daughters and sisters.

English and Anglo-American writers—published and unpublished—continued to evoke "mastery" as the ultimate goal of the military contests before them in the mid-eighteenth century. The epigraph of this chapter demonstrates that men on the western frontier feared the same eventuality, not just for their region but for all of North America: "Who will be Masters of America The French or the English; and grief if it is not desided by a *united* vigorous blow at the Root," asked William Williams of his kinsman Israel Williams in 1756. Seth Pomeroy told a tale from the early days of King George's War, when four unarmed New England men were captured by two French men and one Indian. The captives turned the tables on their captors, when in an unguarded moment they seized their captors' weapons and in one stroke "made themselves Masters of them." Using the same language, Pomeroy writes to his wife in April of 1745 at the beginning of the first Louisbourg expedition, saying, "I Can not But take notice of & I hope with Thankfull ness ye Smiles of Devine Providence in ye affair; & Do not Doubt Except—Providence Should Remarkably Frown upon us we Shall be masters of ye Island of Cape Britton." An anonymous account of the second siege of Louisbourg in 1758 describes the actions of English soldiers heroically: "They instantly attacked the next *Battery* to them in flank with so much Vigour. . . . they had hardly given there a Specimen of true *English* Bravery, before they saw themselves *Masters* of the Shore with all its strong Works." According to this observer, the French knew the jig was up. In contrast to "true *English* Bravery," he notes "the dastardly *Panic* that appeared to slacken the Enemy's Fire as soon as they saw our Men landed pretty near them, now shewed itself very conspicuously by its Effects, the little Resistance they made when their Numbers are compared with ours, and the great Confusion with which they fled every way before our Men into the contiguous Woods." In sum, Louisbourg's "late Masters were in too much Hurry" to flee English military and political supremacy; they left honor and bravery all to the victors. By the early 1760s, Anglo-American writers boasted that French, English, and Indian peoples from Louisbourg to Detroit knew that "the English . . . were Masters of all."[63]

Sometimes the notion of words as a means of waging war became too literal a metaphor, as a few New England writers suggest that guns occasionally (and literally) spoke for themselves. For example, in Samuel Penhallow's history of the Indian wars, he describes a French and Indian attack on a New England ship in Newfoundland in 1704, equipped with "fourteen guns, with twenty-four men." He commends the New England captain for defending himself "with great courage and good conduct, from divers bold and desperate attempts which they made upon him. When he had beat them at small arms, they then brought the Galley to bear upon him with her great guns, which he returned in the like language." Happy with this metaphor, Penhallow uses it again to describe an attack on some English whale boats during Dummer's War in 1724: "Capt. Winslow, who was considerably ahead and out of danger, perceiving the engagement, courageously returned back to their assistance. But before he could give them any relief, was surrounded with about thirty canoes, who made a hideous yelling; but he gave them no answer but from the muzzles of his guns." Apparently, guns could speak in a variety of languages, although the sense of their replies was the same. One anonymous journal of the 1745 siege of Louisbourg reports on an exchange between English and French officials as the English offered a flag of truce—that is, gave the French an opportunity to surrender—before they began their final assault on the city. M. Louis du Chambon, commander in chief of the fort, replied, "that the King his Master having intrusted him with the defence of the Island, he could not hearken to any such proposal, till after the most vigorous Attack, and that he had no Answer to make but by the Mouth of their Cannon." Reversing the equation of words and guns, one anonymous English poet suggests that the English victory in the Seven Years' War would be accomplished in large part with words—specifically, through liberty of the press. The poet argues that with the silencing of the guns, the war would continue after 1760 not by spilling blood but by spilling ink, and the press will work to "clear the Land of Superstition's Weed" (an allusion to Roman Catholicism, of course).[64]

In the end, the last of the intercolonial wars would be won by both words and guns. Upon the capitulation of Québec in 1759 and Montreal in 1760, the Seven Years' War shifted decisively to the English, although as always English mastery of both ally and enemy Indians remained questionable.[65] According to the volumes of pamphlets, books, and newspapers published in New England and London, the outcome of the war was natural, even foreordained. Accounts of Seven Years' War battles are as repetitive in their language as the artillery election sermons described earlier in the chapter, blurring the details of individual encounters to emphasize the triumph of English courage over French cowardice and Indian treachery. One spectator of the 1758 siege of Louisbourg reported that English sailors "instantly attacked the next *Battery* to them in flank with so much Vigour . . . they had hardly given there a Specimen of true *English* Bravery, before they saw themselves *Masters* of the Shore with all its strong Works." Over and over again, English and Anglo-American authors appointed themselves the "masters" of both French and Indian men. The same toxic combination of anti-Catholicism and disgust for Indians appears again and again in celebrations of the English victory. One anonymous poet gloated:

> No more shall *France*, with haughty Strides of Pow'r
> Triumphant move, her Neighbours to devour.
> No more shall Lewis' savage Schemes succeed;
> Schemes big with Death, and ev'ry baneful Seed.
> No more *Te Deums* be sung for Vict'ry gain'd,
> (Her Coffers now, *alas!* are sadly drain'd)

No more, (O may we *prophecy* in Truth!)
Her Priests no more debauch the *Indian* Youth.[66]

Once again, English presses worked overtime to reassure their reading audience of the inevitable outcome of the war, papering over the 140-year struggle that had preceded it.

Epilogue
On the Plains of Abraham

The Plains of Abraham, site of the Battle of Québec just outside the old city walls, today is called le Parc des Champs-de-Battaille (Battlefields Park), and the grounds are now the province of morning joggers, tour buses, and families on outings. Historians of the nineteenth and twentieth centuries have used General James Wolfe's daring surprise attack on Québec on September 13, 1759—and the dramatic coincidence of his death and the death of the French general, the Marquis de Montcalm, later that day—to draw a variety of lessons for their students and readers. Anglophone historians—English, Canadian, and American—write admiringly of Wolfe's troops' determined overnight scaling of the cliffs of Cap Diamant to mass themselves outside the city walls undetected, as if by magic, and some have seen in this strategy clear proof of the superiority (and superior manliness) of English civilization. Francis Parkman, writing at the height of British imperial power in the late nineteenth century, suggested that it was the "fatuity of Louis XV. and his Pompadour that made the conquest of Canada possible." In other words, historians need only look at the corrupt and feminized French to see that their hold on North America was doomed. According to Parkman, "America owes much to the imbecility of Louis XV. and the ambitious vanity and personal dislikes of his mistress." *Cherchez la femme,* indeed.[1]

While Wolfe's success earned him instant (although posthumous) fame and glory in Britain and colonial America, the importance of the Battle of Québec to the outcome of the Seven Years' War has probably been overstated. The British not only had to take Québec, they had to hold it and its restive civilians through the difficult winter of 1760 and beat back a French counterattack the following spring. Victory in Canada was assured only upon the surrender of Governor Vaudreuil in Montreal in August of 1760.[2] Nevertheless, the legend of Montcalm—dying of his wounds inside the city walls and then buried in the Ursuline chapel in a hole blasted by an artillery round—and Wolfe—expiring of his wounds on the battlefield—

Figure 17. View of the Plains of Abraham, now le Parc des Champs-de-Bataille (Battlefields Park), Québec, P.Q. Photo by author.

has proved much harder to kill than the two unlucky generals. More than two hundred years later, "Québec 1759" even became an anglophone Canadian strategy game for older children and interested adults, inviting them to take a side as "Montcalm & Wolfe struggle for North America" in this "unique and exciting game." Significantly, there were only two sides in this version of the story: the Indians in this cardboard battle are reduced to French allies and just two game pieces, although unlike French and British troops the Indian tiles can make more than one board move at a time and thus can appear and disappear at the will of the French player to "conduct raids on the British units." However, the rules specify that "if involved in a battle along with other French units they must be kept in reserve."[3] Indians in this game—as in most nineteenth- and twentieth-century versions of North American history—are reduced quite literally to pawns of the French.

    With men still talking—and writing—about warfare in such gendered terms, and so determined to erase the presence of Indians, what had changed in nearly a century and a half of warfare in the northeastern borderlands? Disease and warfare had dramatically reshaped the human landscape of the region, devastating the overall Native population in the seven-teenth century, and neither the Indians nor the French could keep pace with the successes of English migration and New England's high natural rate of reproduction. By the 1760s, Anglo-Americans had the demographic advantage over their rivals, but by so rapidly expanding its North American empire, England had guaranteed that it would be engaged in almost con-stant efforts to put down both Indian and Anglo-American uprisings over the next two decades.[4] In some ways, however, very little had changed since the Plymouth settlers landed in 1620. On all sides—but particularly so among Anglo-Americans—the same language and ideas appeared over and over again to explain and justify warfare on all sides. Warfare remained a deeply gendered experience for all concerned—soldiers, sailors, officers, magistrates, wives, children, captives, prisoners of war, and so-called "non-combatants" alike. Warfare in the colonial northeastern borderlands had worked to demonstrate that military success and political independence were the conjoined prerogatives of real men—of men who had proved themselves masters rather than dogs, children, women, or slaves to other men, and Indian, French, and English men still agreed on that.

Mid-eighteenth-century imperial warfare changed New England men's identity, encouraging them perhaps to see their identities as English men built around not just the immediate aspects of their lives as Protestant hus-bands, fathers, and independent householders but around more abstract appeals to nation and empire. Anglo-American men in the mainland colo-nies would use this broader vision of nation in the 1770s and 1780s in the American Revolution and the ensuing war for independence, when many of them reluctantly conceded that their efforts to beat back the threat of French and Indian domination had inordinately strengthened the hand of the British. Once again, the same fears that drove Anglo-American men to take up arms against Indians and French Canadians would be exploited, but this time they were used to mobilize Americans against the British. As Cotton Mather had discovered at the end of the previous century, threats to Anglo-American homes and families were particularly useful wartime propaganda.[5]

Colonial warfare and contact with Indians also contributed to the in-vention of a new tradition of Anglo-American political protest. After the Seven Years' War, when Anglo-Americans themselves felt that British pre-sumptions of sovereignty in North America went too far, they explicitly compared themselves to Indians, those other victims of colonial aggression. Masquerading as Indians became a kind of blackface performance of aggrieved New England manhood, from the Boston Tea Party in 1773 to land rioters in Maine in the 1790s and into the nineteenth century. By dressing as Indians, white New England men made the political point that they were being treated like Indians, and that they refused to accept that treatment any longer whether at the hands of colonial officials, local grandees, or the United States' government. Their performances implicitly suggested that their actual identities as free white men ought to have exempted them from such abuse. The fact that their masquerade usually served also to disguise their identities while they engaged in vandalism, threats of violence, and/or the destruction of property helped emphasize that they were deadly serious about their complaints.[6]

Was this masquerade simply a joke, meant to mock the supposed likeness of white men and Indians, or was it another acknowledgment of the similarities of Indians and Anglo-Americans even after the demographic and political advantage had shifted decisively to the latter? Can we see in it a memory of a colonial past where the outcome of these struggles was far from certain? Perhaps these men stood in protest like Roger Chillingworth, Hester Prynne's cuckolded husband in Nathaniel Hawthorne's *The Scarlet Letter* (1850), who first appears before Hester as she stands on the scaffold in Boston. While she awaits her public shaming, she sees "a figure which irresistably took possession of her thoughts. . . . a white man, clad in a strange disarray of civilized and savage costume," an exciting but disturbing reminder of a colonial frontier where Indians and Europeans mixed, borrowed, fought, and reinvented themselves.[7]

Notes

Introduction

1. Samuel Nowell, *Abraham in Arms, or, The First Religious General with his Army Engaging in a War* (Boston, 1678). On reports of the French in southern Maine in the summer of 1676, see Joshua Scottow and Henry Jocelyn, letter to Governor John Leverett, September 15, 1676, Coll. S-888, misc. box 33/21, Maine Historical Society, Portland.

2. John Underhill, *Newes from America* (London, 1638; reprint, 1891), 15–16; ms. copy of depositions of David and Hannah Meade, Cambridge, Mass., 1677, Maine Historical Society, Portland.

3. See, for example, divorce petition of Christopher Lawson, Suffolk Court Files, docket #913, Massachusetts State Archives, Boston; Emma Lewis Coleman, *New England Captives Carried to Canada* (Portland, Maine: The Southworth Press, 1922; reprint, Bowie, Md.: Heritage Books, 1989), vols. 1 and 2, passim.

4. Richard Trexler, *Sex and Conquest: Gendered Violence, Political Order, and the European Conquest of the Americas* (Ithaca, N.Y.: Cornell University Press, 1995); James D. Drake, *King Philip's War: Civil War in New England, 1675–1676* (Amherst: University of Massachusetts Press, 1999); Pauline Turner Strong, *Captive Selves, Captivating Others: The Politics and Poetics of Colonial American Captivity Narratives* (Boulder, Colo.: Westview Press, 1999); Karen Ordahl Kupperman, *Indians and English: Facing Off in Early America* (Ithaca, N.Y.: Cornell University Press, 2000); Joyce Chaplin, *Subject Matter: Technology, the Body, and Science on the Anglo-American Frontier, 1500–1676* (Cambridge, Mass.: Harvard University Press, 2001); John Wood Sweet, *Bodies Politic: Negotiating Race in the American North, 1730–1830* (Baltimore: Johns Hopkins University Press, 2003); Nancy Shoemaker, *A Strange Likeness: Becoming Red and White in Eighteenth-Century North America* (New York: Oxford University Press, 2004).

5. Evelyn Brooks Higginbotham, "African American Women's History and the Metalanguage of Race," *Signs: Journal of Women in Culture and Society* 17 (1992): 251–74; Gerda Lerner, "U.S. Women's History: Past, Present, and Future," Kimberly Springer, "Unexpected: Women, Sources, and Histories," Kathi Kern, "Productive Collaborations: The Benefits of Cultural Analysis to the Past, Present, and Future of Women's History," Jennifer M. Spear, "The Distant Past of North American Women's History," Leslie M. Alexander, "The Challenge of Race: Rethinking the Position of Black Women in the Field of Women's History," and Lerner, "Reply to Responses," all in *Journal of Women's History* 16 (2004): 10–64.

6. Kathleen M. Brown, *Good Wives, Nasty Wenches, and Anxious Patriarchs:*

Gender, Race, and Power in Colonial Virginia (Chapel Hill: University of North Carolina Press, 1996); Kirsten Fischer, *Suspect Relations: Sex, Race, and Resistance in Colonial North Carolina* (Ithaca, N.Y.: Cornell University Press, 2002); Jennifer L. Morgan, *Laboring Women: Reproduction and Gender in New World Slavery* (Philadelphia: University of Pennsylvania Press, 2004).

7. Jill Lepore, *The Name of War: King Philip's War and the Origins of American Identity* (New York: Alfred A. Knopf, 1998); Chris Hedges, *War Is a Force That Gives Us Meaning* (New York: Public Affairs, 2002).

8. Daniel Mandell, *Behind the Frontier: Indians in Eighteenth-Century Eastern Massachusetts* (Lincoln: University of Nebraska Press, 1996); Claudio Saunt, *A New Order of Things: Property, Power, and the Transformation of the Creek Indians, 1733–1816* (Cambridge: Cambridge University Press, 1999); Susan Sleeper-Smith, *Indian Women and French Men: Rethinking Cultural Encounter in the Western Great Lakes* (Amherst: University of Massachusetts Press, 2001).

9. Lyndal Roper, *The Holy Household: Women and Morals in Reformation Augsburg* (Oxford: Oxford University Press, 1989); Merry E. Wiesner, *Women and Gender in Early Modern Europe*, 2nd ed. (Cambridge: Cambridge University Press, 2000); P. Reneé Baernstein, *A Convent Tale: A Century of Sisterhood in Spanish Milan* (New York: Routledge, 2002).

10. Irene Silverblatt, *Moon, Sun, and Witches: Gender Ideologies and Class in Inca and Colonial Peru* (Princeton, N.J.: Princeton University Press, 1987); Ramón Gutiérrez, *When Jesus Came, the Corn Mothers Went Away: Marriage, Sexuality, and Power in New Mexico, 1500–1846* (Stanford, Calif.: Stanford University Press, 1991); John Thornton, *Africa and Africans in the Making of the Atlantic World, 1400–1680* (Cambridge: Cambridge University Press, 1992); Michael Gomez, *Exchanging Our Country Marks: The Transformation of African Identities in the Colonial and Antebellum South* (Chapel Hill: University of North Carolina Press, 1998).

11. Saunt, *A New Order of Things*; Sleeper-Smith, *Indian Woman and French Men.*

12. Colin G. Calloway, *New Worlds for All: Indians, Europeans, and the Remaking of Early America* (Baltimore, Md.: Johns Hopkins University Press, 1997); Peter C. Mancall and James H. Merrell, eds., *American Encounters: Natives and Newcomers from European Contact to Indian Removal, 1500–1850* (New York: Routledge, 2000); Ann Marie Plane, *Colonial Intimacies: Indian Marriage in Early New England* (Ithaca, N.Y.: Cornell University Press, 2000); Daniel Richter, *Facing East from Indian Country: A Native History of Early America* (Cambridge, Mass.: Harvard University Press, 2001).

13. Laurel Thatcher Ulrich, *Good Wives: Image and Reality in the Lives of Women in Northern New England, 1650–1750* (New York: Oxford University Press, 1980); Ann M. Little, "A 'Wel Ordered Commonwealth': Gender and Politics in New Haven Colony, 1636–1690" (Ph.D. diss., University of Pennsylvania, 1996); Mary Beth Norton, *Founding Mothers and Fathers: Gendered Power and the Forming of American Society* (New York: Alfred A. Knopf, 1996).

14. Sleeper-Smith, *Indian Women and French Men*; William Foster, *The Captors' Narrative: Catholic Women and Their Puritan men on the Early American Frontier* (Ithaca, N.Y.: Cornell University Press, 2003).

15. Francis Jennings, *The Invasion of America: Indians, Colonialism, and the Cant of Conquest* (Chapel Hill: University of North Carolina Press, 1975); William Cronon, *Changes in the Land: Indians, Colonists, and the Ecology of New England* (New York: Hill and Wang, 1983); Richard White, *The Middle Ground: Indians, Empires, and Republics in the Great Lakes Region, 1650–1815* (Cambridge: Cambridge University Press, 1991).

16. Fischer, *Suspect Relations*; Thornton, *Africa and Africans*.

17. Linda K. Kerber, *Women of the Republic: Intellect and Ideology in Revolutionary America* (Chapel Hill: University of North Carolina Press, 1980); Christine Stansell, *City of Women: Sex and Class in New York, 1789–1860* (New York: Alfred A. Knopf, 1982); Carol F. Karlsen, *The Devil in the Shape of a Woman: Witchcraft in Colonial New England* (New York: W.W. Norton, 1987); Susan Juster, *Disorderly Women: Sexual Politics and Evangelicalism in Revolutionary New England* (Ithaca, N.Y.: Cornell University Press, 1994); Cornelia Hughes Dayton, *Women Before the Bar: Gender, Law, and Society in Connecticut, 1639–1789* (Chapel Hill: University of North Carolina Press, 1995); Carol Shammas, "Anglo-American Household Government in Comparative Perspective," *William and Mary Quarterly* 3rd ser., 52 (1995): 104–44; Brown, *Good Wives*; Norton, *Founding Mothers and Fathers*; Theda Perdue, *Cherokee Women: Gender and Culture Change, 1700–1835* (Lincoln: University of Nebraska Press, 1998); Marilyn J. Westerkamp, *Women and Religion in Early America, 1600–1850: The Puritan and Evangelical Traditions* (London and New York: Routledge, 1999); Karin Wulf, *Not All Wives: Women of Colonial Philadelphia* (Ithaca, N.Y.: Cornell University Press, 2000); Fischer, *Suspect Relations*; Morgan, *Laboring Women*.

18. Kenneth A. Lockridge, *On the Sources of Patriarchal Rage: The Commonplace Books of William Byrd and Thomas Jefferson and the Gendering of Power in the Eighteenth Century* (New York: New York University Press, 1992); Toby Ditz, "Shipwrecked; or, Masculinity Imperiled: Mercantile Representations of Failure and the Gendered Self in Eighteenth-Century Philadelphia," *Journal of American History* 81 (1994): 51–80; Lisa Wilson, *Ye Heart of a Man: the Domestic Life of Men in Colonial NewEngland* (New Haven, Conn.: Yale University Press, 1999); Foster, *The Captors' Narrative*; Anne Lombard, *Making Manhood: Growing Up Male in Colonial New England* (Cambridge, Mass.: Harvard University Press, 2003).

19. Cronon, *Changes in the Land*; James Axtell, *The Invasion Within: The Contest of Cultures in Colonial North America* (New York: Oxford University Press, 1985); White, *The Middle Ground*; Jean O'Brien, *Dispossession by Degrees: Indian Law and Identity in Natick, Massachusetts, 1650–1780* (Cambridge: Cambridge University Press, 1997); Perdue, *Cherokee Women*; Richter, *Facing East from Indian Country*; Sleeper-Smith, *Indian Woman and French Men*.

20. Recently, other authors have attempted to bridge the gap between women's and gender history and ethnohistory, most notably Trexler, *Sex and Conquest*; Perdue, *Cherokee Women*; Plane, *Colonial Intimacies*; Sleeper-Smith, *Indian Woman and French Men*; and Fischer, *Suspect Relations*. See also Ann Laura Stoler, "Tense and Tender Ties: The Politics of Comparison in North American History and (Post) Colonial Studies," *Journal of American History* 88 (2001): 829–65, and responses by

Ramón A. Gutiérrez, Lori D. Ginzberg, Dirk Hoerder, Mary A. Renda, and Robert J. McMahon, ibid., 866–92.

21. Chaplin, *Subject Matter*; Shoemaker, *Strange Likeness*.

22. On the new western history, see William Cronon, George Miles, and Jay Gitlin, eds., *Under an Open Sky: Rethinking America's Western Past* (New York: W. W. Norton, 1992) and Patricia Nelson Limerick, *Legacy of Conquest: The Unbroken Past of the American West* (New York: W. W. Norton, 1987).

In "From Borderlands to Borders: Empires, Nation-States, and the Peoples in Between in North American History," *American Historical Review* 104 (1999): 814–41, Jeremy Adelman and Stephen Aron attempt to create a distinction without a difference between "frontier history" and "borderlands history." In this study, I use the terms "frontier" and "borderlands" interchangeably to signify regions or spaces in which political and military power is contested. Quality examples of recent borderlands books include Gutiérrez, *When Jesus Came, the Corn Mothers Went Away*; White, *The Middle Ground*; Eric Hinderaker, *Elusive Empires: Constructing Colonialism in the Ohio Valley, 1673–1800* (Cambridge: Cambridge University Press, 1997); Al Hurtado, *Intimate Frontiers: Sex, Gender, and Culture in Old California* (Albuquerque: University of New Mexico Press, 1999); Geoffrey Plank, *An Unsettled Conquest: The British Campaign Against the Peoples of Acadia* (Philadelphia: University of Pennsylvania Press, 2000); Sleeper-Smith, *Indian Women and French Men*.

23. Francis Parkman, *France and England in North America*, vols. 1 and 2 (New York: Literary Classics of the United States, Inc., distributed to the trade by the Viking Press, 1983); Frederick Jackson Turner, *The Frontier in American History* (New York: Henry Holt and Co., 1920).

24. Lepore, *Name of War*; Richter, *Facing East from Indian Country*.

25. Stephen Greenblatt, *Marvellous Possessions: The Wonder of the New World* (Chicago: University of Chicago Press, 1991); Christopher Castiglia, *Bound and Determined: Captivity, Culture-Crossing, and White Womanhood from Mary Rowlandson to Patti Hearst* (Chicago: University of Chicago Press, 1996); Lepore, *Name of War*.

26. Linda Colley, *Captives* (New York: Pantheon Books, 2002).

27. Kathleen J. Bragdon, *The Columbia Guide to the American Indians of the Northeast* (New York: Columbia University Press, 2001), 27–32.

Chapter 1

1. See, for example, Francis Jennings, *The Invasion of America: Indians, Colonialism, and the Cant of Conquest* (Chapel Hill: University of North Carolina Press, 1975); Neal Salisbury, *Manitou and Providence: Indians, Europeans, and the Making of New England* (New York: Oxford University Press, 1982), ch. 7; Ann Kibbey, *The Interpretation of Material Shapes in Puritanism: A Study of Rhetoric, Prejudice, and Violence* (Cambridge: Cambridge University Press, 1986); Alfred A. Cave, *The Pequot War* (Amherst: University of Massachusetts Press, 1996).

2. Virginia DeJohn Anderson, *New England's Generation: The Great Migration*

and the Formation of Society and Culture in the Seventeenth Century (Cambridge: Cambridge University Press, 1991); Gloria L. Main, *Peoples of a Spacious Land: Families and Cultures in Colonial New England* (Cambridge, Mass.: Harvard University Press, 2001).

3. John Mason, *A Brief History of the Pequot War* (London, 1638); John Underhill, *Newes from America, or a New and Experimentall Discoverie of New England* (London, 1638); Lion Gardiner, "Leift. Lion Gardener His Relation of the Pequot Warres," *Collections of the Massachusetts Historical Society*, 3rd ser., 3 (Cambridge, Mass., 1833), 131–60. While Mason and Underhill published two rival accounts in close succession shortly after the war, Gardiner's account was written circa 1660 and remained unpublished until this edition.

4. Underhill, *Newes from America*, 15–16. For the chronology of the Pequot War attacks and skirmishes, see Cave, *Pequot War*, ch. 4.

5. On English and Anglo-American masculinity see Tim Hitchcock and Michèle Cohen, eds., *English Masculinities, 1660–1800* (London: Longman, 1999); Susan Kingsley Kent, *Gender and Power in Britain, 1640–1990* (London: Routledge, 1999); Lisa Wilson, *Ye Heart of a Man: the Domestic Life of Men in Colonial New England* (New Haven, Conn.: Yale University Press, 1999); Anne Lombard, *Making Manhood: Growing Up Male in Colonial New England* (Cambridge, Mass.: Harvard University Press, 2003).

On Native gender roles, see Kathleen M. Brown, *Good Wives, Nasty Wenches, and Anxious Patriarchs: Gender, Race, and Power in Colonial Virginia* (Chapel Hill: University of North Carolina Press, 1996), ch. 2; Brown, "The Anglo-Algonkian Gender Frontier," 26–48, and Lucy Murphy, "Autonomy and the Economic Roles of Indian Women of the Fox-Wisconsin River Region, 1763–1832," 72–89, both in *Negotiators of Change: Historical Perspectives on Native American Women*, ed. Nancy Shoemaker (New York: Routledge, 1995); Theda Perdue, *Cherokee Women: Gender and Culture Change, 1700–1835* (Lincoln: University of Nebraska Press, 1998); Nancy Shoemaker, "An Alliance Between Men: Gender Metaphors in Eighteenth-Century American Indian Diplomacy East of the Mississippi," *Ethnohistory* 46 (1999): 239–63; Karen Ordahl Kupperman, *Indians and English: Facing Off in Early America* (Ithaca, N.Y.: Cornell University Press, 2000), 142–53; Gail D. Danvers, "Dark Clouds Gathering: Anglo-Iroquois Contact, Conflict and Cultural Dislocation on the New York Colonial Frontier, 1740s–1770s" (Ph.D. diss., University of Sussex, 2001), ch. 3; R. Todd Romero, *Making War and Minting Christians: Masculinity, Religion, and Colonialism in Early New England* (forthcoming, University of Massachusetts Press).

6. Shoemaker, "Alliance Between Men"; Joyce Chaplin, *Subject Matter: Technology, the Body, and Science on the Anglo-American Frontier, 1500–1676* (Cambridge, Mass.: Harvard University Press, 2001), ch. 7; Nancy Shoemaker, *A Strange Likeness: Becoming Red and White in Eighteenth-Century North America* (New York: Oxford University Press, 2004), 3–12 and ch. 5.

7. Jennings, *Invasion of America*; William Cronon, *Changes in the Land: Indians, Colonists, and the Ecology of New England* (New York: Hill and Wang, 1983); Richard White, *The Middle Ground: Indians, Empires, and Republics in the Great Lakes Region, 1650–1815* (Cambridge: Cambridge University Press, 1991).

8. Richard Trexler, *Sex and Conquest: Gendered Violence, Political Order, and the European Conquest of the Americas* (Ithaca, N.Y.: Cornell University Press, 1995).

9. On warfare in colonial New England, see Douglas Edward Leach, *Flintlock and Tomahawk: New England in King Philip's War* (New York: Macmillan, 1958); Russell Bourne, *The Red King's Rebellion: Racial Politics in New England, 1675–1678* (New York: Athenaeum, 1990); Harold E. Selesky, *War and Society in Colonial Connecticut* (New Haven, Conn.: Yale University Press, 1990); Ian K. Steele, *Warpaths: Invasions of North America* (New York: Oxford University Press, 1994); Cave, *Pequot War*; Jill Lepore, *The Name of War: King Philip's War and the Origins of American Identity* (New York: Alfred A. Knopf, 1998); James D. Drake, *King Philip's War: Civil War in New England, 1675–1676* (Amherst: University of Massachusetts Press, 1999); Guy Chet, *Conquering the American Wilderness: The Triumph of European Warfare in the Colonial Northeast* (Amherst: University of Massachusetts Press, 2003); and Evan Haefeli and Kevin Sweeney, *Captors and Captives: The 1704 French and Indian Raid on Deerfield* (Amherst: University of Massachusetts Press, 2003).

10. Shoemaker describes the importance of Euro-Indian diplomacy in understanding colonial history in *Strange Likeness*, 3–12 and ch. 4.

11. Daniel K. Richter, *The Ordeal of the Longhouse: The Peoples of the Iroquois League in the Era of European Colonization* (Chapel Hill: University of North Carolina Press, 1992), 21–22; Richter, *Facing East from Indian Country: A Native History of Early America* (Cambridge, Mass.: Harvard University Press, 2001), 98–99. Quotations from William Bradford and Edward Winslow, *Mourt's Relation, or, Journal of the Plantation at Plymouth* (Boston: John Kimball Wiggin, 1865), 106–7, hereafter cited as *Mourt's Relation*; Salisbury, *Manitou and Providence*, 110–19.

12. *Mourt's Relation*, 106–9.

13. Richter, *Facing East from Indian Country*, ch. 4; Shoemaker, *Strange Likeness*, 50–55, 71–72.

14. *Mourt's Relation*, 106–11.

15. Increase Mather, *A Relation of the Troubles which have hapned in New-England* (Boston: John Foster, 1677). For a good recent discussion of the long-standing roots of King Philip's War, see Richter, *Facing East from Indian Country*, 90–105.

16. Quotations from I. Mather, *A Relation of the Troubles*, 14–17. Indians were not the only people to mock Standish for his diminutive stature. Thomas Morton, the enthusiastic reveler at Merrymount, famously gave Standish the derisive nickname "Captain Shrimp" in his account of his conflicts with Standish and Plymouth, in *New English Canaan, or New Canaan* (Amsterdam, 1637), 142–43.

17. Benjamin Church, *The History of the Eastern Expeditions of 1689, 1690, 1692, 1696, and 1704 against the Indians and the French*, ed. Henry Martyn Dexter (Boston: J. K. Wiggin and W. P. Lunt, 1867), xxx.

18. Mahomett's petition, 1736: Ayer Collection #559, Newberry Library, Chicago, Ill. See also Certified Copy of Book of Proceedings Before Commissioners of Review (London, 1769); Calendar of State Papers colonial series: America and West Indies, 42:200–204, 211–12, 223; and Journal of the Commissioners for Trade and Plantations, 45:105–11, 116, 168–71, 184, 265–66, 297, 305–06, 308–10, 312–14, 321, 324–25, for the full records of the Mohegans' case.

19. On gender, English nationalism, and religion, see Anne McLaren, "Gender, Religion, and Early Modern Nationalism: Elizabeth I, Mary Queen of Scots, and the Genesis of English Anti-Catholicism," *American Historical Review* 107 (June 2002): 739–67; and Judith M. Richards, "The English Accession of James VI: 'National' Identity, Gender, and the Personal Monarchy of England," *English Historical Review* 117 (June 2002): 513–35. Examples of sixteenth-century English pamphlets that link masculinity and warfare are: Nicholas Breton, *The Scholler and the Souldier. A disputation pithily passed between them* (London, 1597); Niccolò Machiavelli, *The Arte of Warre*, trans. Peter Withorne (London, 1573).

20. William Haller, *The Rise of Puritanism* (New York: Columbia University Press, 1938), 151 ff.; Edward Turges, *The Christian Souldier, his combat, conquest, and crowne* (London, 1639), 2; *The Souldiers Pocket Bible* (London, Edm. Calamy/G. B. and R. W., ca. 1640s?).

21. John Davenport, *A Royall Edict for Military Exercises* (London, 1629), 3, 15. See 2 Samuel 1:18 ("Also he bade them teach the children of Judah *the use of* the bow: behold, *it is* written in the book of Jasher"). Chaplin discusses English archery and its importance until about 1600 in *Subject Matter*, ch. 3. Although longbows were used by the English in their early encounters with Native people in North America, Davenport's discussion of "the use of the Bow" in 1629 was undoubtedly metaphorical.

22. Davenport, *Royall Edict*, 4–5, 24, 25. The English settlement of the colony Davenport would serve, New Haven, was made possible only by the English victory in the Pequot War.

23. Philip Gura, *A Glimpse of Sion's Glory: Puritan Radicalism in New England, 1620–1660* (Middletown, Conn.: Wesleyan University Press, 1984); Andrew Delbanco, *The Puritan Ordeal* (Cambridge, Mass.: Harvard University Press, 1989); David D. Hall, *Worlds of Wonder, Days of Judgment: Popular Religious Belief in Early New England* (New York: Alfred A. Knopf, 1989); David D. Hall, ed., *The Antinomian Controversy, 1636–1638: A Documentary History* (Durham, N.C.: Duke University Press, 1990); Anderson, *New England's Generation*; Susan Juster, *Disorderly Women: Sexual Politics and Evangelicalism in Revolutionary New England* (Ithaca, N.Y.: Cornell University Press, 1994). On the diversity of Puritanism in America, see Heather Miyano Kopelson, "Performing Faith: Religious Practice and Identity in the Puritan Atlantic, 1660–1720," diss. in progress, University of Iowa.

24. Samuel Nowell, *Abraham in Arms: or, the first religious General with his Army engaging in a War* (Boston, 1678), reprinted in *So Dreadfull a Judgment: Puritan Responses to King Philip's War, 1676–1677*, ed. Richard Slotkin and James K. Folsom (Middletown, Conn.: Wesleyan University Press, 1978), 273. Lombard writes about the connections among manhood, ideals of fatherhood, and politics in colonial New England in *Making Manhood*, ch. 5.

25. Nowell, *Abraham in Arms*, 274, 277. Other scholars have emphasized Nowell's cautions against unjust wars—that is, offensive wars conducted purely for greed or territorial expansion. (See Geoffrey Plank, "Massachusetts, Acadia, and Puritan Anti-Expansionism," unpublished paper presented at the 1996 annual meeting of the American Historical Association, Pacific Coast Branch, San Francisco, Calif.) However, most puritans believed that their conduct in the Pequot War

and King Philip's War had stayed within the bounds of Nowell's prescriptions for a just war: "1. For defence of ourselves, 2. To recover what hath been taken away, 3. To punish for injuries done," 276.

26. Nowell, *Abraham in Arms*, 288–91. In this instance, there is more than an echo of a Jeremiad in Nowell's sermon. On the Jeremiad, see Alan Heimert and Andrew Delbanco, eds., *The Puritans in America: A Narrative Anthology* (Cambridge, Mass.: Harvard University Press, 1985), 229–60.

27. Heather Kopelson, "Christian Soldiers and Singers: Religious Citizenship and Puritan Identity in Early New England, 1660–1690," unpublished paper delivered at the Omohundro Institute of Early American History and Culture Annual Conference, June 2002, College Park, Maryland; Chet, *Conquering the American Wilderness*, 58–59. Quotations from Nowell, *Abraham in Arms*, 284–88.

28. Charles J. Hoadly, ed., *Records of the Colony and Plantation of New Haven, 1638–1649* (Hartford, 1857), 25–26, 33–35, 76, 96–97, 201–5; *The Public Records of the Colony of Connecticut* (Hartford: Lockwood & Brainard Company, 1850–90), 1:542–45. The fines for delinquencies of the watch or training days were between one and five shillings. On the high rates of prosecution and conviction for shirking the watch or training duties in early New Haven, see Ann M. Little, "A 'Wel Ordered Commonwealth': Gender and Politics in New Haven Colony, 1636–1690" (Ph.D. diss., University of Pennsylvania, 1996), 58–59. While here I emphasize the ways in which militias were designed to uphold New England's social order, Louise A. Breen explores the potentially subversive nature of the artillery companies as institutions that nurtured dissenters and gave them social status in *Transgressing the Bounds: Subversive Enterprises Among the Puritan Elite in Massachusetts, 1630–1692* (Oxford: Oxford University Press, 2001).

29. Fred Anderson, *A People's Army: Massachusetts Soldiers and Society in the Seven Years' War* (Chapel Hill: University of North Carolina Press, 1984), chs. 3–4 and 6; Chet, *Conquering the American Wilderness*, 61–63.

30. To the contrary, in *Arming America: The Origins of a National Gun Culture* (New York: Alfred A. Knopf, 2000), Michael Bellesiles presents some suggestive evidence concerning the limited nature of gun ownership in colonial America in ch. 3, "Guns in the Daily Life of Colonial America," which became the most often attacked chapter in his book. His critics have assembled a great deal of evidence to challenge his evidence and interpretations in this chapter. See, for example, "Forum: Historians and Guns," *William and Mary Quarterly* 3rd ser., 59 (2002): 203–68.

31. *Province and Court Records of Maine*, vol. 2: York County Court Records, ca. 1653–79 (Portland: Maine Historical Society, 1931), passim. Of the seventy-three inventories reviewed, eight were very incomplete.

32. New Haven Probate Records, 1647–87; vol. 1, part 1, State Archives, Connecticut State Library, Hartford; *Public Records of the Colony of Connecticut* 1:442–508. Of the seventy-eight men's inventories from New Haven, fifty-eight showed at least one gun, which usually was listed with the other accessories of war. Another three men died in possession of swords and powder, for example, but no guns. Of the twenty men who died completely unarmed, nearly half (nine) were clearly single and did not keep households—probably because they were mariners. Of the thirty-three men's inventories from Connecticut in the 1640s, twenty-four show guns, and

another two show ammunition but no guns. Of the seven men who died unarmed, three did not keep their own households, and four had very young families.

On the uses of probate records, see Peter Benes, ed., *Early American Probate Inventories* (Boston: Boston University, 1989), esp. 5–40, and Gloria Main, "Many Things Forgotten: The Use of Probate Records in *Arming America*," *William and Mary Quarterly* 3rd ser., 59 (2002): 211–16.

33. *Public Records of the Colony of Connecticut* 1:466–468, 492.

34. Patrick Malone, *The Skulking Way of War: Technology and Tactics in New England Indian Warfare* (Baltimore: Johns Hopkins University Press, 1993), ch. 3; Bellesiles, *Arming America*, 70–80. On women, see New Haven Probate Records, 1647–87; vol. 1, part 1; *Public Records of the Colony of Connecticut* 1:442–508. Of six women's inventories in the New Haven and Connecticut records total, not a single household kept guns, ammunition, armor, or other weaponry.

35. Beauchamp Plantagenet, *A Description of the Province of New Albion* (London: James Moxon, 1650), 9–10, 30; Bellesiles, *Arming America*, 93–95 and ch. 4.

36. William Hubbard, *A Narrative of the Troubles with the Indians in New-England* (Boston, 1677), 79, 85.

37. Increase Mather, *A Brief History of the Warr with the Indians in New-England* (Boston, 1676), reprinted in *So Dreadfull a Judgment*, 108, 141.

38. Cotton Mather, *Decennium Luctuosum: an History of Remarkable Occurences in the long war which New England hath had with the Indian Salvages, 1688–1698* (Boston, 1699), 66, 84; Mary Beth Norton, *In the Devil's Snare: The Salem Witchcraft Crisis of 1692* (New York: Alfred A. Knopf, 2002), 105–6.

39. Malone, *Skulking Way of War*, ch. 1; Richter, *Ordeal of the Longhouse*, chs. 2–3; Richter, "War and Culture: The Iroquois Experience," *William and Mary Quarterly* 3rd. ser., 40 (1983): 528–59; Kathleen J. Bragdon, *Native Peoples of Southern New England, 1500–1650* (Norman: University of Oklahoma Press, 1996), 46–53; José António Brandão, ed., *Nation Iroquoise: A Seventeenth-Century Ethnography of the Iroquois* (Lincoln: University of Nebraska Press, 2003), 64–75, 94–95. On the limits of women's political power, see Elisabeth Tooker, "Women in Iroquois Society," in *Extending the Rafters: Interdisciplinary Approaches to Iroquoian Studies*, ed. Michael K. Foster, Jack Campisi, and Marianne Mithun (Albany, N.Y.: SUNY Press, 1984); Nancy Shoemaker, "The Rise or Fall of Iroquois Women," *Journal of Women's History* 2 (1991): 40; and José António Brandão, *"Your fyre shall burn no more": Iroquois Policy Toward New France and Its Native Allies to 1701* (Lincoln: University of Nebraska Press, 1997), 21 and chs. 3–4.

40. I. Mather, *A Brief History of the Warr with the Indians in New-England,* 138–39, 149; Benjamin Church, *Entertaining Passages Relating to Philip's War* (Boston, 1716), in *So Dreadfull a Judgment*, 397–99, 403, 423–32; Ann Marie Plane, "Putting a Face on Colonization: Factionalism and Gender Politics in the Life History of Awashunkes, the 'Squaw Sachem' of Saconet," in *Northeastern Indian Lives, 1632–1816*, ed. Robert S. Grumet (Amherst: University of Massachusetts Press, 1996), 140–65; Carolyn Merchant, *Ecological Revolutions: Nature, Gender, and Science in New England* (Chapel Hill: University of North Carolina Press, 1989), 83–84; Bragdon, *Native Peoples*, 157–59.

41. Underhill, *Newes from America*, 5, 39. Underhill also praises a Pequot dip-

lomat by describing him as "a man of good understanding, portly, carriage grave, and majesticall in his expressions," 10. For a thorough discussion of Indian masculinity and warfare, see Ralph Todd Romero, "Making War and Minting Christians: Masculinity, Religion, and Colonialism in Early New England" (Ph.D. diss., Boston College, 2004), chs. 1, 9, and 11.

42. Underhill, *Newes from America*, 23–24; Mason, *Brief History*, 6; Hubbard, *Narrative of the Troubles*, 14. All emphases in the original documents.

43. Mason, *Brief History*, 4–5.

44. Father Joseph Lafitau, *Customs of the American Indians Compared with the Customs of Primitive Times*, trans. and ed. by William N. Fenton and Elizabeth L. Moore (Toronto: The Champlain Society, 1974), 2:155–162; Richter, "War and Culture."

45. *Travels in New France by J.C.B.*, ed. Sylvester K. Stevens, Donald H. Kent, and Emma Edith Woods (Harrisburg: Pennsylvania Historical Commission, 1941), 72–73; I. Mather, *A Relation of the Troubles*, 13–14.

46. William Foster, *The Captors' Narrative: Catholic Women and Their Puritan Men on the Early American Frontier* (Ithaca, N.Y.: Cornell University Press, 2003), 12; Jabez Fitch, "A Brief Narrative of several things respecting the Province of New Hampshire in New-England," ch. 4, Massachusetts Historical Society, Boston; John Easton, *A Relacion of the Indyan Warre* (1675), in *Narratives of the Indian Wars, 1675–1699*, ed. Charles H. Lincoln (New York: Charles Scribner's Sons, 1913), 9.

For complaints about being treated like dogs, see *Indian Treaties printed by Benjamin Franklin, 1736–1762* (Philadelphia: Historical Society of Pennsylvania, 1938); for example, Canassatego's comments to Conrad Weiser: "the New England People were much worse than Indians, for they make no more of killing an Indian, tho' in Alliance with them, than they do a Dog," 309–11. See also the remarks by an English garrison commander who reported that an Indian threatened "to kill us all like Dogs" in order to take Fort St. George in Maine, in a letter dated July 21, 1724, Coll. S-2029, misc. box 98/7, Maine Historical Society, Portland. (This is a document copied from SC1 45X, Massachusetts Archives Collection, 29:154–57, Massachusetts State Archives, Boston.)

47. Malone, *Skulking Way of War*, 37–64, 80–87; Bellesiles, *Arming America*, 124–36.

48. For examples of colonial usage of the term "parley," see Gardiner, "Leift Lion Gardener His Relation," "demanded the Pequit Sachem to come into parley," 141, and "No, it is not the manner of a parley," 146; C. Mather, *Decennium Luctuosum*, "near the place, where they had urged for a *Parley*," emphasis in the original, 97.

49. Jane Kamensky, "Talk Like a Man: Speech, Power, and Masculinity in Early New England," *Gender and History* 8 (1996): 22–47; Kamensky, *Governing the Tongue: The Politics of Speech in Early New England* (New York: Oxford University Press, 1997); Shoemaker, "Alliance Between Men," and *Strange Likeness*, 61–124.

50. Lafitau, *Customs of the American Indians*, 1:297–99, 2:142; Richter, *Ordeal of the Longhouse*, 46–47. Richter notes that a 1609 battle between the Montagnais and Algonquin against the Mohawks was preceded by "both sides hastily erect[ing] fortifications, from which they hurled taunts at each other through the night," 54.

See also Inga Clendinnen "'Fierce and Unnatural Cruelty': Cortés and the Conquest of Mexico," in *New World Encounters*, ed. Stephen Greenblatt (Berkeley: University of California Press, 1993), 12–47.

51. Underhill, *Newes from America*, 9. Underhill thinks that this first greeting was meant "cheerfully," although in the context of the other taunts the English receive from Indians, I think they meant to taunt or intimidate him with their greeting. This was also their goal with their "most dolefull and wofull cryes all the night," which kept Underhill awake.

52. Mason, *Brief History*, 7; Underhill, *Newes from America*, 16.

53. Underhill, *Newes from America*, 22. See also, for example, Underhill's discussion of "this insolent Nation" and their "proud challenges" to English manhood, 15; the "insolencie of the enemie," 16; their "boldnesse," 22. Mason in his *Brief History* describes the Indians' "great pride and Insolency," x; their "great Pride, threatening and resolving the utter ruin and Destruction of all the *English*," 9.

54. Hubbard, *Narrative of the Troubles*, 75–76.

55. Hubbard, *Narrative of the Troubles*, 75–76; Kamensky, "Talk Like a Man."

56. I. Mather, *Brief History*, 136.

57. Quotations in this and the preceding paragraph taken from C. Mather, *Decennium Luctuosum*, 92–97. See also Kenneth Silverman, *The Life and Times of Cotton Mather* (New York: Columbia University Press, 1984), 74–76.

58. I. Mather, *Brief History*, 113–14.

59. Depositions of David and Hannah Meade of Cambridge, Mass., October 8, 1677; Coll. 77, Box 1, folder 38, Maine Historical Society, Portland.

60. Adam J. Hirsch, in "The Collision of Military Cultures in Seventeenth-Century New England," *Journal of American History* 74 (1988): 1187–1212, provides a brilliant analysis of styles of warfare as central to the cultural clash between Native Americans and the English. Although he does not specifically identify his subject as a gendered one, he demonstrates the importance of warfare to men of both cultures. James Axtell, in *The European and the Indian: Essays in the Ethnohistory of Colonial North America* (New York: Oxford University Press, 1981), 138–42, provides a more detailed illustration of the cultural clash evident in warfare, but differs from Hirsch in his claim that the experience of the Pequot War was too brief for the English to learn much about Indian styles of warfare. On Iroquois warfare, see Brandão, "*Your fyre shall burn no more*," chs. 3–4; Richter, "War and Culture"; and Richter, *Ordeal of the Longhouse*, ch. 3. Clendinnen also notes the different approaches to war in "'Fierce and Unnatural Cruelty'".

For further discussion of eastern Indian styles of warfare, see Leroy V. Eid, "'National' War Among the Indians of Northeastern North America," *Canadian Review of American Studies* 16 (1985): 125–54; Eid, "'A Kind of Running Fight': Indian Battlefield Tactics in the Late Eighteenth Century," *Western Pennsylvania Historical Magazine* 71 (1988): 147–71; Malone, *Skulking Way of War*; Peter Way, "The Cutting Edge of Culture: British Soldiers Encounter Native Americans in the French and Indian War," in *Empire and Others: British Encounters with Indigenous Peoples, 1600–1850*, ed. Martin Daunton and Rick Halpern (Philadelphia: University of Pennsylvania Press, 1999).

61. Underhill, *Newes from America*, 14–15; Mason, *Brief History*, 19.

62. Hubbard, *Narrative of the Troubles*, 10; Richter, "War and Culture"; Lepore, *Name of War*, chs. 3–4.

63. For example, Gardiner urged the English not to begin a war in 1636, noting that "war is like a three-footed Stool, want one foot and down comes all; and these three feet are men, victuals, and munition." From his position at the fledgling Fort Saybrook, he writes "therefore, seeing in peace you are like to be famished, what will or can be done if war?" When several officers, including Underhill, appeared at the Fort to being journeying into Pequot country, Gardiner reports that this was "to my great grief, for, said I, you come hither to raise these wasps about my ears, and then you will take wing and flee away." But, "seeing you will [pursue war with the Pequots], I pray you, if you don't load your Barks with Pequits, load them with corn, for that is now gathered with them, and dry, ready to put into their barns, and both you and we will have need of it," Gardiner, "Leift. Lion Gardiner His Relation," 138–40.

64. Underhill, *Newes from America*, 36–44; Mason, *Brief History*, 4–10.

65. Underhill, *Newes from America*, 39–40; Mason, *Brief History*, 9–10. Underhill would lead a similar attack by Dutch forces in Keift's War against the Weequaesgeek fort near Greenwich, Connecticut, in 1644. At least three hundred, and possibly as many as seven hundred men, women, and children were torched in their village. See Evan Haefeli, "Kieft's War and the Cultures of Violence in Colonial America," in *Lethal Imagination: Violence and Brutality in American History*, ed. Michael A. Bellesiles (New York: New York University Press, 1999), 32; Chet, *Conquering the American Wilderness*, 27–29.

66. Underhill, *Newes from America*, 41–42; William Bradford, *Bradford's History of Plymouth Plantation, 1600–1646*, ed. William T. Davis (New York: Charles Scribner's Sons, 1908), 340.

67. Mason, *Brief History*, 11; Underhill, *Newes from America*, 42–43.

68. James Shepard, *Connecticut Soldiers in the Pequot War of 1637* (Meriden, Conn.: Journal Pub. Co., 1913). Aside from the officers, eighteen enlisted men went on to help found or settle in New Haven Colony's towns: John Clark, John Hall, Nicholas Jennings/Gennings, Nathaniel Merriman, Richard Osborne, Edward Pattison, Robert Seely, and Samuel Whitehead settled in New Haven Town; Thomas Blatchley/Blakesley, John Plumb, Robert Rose, and Robert Rose, Jr., settled in Branford; Jeremy Jagger and Samuel Sherman settled in Stamford; John Johnson and John Stone settled in Guilford; and James Roggers and Thomas Tibbals settled in Milford.

69. "Relation of the Plott—Indian," *Collections of the Massachusetts Historical Society*, 3rd ser., 3 (Cambridge, 1833), 161–64.

70. "Relation of the Plott—Indian" reveals that New Haven's governor Theophilus Eaton had been promptly informed of the plot, 161, 164. For New Haven's and Connecticut's preparations for war, see Hoadly, *Records of the Colony and Plantation of New Haven, 1638–1649*, 69–70, 78; *Public Records of the Colony of Connecticut* 1:74–106.

On the United Colonies of New England, see Ann M. Little, "'Wel Ordered Commonwealth,'" 63–68; *Records of the Colony of New Plymouth*, vol. 14, *Acts of the Commissioners of the United Colonies of New England*, vol. 1, *1643–51* (Boston,

1859), 10–12; Hoadly, *Records of the Colony and Plantation of New Haven, 1638–1649*, 110.

71. See, for example, *Public Records of the Colony of Connecticut*, 1:1, 46–47, 52, 73–74, 79, 106, 138, 197, 235, 240, 263, 284, 294, 351, 353, 402, quotation from 576–77; Hoadly, *Records of the Colony and Plantation of New Haven, 1638–1649*, 60, 206; Charles J. Hoadly, ed., *Records of the Colony or Jurisdiction of New Haven from May 1653 to the Union* (Hartford, 1858), 67, 195, 217, 219, 299, 593–95. For more on Indians and English law in New England, see Yasuhide Kawashima, *Puritan Justice and the Indian: White Man's Law in Massachusetts, 1630–1763* (Middletown, Conn.: Wesleyan University Press, 1986).

72. Connecticut Archives, *Indians*, 1:1, docs. 10–23, at the Connecticut State Library, Hartford. Quotation from a letter to Captain John Allyn, July 8, 1669.

73. Chet, *Conquering the American Wilderness*, ch. 3.

74. Hubbard, *Narrative of the Troubles*, 19.

75. Hubbard, *Narrative of the Troubles*, 38–39.

76. C. Mather, *Decennium Luctuosum*, 92, 96.

77. Chaplin calls this practice "ventriloquizing" the Indians in *Subject Matter*, 26–27.

78. Church, *Entertaining Passages*, 419, 406–8.

79. Kirsten Fischer describes the ways in which free and enslaved African Americans come to be identified with animals, subject to laws and forms of corporal punishment that white colonists were not, in *Suspect Relations*, chs. 4–5.

80. I. Mather, *Brief History*, 108, 134–35; *An Essay for the Recording of Illustrious Providences* (Boston, 1684), preface and chs. 1, 3–4, 10. The elder Mather also uses the term "wolves" once in his *An Earnest Exhortation to the Inhabitants of New-England* (Boston, 1676), reprinted in *So Dreadfull a Judgment*, 176.

81. C. Mather, *Humiliations follow'd with Deliverances* (Boston, 1697), 4–5, 33.

82. C. Mather, *Decennium Luctuosum*, 34, 37, 77, 83–86, 89, 99, 123–26; *Humiliations follow'd with Deliverances*, 42.

83. Fischer, *Suspect Relations*; Shoemaker, *Strange Likeness*.

84. Chaplin, *Subject Matter*; Main, *Peoples of a Spacious Land*, especially chs. 4, 5, and 8. On variola in North America, see Elizabeth A. Fenn, *Pox Americana: The Great Smallpox Epidemic of 1775–1783* (New York: Hill and Wang, 2001). See also David S. Jones's warning against an overly-determined approach to the effects of European diseases among Native Americans in "Virgin Soils Revisited," *William and Mary Quarterly* 3rd ser. 60 (2003): 703–41.

85. See, for example, SC1 45X, Massachusetts Archives Collection, 70:1, 10–11, 12, 131, 132, 134, 266, 277, 381, 386, Massachusetts State Archives, Boston. See also vol. 73, passim.

Chapter 2

1. Richard Slotkin, *Regeneration through Violence: The Mythology of the American Frontier, 1600–1860* (Middletown, Conn.: Wesleyan University Press, 1973);

Francis Jennings, *The Invasion of America: Indians, Colonialism, and the Cant of Conquest* (Chapel Hill: University of North Carolina Press, 1975); Neal Salisbury, *Manitou and Providence: Indians, Europeans, and the Making of New England* (New York: Oxford University Press, 1982); Jill Lepore, *The Name of War: King Philip's War and the Origins of American Identity* (New York: Knopf, 1998).

On the conflict of warrior cultures, see Patrick Malone, *The Skulking Way of War: Technology and Tactics in New England Indian Warfare* (Baltimore: Johns Hopkins University Press, 1993); Adam J. Hirsch, "The Collision of Military Cultures in Seventeenth-Century New England," *Journal of American History* 74 (1988): 1187–1212; and Daniel Richter, "War and Culture: The Iroquois Experience," *William and Mary Quarterly* 3rd ser., 40 (1983): 528–59.

2. John Underhill, *Newes from America* (London, 1638), 7. Inga Clendinnen has written about the essential and unavoidable confusions of the colonial encounter in *Ambivalent Conquests: Maya and Spaniard in Yucatan, 1517–1570* (Cambridge: Cambridge University Press, 1987), and " 'Fierce and Unnatural Cruelty': Cortés and the Conquest of Mexico," in *New World Encounters,* ed. Stephen Greenblatt (Berkeley: University of California Press, 1993), 12–47.

3. Lion Gardiner, "Leift. Lion Gardener His Relation of the Pequot Warres," *Collections of the Massachusetts Historical Society,* 3rd ser. 3 (Cambridge, Mass., 1833), 144–46.

4. Linda R. Baumgarten, "Leather Stockings and Hunting Shirts," in *American Material Culture: The Shape of the Field,* ed. Ann Smart Martin and J. Ritchie Garrison (Winterthur, Del.: Henry Francis du Pont Winterthur Museum; Knoxville: University of Tennessee Press, 1997), 251–76; Timothy J. Shannon, "Dressing for Success on the Mohawk Frontier: Hendrick, William Johnson, and the Indian Fashion," *William and Mary Quarterly* 3rd ser., 53 (1996), 13–42. Art historian Beth Fowkes Tobin uses the term "cultural cross-dressing" in a chapter on portraits of British officer and Mohawk warriors in *Picturing Imperial Power: Colonial Subjects in Eighteenth-Century British Painting* (Durham, N.C.: Duke University Press, 1999), as do Erin Skye Mackie, "Cultural Cross-Dressing: The Colorful Case of the Caribbean Creole," 250–70, and Joe Snader, "The Masquerade of Colonial Identity in Frances Brooke's *Emily Montague* (1769)," 119–42, both in *The Clothes that Wear Us: Essays on Dressing and Transgressing in Eighteenth-Century Culture,* ed. Jessica Muns and Penny Richards (Newark: University of Delaware Press; London: Associated University Presses, 1999).

5. Lepore explores English anxieties provoked by Indian "attacks on bounded systems" in King Philip's War and suggests that attacks on English homes and farms were experienced as attacks on Englishness, *Name of War,* ch. 3.

6. On the transformative power of clothing in the early modern period, see Vern L. Bullough and Bonnie Bullough, *Cross Dressing, Sex, and Gender* (Philadelphia: University of Pennsylvania Press, 1993), ch. 4; Marjorie Garber, *Vested Interests: Cross-Dressing and Cultural Anxiety* (New York: Routledge, 1992), ch. 1; Laura Levine, *Men in Women's Clothing: Anti-Theatricality and Effeminization, 1579–1642* (Cambridge: Cambridge University Press, 1994); and Muns and Richards, eds., *Clothes that Wear Us.*

7. Valerie Traub, "Mapping the Global Body," in *Early Modern Visual Cul-*

ture, ed. Peter Erickson and Clarke Hulse (Philadelphia: University of Pennsylvania Press, 2000), 44–97; Helen Callaway, "Dressing for Dinner in the Bush: Rituals of Self-Definition and British Imperial Authority," in *Dress and Gender: Making and Meaning in Cultural Contexts*, ed. Ruth Barnes and Joanne B. Eicher (New York: St. Martin's Press, 1992), 232–47.

8. Garber's notion of the "category crisis" transvestism causes seems useful here: "'category crisis' . . . is not the exception but rather the ground of culture itself. By 'category crisis' I mean a failure of definitional distinction, a borderline that becomes permeable, that permits of border crossing from one (apparently distinct) category to another: black/white, Jew/Christian, noble/bourgeois, master/servant, master/slave. The binarism male/female, one apparent ground of distinction (in contemporary eyes, at least) between 'this' and 'that,' 'him' and 'me,' is itself put into question or under erasure in transvestism, and a transvestite figure, or a transvestite mode, will always function as a sign of overdetermination—a mechanism of displacement from one blurred boundary to another," *Vested Interests*, 16.

9. Ann Rosalind Jones and Peter Stallybrass, *Renaissance Clothing and the Materials of Memory* (Cambridge: Cambridge University Press, 2000), especially chs. 1 and 7–9; Levine, *Men in Women's Clothing*; Garber, *Vested Interests*, ch. 1.

10. Carole Shammas, "How Self-Sufficient Was Early America?" *Journal of Interdisciplinary History* 13 (1982): 247–72; Peter Benes, ed., *Textiles in Early New England: Design, Production, and Consumption* (Boston: Boston University, 1999); Peter Benes, ed., *Textiles in New England II: Four Centuries of Material Life* (Boston: Boston University, 2001); Adrienne D. Hood, *The Weaver's Craft: Cloth, Commerce, and Industry in Early Pennsylvania* (Philadelphia: University of Pennsylvania Press, 2003), 1–14.

11. Ann M. Little, "A 'Wel Ordered Commonwealth': Gender and Politics in New Haven Colony, 1636–1690" (Ph.D. diss., University of Pennsylvania, 1996), 186–93; Patricia Trautman, "Dress in Seventeenth Century Cambridge," in *Early American Probate Inventories*, vol. 12, ed. Peter Benes (Boston: Boston University, 1989), 62–63; *New England Begins: The Seventeenth Century*, vol. 2, *Mentality and Environment* (Boston: Museum of Fine Arts, 1982).

12. Lt. Colonel Massy at Fort Stanwix, November 17, 1759, to General Jeffrey Amherst, the Jeffrey Amherst Papers, vol. 4, The Clements Library, Ann Arbor, Mich; Joanna Cotton of Salisbury, Mass., to Increase Mather, March 13, 1697, SC1 45X, Massachusetts Archives Collection, 57: 67, Massachusetts State Archives, Boston.

13. Joshua Scottow, *Old Men's Tears for their own Declensions, mixed with Fears of their and posterities further falling off from New England's Primitive Constitution* (Boston, 1691), 5; Scottow was himself a veteran of the Maine frontier's Indian wars. On sumptuary laws, see Alice Morse Earle, *Two Centuries of Costume in America, 1620–1820* (New York: Macmillan Company, 1903; reprint, Williamstown, Mass.: Corner House Publishers, 1974), 1:61–68.

14. *The Infortunate: The Voyage and Adventures of William Moraley, an Indentured Servant*, ed. Susan E. Klepp and Billy G. Smith (University Park: Pennsylvania State University Press, 1992), 50–53. When he arrived at his master's residence, he writes, "I was stripp'd of my Rags, and received in lieu of them a torn Shirt, and an

old Coat. They tell me, it was only for the present, for I might expect better," 77. Moraley notes that during his stay in the Delaware Valley, "The Negroes and bought Servants, are clad in coarse Osnabrigs, both Coat, Waistcoat, Breeches, and Shirt, being of the same Piece, and so rough, that the Shirt occasions great Uneasiness to the Body," 71. *The Autobiography of Benjamin Franklin*, ed. Leonard W. Labaree, Ralph L. Ketcham, Helen C. Boatfield, and Helen H. Fineman (New Haven, Conn.: Yale University Press, 1954), 73.

15. Several scholars have noted the increasing anxiety over cross-dressing in early modern England. See, for example, Bullough and Bullough, *Cross Dressing, Sex, and Gender*, ch. 4; Garber, *Vested Interests*, ch. 1; and Levine, *Men in Women's Clothing*.

16. Lois G. Carr and Lorena S. Walsh, "The Planter's Wife: The Experience of White Women in Seventeenth-Century Maryland," *William and Mary Quarterly* 3rd ser., 34 (1977): 542–71; Kathleen M. Brown, *Good Wives, Nasty Wenches, and Anxious Patriarchs: Gender, Race, and Power in Colonial Virginia* (Chapel Hill: University of North Carolina Press, 1996), ch. 3.

17. Cornelia Hughes Dayton, *Women Before the Bar: Gender, Law, and Society in Connecticut, 1639–1789* (Chapel Hill: University of North Carolina Press, 1995); Carole Shammas, "Anglo-American Household Government in Comparative Perspective," *William and Mary Quarterly* 3rd ser., 52 (1995): 104–44; Brown, *Good Wives*; Mary Beth Norton, *Founding Mothers and Fathers: Gendered Power and the Forming of American Society* (New York: Alfred A. Knopf, 1996); Ann M. Little, "'Shee would bump his mouldy britch': Authority, Masculinity, and the Harried Husbands of New Haven Colony, 1638–1670," in *Lethal Imagination: Violence and Brutality in American History*, ed. Michael Bellesiles (New York: New York University Press, 1999), 43–66; Little, "A 'Wel Ordered Commonwealth,'" 69–117, 236–305.

18. Kathleen M. Brown, "'Changed . . . into the Fashion of a Man': The Politics of Sexual Difference in a Seventeenth-Century Anglo-American Settlement," *Journal of the History of Sexuality* 6 (1995): 171–93; Brown, *Good Wives*, 75–80; Norton, *Founding Mothers and Fathers*, 183–97.

19. English tradesmen sometimes wore leather aprons to protect themselves from the hazards of their occupations. Earle, *Two Centuries of Costume in America*, 1:80; Alice Morse Earle, *Costume of Colonial Times* (New York: Charles Scribner's Sons, 1894), 47–48.

20. Karen Ordahl Kupperman, "Presentment of Civility: English Reading of American Self-Presentation in the Early Years of Colonization," *William and Mary Quarterly* 3rd ser., 54 (1997): 193–228; and Karen Ordahl Kupperman, *Indians and English: Facing Off in Early America* (Ithaca, N.Y.: Cornell University Press, 2000), ch. 2.

21. Thomas Morton, *New English Canaan, or New Canaan* (Amsterdam, 1637), 29–31. Morton's emphasis on the sameness of purpose of English and Indian costume is perhaps not surprising, given the fact that he was the founder of the short-lived colony at Mount Wollaston known as "Merrymount." In 1628, Plymouth Colony accused Morton of enticing their servants away with his leveling visions of an interracial society and ultimately marched against Morton and forced Merrymount to disband. The separatists accused him of all manner of dangerous

boundary blurring, between Christian and Pagan, English and Indian, master and servant, and so on: "set[ting] up a May-pole, drinking and dancing aboute it many days togeather, inviting the Indean women, for their consorts, dancing and frisking togither, (like so many fairies, or furies rather,) and worse practises," William Bradford, *Bradford's History of Plymouth Plantation, 1600–1646*, ed. William T. Davis (New York: Charles Scribner's Sons, 1908), 237–38. For his part, Morton wrote that "This harmeles mirth made by yonge men (that lived in hope to have wives brought over to them, that would save them a laboure to make a voyage to fetch any over) was much distasted, of the precise Seperatists: that keepe much a doe, about the tyth of Muit and Cummin; troubling their braines more then reason would require about things that are indifferent: and from that time sought occasion against my honest Host of Ma-re Mount to overthrow his ondertakings, and to destroy his plantation quite and cleane," *New English Caanan*, Book 3, 135–36. See also Michael Zuckerman, "Pilgrims in the Wilderness: Community, Modernity, and the Maypole at Merry Mount," *New England Quarterly* 50 (1977): 255–77.

22. Kathleen J. Bragdon, *Native Peoples of Southern New England, 1500–1650* (Norman: University of Oklahoma Press, 1996), 171–72; Christopher Levett, *A Voyage Into New England* (London, 1628), reprinted in *Maine in the Age of Discovery: Christopher Levett's Voyage, 1623–24, and a Guide to Sources* (Portland: Maine Historical Society, 1988), 54.

23. Bragdon, *Native Peoples*, 171–73; Malone, *Skulking Way of War*, 25–26; Richter, *The Ordeal of the Longhouse* (Chapel Hill: University of North Carolina Press, 1992), 33; José António Brandão, ed., *Nation Iroquoise: A Seventeenth-Century Ethnography of the Iroquois* (Lincoln: University of Nebraska Press, 2003), 100–101; William Pote, Jr., original ms. journal kept by him 1745–47 during captivity among the French & Indians, Ayer Collection ms. 733, 109–10, Newberry Library, Chicago, Ill.

24. "The Captivity Narrative of Joseph Bartlett," in *A Sketch of the History of Newbury, Newburyport, and West Newbury from 1635 to 1845*, ed. Joshua Coffin (Boston: S. G. Drake, 1845), 332; Pote, 20–21, 108, 195; Robert Eastburn, *A Faithful Narrative* (Philadelphia, 1758), 17–18; Thomas Brown, *A Plain Narrative* (Boston, 1760), 15.

25. Lepore, *Name of War*, xix, 79–83; Morton, *New English Canaan*, title page. Kupperman argues that Indian "nakedness" was a complex concept for English observers as it was read both positively and negatively by them, *Indians and English*, 49–53.

26. Benjamin Thompson, *New England's Crisis* (Boston, 1676), reprinted in *So Dreadfull a Judgment: Puritan Responses to King Philip's War, 1676–1677*, ed. Richard Slotkin and James K. Folsom (Middletown, Conn.: Wesleyan University Press, 1978), 219; Benjamin Church, *Entertaining Passages Relating to Philip's War* (Boston, 1716), reprinted in *So Dreadfull a Judgment*, 418, 451; Elizabeth Hanson, *God's Mercy Surmounting Man's Cruelty* (Philadelphia, 1729), 5, 12. "Small breeches" or "small clothes" were a kind of men's undergarment. It is unclear here if Philip was wearing an item of European manufacture, or if this is the term Church uses to mean "breechclout."

27. Richter, *Ordeal of the Longhouse*, chs. 2–3; Richter, "War and Culture";

James Axtell, *The Invasion Within: The Contest of Cultures in Colonial North America* (New York: Oxford University Press, 1985), 302–27; Lepore, *Name of War*, 116–18.

28. "Joseph Bartlett," 332.

29. "Joseph Bartlett," 332; Richter, "War and Culture." Bartlett adds that he placed little faith in the English woman's words: "she being a papist, I placed little reliance on her assertions." Nevertheless her counsel was accurate; as Bartlett remembered, "the old squaw was very kind to me," 332.

30. Pierre Millet, Account of his Captivity with the Oneidas, 1690–91, Ayer Collection 605, 9–12, 15, Newberry Library, Chicago, Ill. The Newberry manuscript is not a seventeenth-century document, but a nineteenth-century translation by Mrs. E. E. Ayer, in a bound notebook circa 1894.

31. T. Brown, *Plain Narrative*, 14–24; Ian K. Steele, *Betrayals: Fort William Henry and the "Massacre"* (New York: Oxford University Press, 1990), 74–75.

32. Cotton Mather, *Decennium Luctuosum: an History of Remarkable Occurences in the long war which New England hath had with the Indian Salvages, 1688–1698* (Boston, 1699), 224; John Gyles, *Memoirs of Odd Adventures, Strange Deliverances, &c* (Boston, 1736), 16; Increase Mather, *Humiliations follow'd with Deliverances* (Boston, 1697), 53; Pote, 174–75.

33. Richter, "War and Culture"; Inga Clendinnen, "The Cost of Courage in Aztec Society," *Past and Present* 107 (1985): 44–89; Inga Clendinnen, *Aztecs: An Interpretation* (Cambridge: Cambridge University Press, 1991), 87–98, 111–52. In *Aztecs*, Clendinnen makes a connection between Iroquois and Aztec ritual torture and execution, 87–88, 93. Richter describes the ritual cannibalism of the Iroquois execution feast but demurs to interpret it, claiming that it "carried great religious significance for the Iroquois, but its full meaning is irretrievable," 534.

34. I do not mean to suggest that Natives always wished to dress like and identify with Europeans. In other places and times, Indians associated European clothing with a loss of status. See, for example, Rebecca Kugel, "'To Work Like a Frenchman': Ojibwe Men's Definitions of Metis Men's Ethinicity in the Early Nineteenth Century," presented at the American Society for Ethnohistory Annual Conference, 1999.

35. Gyles, 32–34. Gyles writes this memoir as a middle-aged man looking back on his adolescence in captivity. Accordingly, he may have consciously or unconsciously shaped his narrative to reflect the politics of the 1730s.

36. John Norton, *The Redeemed Captive* (Boston, 1748), 9, 28; Pote, 116–17.

37. T. Brown, *Plain Narrative*, 19–20.

38. James Axtell, "The White Indians of Colonial America," *William and Mary Quarterly* 3rd ser., 32 (1975): 55–88; reprinted in *The European and the Indian: Essays in the Ethnohistory of Colonial North America* (New York: Oxford University Press, 1981), 168–206; Alden T. Vaughan and Daniel K. Richter, "Crossing the Cultural Divide: Indians and New Englanders, 1605–1763," *American Antiquarian Society Proceedings* 90 (April 16, 1980): 23–99; especially tables 6 and 7. Vaughan and Richter estimate that a quarter of captive men's fates are entirely unknown. For an in-depth look at one family's experience when a captive daughter remained with

and married among the Indians, see John Demos, *The Unredeemed Captive: A Family Story from Early America* (New York: Alfred A. Knopf, 1994).

39. Emma Lewis Coleman, *New England Captives Carried to Canada, between 1677 and 1760 during the French and Indian Wars* (Portland, Maine: The Southworth Press, 1925; reprint, Bowie, Md.: Heritage Books, 1989), vols. 1 and 2.

40. As Anne McClintock argues in *Imperial Leather: Race, Gender, and Sexuality in the Colonial Contest* (New York and London: Routledge, 1995), "cross-dressing can likewise be mobilized for a variety of political purposes," radical and reactionary, 67. Tobin also argues that "positionality is crucial, therefore, in determining the political effect of cross-dressing," *Picturing Imperial Power*, 90.

41. Bradford, 117–18; Usher, as quoted by Axtell, *Invasion Within*, 145. On Robin Cassicinamon's service to and rewards from the English, see *The Public Records of the Colony of Connecticut* (Hartford: Lockwood & Brainard Company, 1850–90), 2:289, 336, 346, 406, 431, 441.

42. *The Public Records of the Colony of Connecticut*, 2:310, 369, 370, 408, 441.

43. *The Public Records of the Colony of Connecticut* (Hartford: Lockwood & Brainard Company, 1850–90), 8:72–73. The clothing offered Ben Uncas and his wife was doubtlessly a sign of their status as well as of their newfound Christian aspirations. When a more obscure Indian, Atchetoset, requested that he and his family be instructed in Christianity, "and that his children may be taught to read, and that thereby they may with greater ease understand the principles of said religion," no clothing was forthcoming from the governor. However, the Assembly voted that twenty pounds be raised to pay for the schooling and instruction required.

44. Axtell, *Invasion Within*, chs. 7–9, especially 169–77; Daniel Gookin, *Historical Collections of the Indians in New England, Massachusetts Historical Society Collections*, 1st ser., 1 (1792), 165; *The Public Records of the Colony of Connecticut* 3:497. The United Colonies of New England was a military and political alliance among the orthodox puritan colonies founded in 1643 in the wake of Miantonomi's threatened uprising against all English settlements in New England, and it included the colonies of Massachusetts, Plymouth, Connecticut, and New Haven.

Taking on European-style clothing became a sign of conversion not just for Indians in colonial America but for others as well. Jon F. Sensbach, in *A Separate Canaan: The Making of an Afro-Moravian World in North Carolina, 1763–1840* (Chapel Hill: University of North Carolina Press, 1998), notes that African American Moravians were clothed as white Moravians, 136–37.

45. James Axtell, "The English Colonial Impact on Indian Culture," in *The European and the Indian*, 245–71; William Cronon, *Changes in the Land: Indians, Colonists, and the Ecology of New England* (New York: Hill and Wang, 1983), 92–95; Shannon, "Dressing for Success."

46. John Williams, *The Redeemed Captive, Returning to Zion* (Boston, 1707), 5; Pote, 20–21; Nehemiah How, *A Narrative of the Captivity of . . . who was taken by the Indians at the Great Meadow-Fort above Fort-Dummer . . . October 11, 1745* (Boston, 1748), 6–7. Baumgarten documents the continuing preference for Indian shoes and leggings for Anglo-American soldiers in the Seven Years' War and the Revolutionary War in "Leather Stockings and Hunting Shirts," 260–63.

47. As quoted by Axtell, *Invasion Within*, 309.

48. Doggett family collection, Minot Family Correspondence, 1708–52: Letter 5: Col. Harmor's & Capt. Heath's letter to Col. Wm. Goffe, January 21, 1721/22, at the Maine Historical Society, Portland.

49. Richter, *Ordeal of the Longhouse*, 79–87; Paul J. Lindholdt, ed., *John Josselyn, Colonial Traveler: A Critical Edition of Two Voyages to New-England* (Hanover, N.H.: University Press of New England, 1988), 92–93; Mary Rowlandson, *The Sovereignty & Goodness of God . . . being a Narrative of the Captivity and Restoration of Mrs. Mary Rowlandson* (Boston, 1682), reprinted in *So Dreadfull a Judgment: Puritan Responses to King Philip's War, 1676–1677*, ed. Richard Slotkin and James K. Folsom (Middletown, Conn.: Wesleyan University Press, 1978), 333, 337–38, 342, 345, 351–52, 354. Increase Mather, in *An Essay for the Recording of Illustrious Providences* (Boston, 1684), reports that a male captive, Quinton Stockwell, was also asked to sew a shirt for his Indian masters, 45.

50. Jean O'Brien, *Disposession by Degrees: Indian Land and Identity in Natick, Massachusetts, 1650–1790* (Cambridge: Cambridge University Press, 1997), 61–90; Lepore, *Name of War*, 28–41, 136–49; Kristina Bross, "'That Epithet of Praying': The Villification of Praying Indians during King Philip's War," in *Fear Itself: Enemies Real and Imagined in American Culture*, ed. Nancy Lusignan Schultz (West Lafayette, Ind.: Purdue University Press, 1999), 53–67. Bross also notes English anxiety about Indians wearing European-style clothing during King Philip's War in "'That Epithet of Praying': The Praying Indian in Early New England Literature" (Ph.D. diss., University of Chicago, 1997), 193–94.

51. Hanson, *God's Mercy*, 5–6; copies of four documents on Fort St. George from SC1 45X, Massachusetts Archives Collection 29:154–57, Massachusetts State Archives, Boston, in Coll. S-2029, Maine Historical Society, Portland; Eastburn, *Faithful Narrative*, 24.

52. The only restrictions put on plunder were on raping "virgins" and killing women, children, and unarmed men. No moral or ethical limits were put on the plundering of property—in fact, the authors of these treatises spend much more time emphasizing that soldiers must pool their plunder and let the officers divide it. Their chief concern was preventing the breakdown of morale and military hierarchies that resulted from soldiers keeping the spoils of war to themselves. See, for example, Francis Markham, *Five decades of epistles of warre* (London, 1622); and William Freke, *Select Essays tending to the universal reformation of learning: concluded with the art of war, or a summary of the martial precepts necessary for an officer* (London, 1693).

53. Axtell, "English Colonial Impact."

54. Rowlandson, *Soveraignty & Goodness of God*, 344. Teresa A. Tolouse, in "'My Own Credit': Strategies of (E)Valuation in Mary Rowlandson's Captivity Narrative," *American Literature* 64 (1992): 655–76, portrays Rowlandson as acutely sensitive to slights to her status as a Christian and as an elite English woman. On Indian versus English gender roles, see Kathleen M. Brown, "The Anglo-Algonquian Gender Frontier," in *Negotiators of Change: Historical Perspectives on Native American Women*, ed. Nancy Shoemaker (New York: Routledge, 1995), 26–48; and Brown, *Good Wives*, chs. 1–2. Michael L. Fickes suggests that Native women would have been equally frustrated with English expectations of them in captivity in "'They

Could Not Endure That Yoke': The Captivity of Pequot Women and Children After the War of 1637," *New England Quarterly* 73 (March 2000): 58–81.

55. Thompson, *New England's Crisis*, 218; Brown, *Good Wives*, ch. 2; David Kuchta, "The Making of the Self-Made Man: Class, Clothing, and English Masculinity, 1688–1832," in *The Sex of Things: Gender and Consumption in Historical Perspective* (Berkeley: University of California Press, 1996), 54–78; Joan Pong Linton, "*Jack of Newbery* and Drake in California: Domestic and Colonial Narratives of English Cloth and Manhood," *ELH* 59 (1992): 23–51.

56. Increase Mather, *A Brief History of the Warr with the Indians in New-England* (Boston, 1676), reprinted in *So Dreadfull a Judgment*, 90.

57. Lepore makes this point for King Philip's War, *Name of War*, 79–83.

58. Rowlandson, *Soveraignty & Goodness of God*, 323–25; 354.

59. Axtell, "The Unkindest Cut, or Who Invented Scalping," in *The European and the Indian*, 16–38.

60. I. Mather, *Brief History*, 98, 100, 116, 120; William Hubbard, *A Narrative of the Troubles with the Indians in New-England* (Boston, 1677), 73–75; I. Mather, *Humiliations*, 45. I have never seen any evidence that English puritans circumcised their boy children, so Increase Mather's use of the term "uncircumcised" to describe the Indians is probably metaphorical. It is significant, however, that his basis of comparison for Indian and English men is penile.

61. Williams, *The Redeemed Captive*, 11; Memorial of James Whidden, SC1 45X, Massachusetts Archives Collection, 74:13, Massachusetts State Archives, Boston; How, *Narrative of the Captivity*, 4; Henry Grace, *History of the Life and Sufferings of Henry Grace* (Basingstoke, 1764), 13; Eastburn, *Faithful Narrative*, 6–7, 10, 17; James Derkinderen, *A narrative of the sufferings of James Derkinderen* (Philadelphia, 1796), 3–4. For more examples, see C. Mather, *Decennium Luctuosum*, 36, 51, 70–71.

62. Underhill, *Newes from America*, 17.

63. Church, *Entertaining Passages*, 460. In their introductory essay to Church's narrative, Slotkin and Folsom note that rather than Philip's death, this rendering of tribute is the climax of Church's narrative, and they argue that the wampum belts represent the transfer of power from Philip "to a proven worthy successor. The King of the Woods has died, and his slayer is crowned in his place," 384–85. Lepore says that "Philip's royalties" ultimately were sent to King Charles II, *Name of War*, 174.

64. Rowlandson, *Soveraignty & Goodness of God*, 349; C. Mather, *Decennium Luctuosum*, 85. See Samuel Sewall's commentary on the death of Dummer in a letter to John Ive dated February 19, 1691/92: "Major Hutchinson sets forward this day, being chief Commander of Souldiers and Inhabitants for the Eastern parts. Twas an amazing stroke that was given us. when York, a Town two days journey from hence, was in a great measure destroy'd about fifte persons kill'd and near ninty captivated. The Reverend Mr. Shubael Dummer, their godly learned pastor, was shot dead, off his horse, as is suppos'd; which is the more sorrowfull to me, because my Mothers Cousin german and my very good friend. This was on the 25th of Janr., the poor people being wretchedly secure because no hurt had been done since the 25th. October till that time. Mr. D. writt me a Letter of the 19th. Janr. full of love, the last words of which were. 'The Lord grant a gracious effect to the desires of the last Fast.

Send good news from O.E.' The News from England by Dolbery, and of this horrid Tragedy, came to us, as it were, in one moment," Samuel Sewall, *Letter-book,* in the *Collections of the Massachusetts Historical Society* (Boston: Massachusetts Historical Society, 1886–88), 6th ser., 1:129. Many thanks to Mark Peterson for this reference.

65. Captain Cyprian Southack to Dudley, May 17, 1703, in *Collections of the Maine Historical Society,* ser. 1, vol. 3 (Portland: Maine Historical Society, 1853), 347; petition of Samuel Whitney, SC1 45X, Massachusetts Archives Collection, 74:46–47, Massachusetts State Archives, Boston, as quoted in the Coleman papers, Massachusetts Historical Society, Boston, Mass.; T. Brown, *Plain Narrative,* 14.

66. Dianne Dugaw, *Warrior Women and Popular Balladry, 1650–1850* (Cambridge: Cambridge University Press, 1989), chs. 5–7. Dugaw notes that she has found more than a hundred popular ballads in the English and American traditions, 2; Dianne Dugaw, ed., *The Female Soldier; Or, the Surprising Life and Adventures of Hannah Snell* (London, 1750; reprinted by the Augustan Reprint Society, 1989), 1–2. Dugaw says that Snell's story was taken up by both *Gentleman's Magazine* and *Scots Magazine* in July of 1750, xii; Anne Spencer Lombard, in "Playing the Man: Conceptions of Masculinity in Anglo-American New England, 1675 to 1765" (Ph.D. diss., University of California, Los Angeles, 1998), notes that Snell's story was republished in the *Boston Weekly News Letter,* December 6, 1750.

67. Dugaw, *Warrior Women,* 52–53.

68. Similarly, Patricia U. Bonomi has shown how allegations of transvestism were used to impugn the historical reputation of an early eighteenth-century royal governor of New York and New Jersey. *The Lord Cornbury Scandal: The Politics of Reputation in British America* (Chapel Hill: University of North Carolina Press, 1998), especially chs. 5–7.

69. C. Mather, *Decennium Luctuosum,* 94; Jabez Fitch, "A Brief Narrative of several things respecting the Province of New Hampshire in New-England," 1728–29, Massachusetts Historical Society, Boston; Samuel Penhallow, *The History of the Wars of New-England with the Eastern Indians* (Cincinnati: J. Harpel, 1859), 41–42. Cotton Mather in *Decennium Luctuosum* reported that a skillful use of English clothing by just one man could similarly enhance his fighting abilities. He tells the story of Thomas Bickford, who sent his family away to safety and stayed at his home alone to defend it against the Indians at Oyster River: "His main *Strategem* was, to Change his *Livery* as frequently as he could; appearing Sometimes in one *Coat,* Sometimes in a *Cap*; which caused his Beseigers, to mistake this *One* for *Many* Defendents. In fine, The pittiful Wretches, despairing to *Beat* him out of his House, e'en left him in it; whereas many that opened unto them, upon their Solemn Engagements of giving them Life and Good Quarter, were barbarously butchered by them," 122.

70. Underhill, *Newes from America,* 18; How, *Narrative of the Captivity,* 6.

Chapter 3

1. Alden T. Vaughan and Daniel K. Richter, in "Crossing the Cultural Divide: Indians and New Englanders, 1605–1763," *American Antiquarian Society Proceedings*

90 (April 16, 1980): 23–99, estimate that at least 1,579 English men, women, and children were taken between 1675 and 1763.

2. John Gyles, *Memoirs of Odd Adventures* (Boston, 1736), 4–5; Mary Rowlandson, *The Soveraignty & Goodness of God . . . being a Narrative of the Captivity and Restoration of Mrs. Mary Rowlandson* (Boston, 1682), reprinted in *So Dreadfull a Judgment: Puritan Responses to King Philip's War, 1676–1677*, ed. Richard Slotkin and James K. Folsom (Middletown, Conn.: Wesleyan University Press, 1978), 329, 341; Emma Lewis Coleman, *New England Captives Carried to Canada* (Portland, Maine: The Southworth Press, 1925; reprint, Bowie, Md.: Heritage Books, 1989), 1:169.

3. Ann Marie Plane has shown how English missionaries focused on reforming Indian families by attempting to replace linear kinship ties with monogamous marriage in *Colonial Intimacies: Indian Marriage in Early New England* (Ithaca, N.Y.: Cornell University Press, 2000), especially introduction and chs. 1–3.

4. James Axtell, "The White Indians of Colonial America," *William and Mary Quarterly* 3rd ser., 32 (1975): 55–88, reprinted in his *The European and the Indian: Essays in the Ethnohistory of Colonial North America* (New York: Oxford University Press, 1981); Axtell, *The Invasion Within: The Contest of Cultures in Colonial North America* (New York: Oxford University Press, 1985), especially chs. 12–13; June Namias, *White Captives: Gender and Ethnicity on the American Frontier* (Chapel Hill: University of North Carolina Press, 1993); John Demos, *The Unredeemed Captive: A Family Story from Early America* (New York: Knopf, 1994). A recent exception to this rule is Evan Haefeli and Kevin Sweeney, *Captors and Captives: The 1704 French and Indian Raid on Deerfield* (Amherst: University of Massachusetts Press, 2003), as its analysis is grounded in the history and experiences of French, Indian, and English peoples alike.

5. The cases of soldiers taken into captivity from military installations or in battle in the wars of the 1740s and 1750s is considered more fully in Chapter 5.

6. Pauline Turner Strong, in *Captive Selves, Captivating Others: The Politics and Poetics of Colonial American Captivity Narratives* (Boulder, Colo.: Westview Press, 1999), 4, describes the "hegemonic tradition" of Anglo-American captivity narratives. Quotations from Elizabeth Hanson, *God's Mercy Surmounting Man's Cruelty* (Philadelphia, 1729), passim.

7. Peter Wood, *Black Majority: Negroes in Colonial South Carolina from 1670 through the Stono Rebellion* (New York: W. W. Norton & Co., 1974); Edmund Morgan, *American Slavery, American Freedom: the Ordeal of Colonial Virginia* (New York: W. W. Norton & Co., 1975); Allan Kulikoff, *Tobacco and Slaves: The Development of Southern Cultures in the Chesapeake, 1680–1800* (Chapel Hill: University of North Carolina Press, 1986); Kathleen M. Brown, *Good Wives, Nasty Wenches, and Anxious Patriarchs: Gender, Race, and Power in Colonial Virginia* (Chapel Hill: University of North Carolina Press, 1996).

8. *The Journal of John Winthrop, 1630–1649*, abridged edition, ed. Richard S. Dunn and Laetitia Yeandle (Cambridge, Mass.: Belknap Press of Harvard University Press, 1996), 1–2.

9. John Demos, *A Little Commonwealth: Family Life in Plymouth Colony* (London: Oxford University Press, 1970); Susan D. Amussen, *An Ordered Society:*

Gender and Class in Early Modern England (Oxford: Oxford University Press, 1988); Brown, *Good Wives*, ch. 1; Mary Beth Norton, *Founding Mothers and Fathers: Gendered Power and the Forming of American Society* (New York: Alfred A. Knopf, 1996), 1–137.

10. Melvin Yazawa, *From Colonies to Commonwealth: Familial Ideology and the Beginnings of the American Republic* (Baltimore: Johns Hopkins University Press, 1985); Lynn Hunt, *The Family Romance of the French Revolution* (Berkeley: University of California Press, 1992).

11. Edmund S. Morgan, *The Puritan Family: Religion and Domestic Relations in Seventeenth-Century New England* (Boston: Trustees of the Public Library, 1944; reprint, New York: Harper and Row, 1966); Demos, *Little Commonwealth*.

12. Cornelia Hughes Dayton, *Women Before the Bar: Gender, Law, and Society in Connecticut, 1639–1789* (Chapel Hill: University of North Carolina Press, 1995); Brown, *Good Wives*; Norton, *Founding Mothers and Fathers*; Ann M. Little, "A 'Wel Ordered Commonwealth': Gender and Politics in New Haven Colony, 1636–1690" (Ph.D. diss., University of Pennsylvania, 1996), chs. 2, 4–5; Little, "'Shee would bump his mouldy britch': Authority, Masculinity, and the Harried Husbands of New Haven Colony, 1638–1670," in *Lethal Imagination: Violence and Brutality in American History*, ed. Michael Bellesiles (New York: New York University Press, 1999), 43–66; Kirsten Fischer, *Suspect Relations: Sex, Race, and Resistance in Colonial North Carolina* (Ithaca, N.Y.: Cornell University Press, 2002).

13. Amussen, *Ordered Society*; Lyndal Roper, *The Holy Household: Women and Morals in Reformation Augsburg* (Oxford: Oxford University Press, 1989).

14. Philip Gura, *A Glimpse of Sion's Glory: Puritan Radicalism in New England, 1620–1660* (Middletown, Conn.: Wesleyan University Press, 1984); Carla Gardina Pestana, *Quakers and Baptists in Colonial Massachusetts* (Cambridge: Cambridge University Press, 1991); Susan Juster, *Disorderly Women: Sexual Politics & Evangelicalism in Revolutionary New England* (Ithaca, N.Y.: Cornell University Press, 1994); Michael P. Winship, *Making Heretics: Militant Protestantism and Free Grace in Massachusetts, 1636–1641* (Princeton, N.J.: Princeton University Press, 2002).

15. Cotton Mather, *Decennium Luctuosum: an History of Remarkable Occurences in the long war which New England hath had with the Indian Salvages, 1688–1698* (Boston, 1699), 217. Mather takes his metaphor of the rod and the strokes of Heaven from Micah 6:9. See also Richard Trexler, *Sex and Conquest: Gendered Violence, Political Order, and the European Conquest of the Americas* (Ithaca, N.Y.: Cornell University Press, 1995).

16. C. Mather, *Decennium Luctuosum*, 217–18.

17. Ibid., 218–20.

18. Ibid., 220–21.

19. Ibid., 221–22.

20. On Algonquian work and gender roles, see Robert Steven Grumet, "Sunksquaws, Shamans, and Tradeswomen: Middle Atlantic Coastal Algonquian Women during the 17th and 18th Centuries," in *Women and Colonization: Anthropological Perspectives*, ed. Mona Etienne and Eleanor Leacock (New York: Praeger, 1980), 43–62; William Cronon, *Changes in the Land: Indians, Colonists, and the Ecology of New England* (New York: Hill and Wang, 1983), ch. 3; Kathleen J. Bragdon, *Native*

Peoples of Southern New England, 1500–1650 (Norman: University of Oklahoma Press, 1996), ch. 3; Plane, *Colonial Intimacies,* 18–26.

On Iroquois work and gender roles, see Elisabeth Tooker, "Women in Iroquois Society," in *Extending the Rafters: Interdisciplinary Approaches to Iroquoian Studies,* ed. Michael K. Foster, Jack Campisi, and Marianne Mithun (Albany, N.Y.: SUNY Press, 1984), 109–23; Daniel K. Richter, *The Ordeal of the Longhouse: The Peoples of the Iroquois League in the Era of European Colonization* (Chapel Hill: University of North Carolina Press, 1992), 22–23, 33–35, 42–49; and Nancy Shoemaker, "The Rise or Fall of Iroquois Women," *Journal of Women's History* 2 (1991): 39–57.

21. Bragdon makes this point for Native women as well: "Women's work among the Ninnimissinuaok profoundly shaped the social relations, political structure, and ideology of their societies. However, in coastal communities at least, women were sometimes devalued in spite of their great contributions to economy," *Native Peoples of Southern New England,* 51.

22. Tooker, "Women in Iroquois Society"; Richter, *Ordeal of the Longhouse,* 42–49; Plane, *Colonial Intimacies,* 18–26. Tooker argues that the role women played in choosing sachems was very limited, and probably had more to do with the fact that the women who exercised this privilege came from elite families than any recognition of women's political power.

23. *Travels in New France by J.C.B.,* ed. Sylvester K. Stevens, Donald H. Kent, and Emma Edith Woods (Harrisburg: Pennsylvania Historical Commission, 1941), 140–45; *Nation Iroquoise: A Seventeenth-Century Ethnography of the Iroquois,* ed. José António Brandão (Lincoln: University of Nebraska Press, 2003), 66–67.

24. Richter, *Ordeal of the Longhouse,* 20; Bragdon, *Native Peoples of Southern New England,* ch. 7, and "Gender as a Social Category in Native Southern New England," *Ethnohistory* 43 (1996): 573–592. In *Colonial Intimacies,* Plane suggests that female lineage was important among Algonquians too, and that women's influence in family life remained great even after the conversion and settling of praying Indians, 18–26, 111–15.

25. Increase Mather, *A Relation of the Troubles which have hapned in New-England* (Boston, 1677), 9; Samuel Penhallow, *The History of the Wars of New-England with the Eastern Indians* (Cincinnati: J. Harpel, 1859), 47–49.

26. *Travels in New France by J.C.B.,* 72.

27. Paul J. Lindholdt, ed., *John Josselyn, Colonial Traveler: a Critical Edition of Two Voyages to New-England* (Hanover, N.H.: University Press of New England, 1988), 92; Axtell, *European and the Indian,* 160; Axtell, *Invasion Within,* 209.

28. Richter, *Ordeal of the Longhouse,* 19–22; Cronon, *Changes in the Land,* 52–56; Plane, *Colonial Intimacies,* chs. 2 and 4.

29. Thomas Morton, *New English Canaan, or New Canaan* (Amsterdam, 1637), 32. See Plane's treatment of this anecdote in Plane, *Colonial Intimacies,* 14–17.

30. Gyles, *Memoirs of Odd Adventures,* 1–2; Nehemiah How, *A narrative of the captivity of . . . who was taken by the Indians at the Great Meadow-Fort above Fort-Dummer . . . October 11, 1745* (Boston, 1748), 3; Henry Grace, *History of the Life and Sufferings of Henry Grace* (Basingstoke, 1764), 10–11; Bunker Gay, *A genuine and correct account of the captivity, sufferings & deliverance of Mrs. Jemima Howe, of Hinsdale in New-Hampshire* (Boston, 1792), 3. On the Western Abenaki, see Colin G.

Calloway, *The Western Abenakis of Vermont, 1600–1800: War, Migration, and the Survival of an Indian People* (Norman: University of Oklahoma Press, 1990).

31. Rowlandson, *Soveraignty & Goodness of God*, 324, 326.

32. Cotton Mather, *Humiliations follow'd with Deliverances* (Boston, 1697), 41–42, 51; Hanson, *God's Mercy*, 4–5; Gay, *Genuine and correct account*, 4. Some scholars have argued that as a Quaker, Hanson's narrative is qualitatively different from those written by puritans—see for example, Strong, *Captive Selves*, 161–66, and Laurel Thatcher Ulrich, *Good Wives: Image and Reality in the Lives of Women in Northern New England, 1650–1750* (New York: Oxford University Press, 1980), 226–34. However, the similarities in the ways in which they undermine Indian mastery are much more striking than their differences.

33. Hanson, *God's Mercy*, 9–10, 13–14; 24–25; Susanna Johnson, *A Narrative of the Captivity of Mrs. Johnson, together with a Narrative of James Johnson*, 3rd edition (Windsor, Vt.: 1814; reprint, Bowie, Md.: Heritage Books, 1990), 35–37; Rowlandson, *Soveraignty & Goodness of God*, 326–27; John Norton, *The Redeemed Captive* (Boston, 1748), 14. Johnson's story was first published by John C. Chamberlain in 1796, but she wrote and published her own captivity narrative in 1807 and completed a third edition of her story just before her death in 1810 that was published in 1814. An early twentieth-century editor of the third edition assures us that "the last two editions are largely Mrs. Johnson's own handiwork, and were revised and edited at her request," *Narrative of the Captivity*, xiii.

34. John Williams, *The Redeemed Captive, Returning to Zion* (Boston, 1707), 11–13; Demos, *Unredeemed Captive*.

35. C. Mather, *Decennium Luctuosum*, 52–57, 89–90.

36. Rowlandson, *Soveraignty & Goodness of God*, 326, 336; Johnson, *Narrative of the Captivity*, 32.

37. Daniel K. Richter, "War and Culture: The Iroquois Experience," *William and Mary Quarterly* 3rd ser., 40 (1983): 528–59; Strong, *Captive Selves*, 77–83; Haefeli and Sweeney, *Captors and Captives*, 125–63.

38. Rowlandson, *Soveraignty & Goodness of God*, 328–29; Hanson, *God's Mercy*, 8–10; Johnson, *Narrative of the Captivity*, 31.

39. Stephen Williams's captivity narrative is published in *A Biographical Memoir of the Rev. John Williams* (Greenfield, Mass.: C. J. J. Ingersoll, 1837), 103; Gyles, *Memoirs of Odd Adventures*, 4–5. Their birth dates are confirmed by Coleman, *New England Captives*, 1:169, 2:52.

40. Gay, *Genuine and correct account*, 7, 9–10, 13–14; "Captivity Narrative of Joseph Bartlett," in Joshua Coffin, *A Sketch of the History of Newbury, Newburyport, and West Newbury from 1635 to 1845* (Boston: S. G. Drake, 1845), in appendix, 331–34.

41. How, *narrative of the captivity*, 5; Norton, *Redeemed Captive*, 12–13; John Williams, *Redeemed Captive*, 23–25; C. Mather, *Humiliations follow'd with Deliverances* (the narratives of Hannah Duston and Hannah Swarton, 41–72, passim), *Decennium Luctuosum*, 52–57, and *A Memorial of the Present Deplorable State of New-England* (Boston, 1707), 32ff; Increase Mather, *An Essay for the Recording of Illustrious Providences* (Boston, 1684), 39–57, passim. Other examples of English men referring to their Indian "masters": William Pote, Jr., original ms. journal kept by him 1745–47 during captivity among the French & Indians, Ayer Collection, New-

berry Library, Chicago, Ill., 25–26, 29, 31, 39, 43, and passim; Robert Eastburn, *A Faithful Narrative* (Philadelphia, 1758), 10.

42. Haefeli and Sweeney present an admirably complex discussion of the calculations involved in deciding whether to adopt or sell English captives to the French in *Captors and Captives*, 147–51.

43. Richard White, *The Middle Ground: Indians, Empires, and Republics in the Great Lakes Region, 1650–1815* (Cambridge: Cambridge University Press, 1991), 240–68; Fred Anderson, *Crucible of War: The Seven Years' War and the Fate of Empire in British North America, 1754–1766* (New York: Alfred A. Knopf, 2000), 237–38; Haefeli and Sweeney, *Captors and Captives*, 147–51.

44. Namias remarks pithily on this feature of colonial captivity narratives in *White Captives*: "Colonial women were repulsed by native food; mid- to late nineteenth-century women were repulsed by dirt," 100.

45. Cronon, *Changes in the Land*, 33–35, 53–57; Christopher Hill, *The World Turned Upside Down: Radical Ideas During the English Revolution* (New York: Viking Press, 1972), 107–50. On New England's particular resentment and fear of poverty and its efforts to "warn out" the undeserving poor, see Ruth Herndon, *Unwelcome Americans: Living on the Margin in Early New England* (Philadelphia: University of Pennsylvania Press, 2001). On poverty in colonial Anglo-America, see Billy G. Smith, *Down and Out in Early America* (University Park: Pennsylvania State University Press, 2004).

46. Rowlandson, *Soveraignty & Goodness of God*, 333, 337, 339, 347, 359; Hanson, *God's Mercy*, 12–13, 24; Gay, *Genuine and correct account*, 8–9, 12. Strong, in *Captive Selves*, has also noted Elizabeth Hanson's fascination with food, 163, and Ulrich notes the interest Rowlandson took in her diet in captivity, *Good Wives*, 227–30. On English anxieties about food and identity in colonial America, see Trudy Eden, "Food, Assimilation, and the Malleability of the Human Body in Early Virginia," in *A Centre of Wonders: The Body in Early America*, ed. Janet Moore Lindman and Michelle Lise Tarter (Ithaca, N.Y.: Cornell University Press, 2001), 29–42.

47. *Memoir of the Rev. John Williams*, 105; Gyles, *Memoirs of Odd Adventures*, 8; Grace, *History of the Life*, 16–17; Hanson, *God's Mercy*, 22–23. See Strong's discussion of Gyles in *Captive Selves*, 166–72. (Alternative spellings for Maliseet include Malecite and Maliceet.)

48. Cronon, *Changes in the Land*, chs. 3–4; Axtell, *Invasion Within*, 166–67; Quinton Stockwell's captivity narrative in I. Mather, *Illustrious Providences*, 49ff.; Gay, *Genuine and correct account*, 12–13.

49. Lisa Wilson, *Ye Heart of a Man: The Domestic Life of Men in Colonial New England* (New Haven, Conn.: Yale University Press, 1999), ch. 4.

50. Hanson, *God's Mercy*, 19–20.

51. Ibid., 20–21; Little, "'Shee would bump his mouldy britch.'"

52. Hanson, *God's Mercy*, 22.

53. Ibid., 20–22.

54. Ibid., 24–30.

55. Gay, *Genuine and correct account*, 13–15.

56. Penhallow, *History of the Wars*, 47. The child allegedly saved from being

roasted and eaten, who like her mother was named Hannah Parsons, was baptized Catholic in Montreal, became a naturalized French citizen, married a French Canadian man, and gave birth to ten children in Montreal and Québec (Coleman, *New England Captives*, 1:410–13).

57. Hanson, *God's Mercy*, 26.

58. On Rowlandson's narrative, see Teresa A. Tolouse, "'My Own Credit': Strategies of (E)Valuation in Mary Rowlandson's Captivity Narrative," *American Literature* 64 (1992): 655–76; Neal Salisbury, ed., *The Sovereignty and Goodness of God, Together with the Faithfulness of His Promises Displayed, Being a Narrative of the Captivity and Restoration of Mrs. Mary Rowlandson and Related Documents* (Boston: Bedford Books, 1997), 1–60. Christopher Castiglia sees Rowlandson's narrative as having much more subversive potential than Tolouse, Salisbury, or I, as he argues in *Bound and Determined: Captivity, Culture-Crossing, and White Womanhood from Mary Rowlandson to Patti Hearst* (Chicago: University of Chicago Press, 1996).

59. Rowlandson, *Soveraignty & Goodness of God*, 333–34.

60. Ibid., 336–37.

61. Ibid., 337.

62. I. Mather, *Illustrious Providences*, 42, 45.

63. Johnson, *Narrative of the Captivity*, 65–70. On Odanak and other mission towns in the St. Lawrence river valley, see Haefeli and Sweeney, *Captors and Captives*, ch. 3 , especially 73–77.

64. Gay, *Genuine and correct account*, 15; Namias, *White Captives*, ch. 3.

Chapter 4

1. Frances E. Dolan, *Whores of Babylon: Catholicism, Gender, and Seventeenth-Century Print Culture* (Ithaca, N.Y.: Cornell University Press, 1999).

2. C. Alice Baker, *True Stories of New England Captives Carried to Canada during the Old French and Indian Wars* (Cambridge, Mass.: E. A. Hall, 1897; reprint, Bowie, Md.: Heritage Books, 1990); James Axtell, *The Invasion Within: The Contest of Cultures in Colonial North America* (New York: Oxford University Press, 1985), 287–301; Barbara E. Austen, "Captured . . . Never Came Back: Social Networks Among New England Female Captives in Canada, 1689–1763," and Alice N. Nash, "Two Stories of New England Captives: Grizel and Christine Otis of Dover, New Hampshire," both in *New England/New France, 1600–1850*, ed. Peter Benes (Boston: Boston University, 1992), 28–48; William Foster, *The Captors' Narrative: Catholic Women and Their Puritan Men on the Early American Frontier* (Ithaca, N.Y.: Cornell University Press, 2003); Evan Haefeli and Kevin Sweeney, *Captors and Captives: The 1704 French and Indian Raid on Deerfield* (Amherst: University of Massachusetts Press, 2003), 1–7, 145–63, 232–49.

3. On women's alleged vulnerability to the devil's blandishments, see Carol Karlsen, *The Devil in the Shape of a Woman: Witchcraft in Colonial New England* (New York: Norton, 1987), especially chs. 4 and 5; Elizabeth Reis, *Damned Women: Sinners and Witches in Puritan New England* (Ithaca, N.Y.: Cornell University Press,

1997); Dolan, *Whores of Babylon*, 27. On the mission towns, see Haefeli and Sweeney, *Captors and Captives*, ch. 3.

4. For the most part, family history for colonial New France must be reconstructed through public and church records—court, colonial, and notarial records—as diaries, journals, letters, and personal papers are virtually nonexistent. On the lack of sources for family history, see Louise Dechêne, *Habitants and Merchants in Seventeenth Century Montreal* (Paris: Plons, 1974; English translation, Montreal: McGill-Queen's University Press, 1992), 237. On the lack of a printing press in Canada, see William J. Eccles, *The French in North America, 1500–1783*, revised edition (East Lansing: Michigan State University Press, 1998), 146–48.

5. John Demos, *The Unredeemed Captive: A Family Story from Early America* (New York: Alfred A. Knopf, 1994).

6. For reports of French collaboration with the Abenaki during King Philip's War, see Henry Jocelyn and Joshua Scottow to Gov. John Leverett, September 15, 1676, Coll. S-888, misc. box 33/21, Maine Historical Society, Portland; *Documentary History of the State of Maine* (Portland, Maine: Lefavor-Tower, 1869–1916), 4:377–79; Geoffrey Plank, *An Unsettled Conquest: The British Campaign Against the Peoples of Acadia* (Philadelphia: University of Pennsylvania Press, 2000), 17–18.

7. Francis D. Cogliano, *No King, No Popery: Anti-Catholicism in Revolutionary New England* (Westport, Conn.: Greenwood Press, 1995), introduction and chs. 1–2.

8. Linda Colley, *Britons: Forging the Nation, 1707–1837* (New Haven, Conn.: Yale University Press, 1992); Anne McLaren, "Gender, Religion, and Early Modern Nationalism: Elizabeth I, Mary Queen of Scots, and the Genesis of English Anti-Catholicism," *American Historical Review* 107 (June 2002): 739–67; Dolan, *Whores of Babylon*, 6–27; Ana M. Acosta, "Hotbeds of Popery: Convents in the English Literary Imagination," *Eighteenth-Century Fiction* 15:3–4 (2003): 615–42.

9. Cotton Mather, *Humiliations follow'd with Deliverances* (Boston, 1697), 30–31. He made the same historical argument a few years later in *Decennium Luctuosum: an History of Remarkable Occurences in the long war which New England hath had with the Indian Salvages, 1688–1698* (Boston, 1699), but put more emphasis on the failings of the Israelites/New Englanders: "The Grand crime of the Jews, was in relation to the Romans, and God made the Romans the Destroyers of the Jews," 215.

See also Joshua Scottow, *Old Men's Tears for their own Declensions, mixed with Fears of their and posterities further falling off from New England's Primitive Constitution* (Boston, 1691), 16–17, 19. According to the index of Early American Imprints, Series I: Evans, 1639–1800, this pamphlet was reprinted four times, in 1715, 1722, 1749, and 1769, perhaps because its anti-Catholic and anti-French message resonated so well with New Englanders through the eighteenth century.

10. Jeremiah Dummer, *A Letter to a Noble Lord, Concerning the Late Expedition to Canada* (London: A. Baldwin, 1712), 8–9; doc. 5 (anonymous, undated), Israel William Papers, Massachusetts Historical Society, Boston; Francis Jennings, *The Invasion of America: Indians, Colonialism, and the Cant of Conquest* (Chapel Hill: University of North Carolina Press, 1975), 228–53.

On the praying Indians more generally, see Jean O'Brien, *Disposession by Degrees: Indian Land and Identity in Natick, Massachusetts, 1650–1790* (Cambridge:

Cambridge University Press, 1997); and Ann Marie Plane, *Colonial Intimacies: In-dian Marriage in Early New England* (Ithaca, N.Y.: Cornell University Press, 2000).

Many English officials recognized their disadvantage at forging Indian alliances, but they were never able to make mission work central to English colonial policy. See, for example, the letter of John Nelson to Charles Talbot, the Earl of Shrewsbury, 1695, Massachusetts Historical Society, Boston. For more on Nelson, see Richard R. Johnson, *John Nelson, Merchant Adventurer: A Life Between Empires* (New York: Oxford University Press, 1991); and Emerson W. Baker and John G. Reid, *The New England Knight: Sir William Phips, 1651–1695* (Toronto: University of Toronto Press, 1998), 157–59, 250–51.

11. C. Mather, *Decennium Luctuosum*, 81, 215–16.

12. C. Mather, *Humiliations follow'd with Deliverances*, 59–71; Dolan, *Whores of Babylon*, 27; Lorrayne Carroll, "'My *Outward Man'*: The Curious Case of Hannah Swarton," *Early American Literature* 31 (1996): 45–73.

13. "The Captivity Narrative of Joseph Bartlett," in *A Sketch of the History of Newbury, Newburyport, and West Newbury from 1635 to 1845*, ed. Joshua Coffin (Boston: S. G. Drake, 1845), 331–34; Emma Lewis Coleman, *New England Captives Carried to Canada* (Portland, Maine: The Southworth Press, 1925; reprint, Bowie, Md.: Heritage Books, 1989), vols. 1 and 2, passim; *Dictionary of Canadian Biography* (Toronto: University of Toronto Press, 1966–98), 2:467–68 (hereafter cited as *DCB*); C. Alice Baker, *True Stories*, 320–21; letter from Meriel at Montreal, June 25, 1711, to Capt. Johnson Harmon, SC1 45X, Massachusetts Archives Collection, 51:212–13, Massachusetts State Archives, Boston.

14. "Joseph Bartlett," 331–34. For another account of an English man describing and mocking Catholic Mass, see William Pote, Jr., original ms. journal kept by him 1745–47 during captivity among the French & Indians, Ayer Collection, Newberry Library, Chicago, Ill., 40, 75–76. John Gyles also portrays himself as fending off the advances of a French priest successfully, boasting that "dismiss'd and never call'd me to Confession more," in *Memoirs of Odd Adventures* (Boston, 1736), 32–36.

15. C. Mather, *Humiliations follow'd with Deliverances*, 72; Coleman, *New England Captives*, 1:204–8. In her narrative as rendered by Mather, Swarton writes that she also hasn't seen or heard from "a Son of Nineteen years old, whom I never saw since we parted, the next morning after we were taken," (C. Mather, *Humiliations*, 72). Coleman says that there is no further trace of this son, John, in the Canadian records (Coleman 1: 205–6).

16. Elizabeth Hanson, *God's Mercy Surmounting Man's Cruelty* (Philadelphia, 1729), 34; Coleman, *New England Captives*, 2:163.

17. Gyles, *Memoirs of Odd Adventures*, 4–5. For a thorough biography of Gyles and his experiences with the Abenaki and French Catholics, see Foster, *Captors' Narrative*, 110–30.

18. Dolan, *Whores of Babylon*, 85–93.

19. Gyles, 4–5.

20. French Canada's rural isolation, widespread illiteracy, and lack of a printing press mean that surviving colonial records are largely government and court records, parish records of births, deaths, and marriages, and other church records.

Dechêne, *Habitants and Merchants*, 237, 270–72; Allan Greer, "The Pattern of Literacy in Québec, 1745–1899," *Histoire Sociale/Social History* 11 (1978): 295–335.

21. Alden T. Vaughan and Daniel K. Richter, in "Crossing the Cultural Divide: Indians and New Englanders, 1605–1763," *American Antiquarian Society Proceedings* 90 (April 16, 1980): 23–99; author's database compiled from the cases documented by Coleman, *New England Captives*, vols. 1 and 2.

22. Pote, 155. Most captives had to walk themselves to Canada, so it's not surprising that there is only one infant of the thirty-four taken into captivity up to age twelve. There is no reliable birth date available for eleven of the sixty-five females who stayed in Canada. This suggests that they were probably children when taken into captivity, so the actual number of preadolescent captives might be as high as forty-five.

23. See Nash, "Two Stories," and C. Alice Baker, *True Stories*, 5–34, for an interesting example of mother and daughter captives whose decisions contradict the trends described in this chapter. Grizel Otis, widowed in a 1689 attack on Dover, New Hampshire, remained in Canada, converted to Catholicism, and remarried, while her infant daughter, Christine, grew up as a French Catholic only to return to New England as a grown widow, leaving her children behind in Canada. The struggle over her fate was related in a pamphlet published in Boston meant to fan the flames of New England anti-Catholicism: François Seguenot, *A Letter from a Romish Priest in Canada, To One who was taken Captive in her Infancy, and Instructed in the Romish Faith, but some time ago returned to this her Native Country* (Boston, 1729).

24. Axtell, *Invasion Within*, 291–94; Laurel Thatcher Ulrich, *Good Wives: Image and Reality in the Lives of Women in Northern New England, 1650–1750* (New York: Oxford University Press, 1980), 208–13.

25. Dechêne, *Habitants and Merchants*, 240–49.

26. Trevor Burnard and Ann M. Little, "Where the girls aren't: women as reluctant migrants but rational actors in early America," in *Re-envisioning U.S. Women's History*, ed. Eileen Boris, Jay Kleinberg, and Vicki Ruiz (forthcoming, Rutgers University Press).

27. Peter Moogk, "Manon's Fellow Exiles: Emigration from France to North America before 1763," in *Europeans on the Move: Studies on European Migration, 1500–1800*, ed. Nicholas Canny (Oxford: Clarendon Press, 1994), 236–60; Leslie Choquette, *Frenchmen into Peasants: Modernity and Tradition in the Peopling of French Canada* (Cambridge, Mass.: Harvard University Press, 1997), 175–77, 235–37, 271–73; *Collection de Manuscrits contenant Lettres, Memoires, et Autres Documents Historiques Relatifs a la Nouvelle France* (Québec, 1883–84), 1:350–51, 389–90. Dechêne suggests that the situation for unmarried men in Montreal from 1666–81 was even worse than these numbers suggest, claiming that there were ten bachelors for every unmarried woman in a given age group in 1681 (*Habitants and Merchants*, 18, 47).

For a good comparison of immigration to North America, see Leslie Choquette, "French and British Emigration to the North American Colonies: A Comparative Overview," *New England/New France, 1600–1850*, ed. Peter Benes (Boston: Boston University, 1992), 49–59.

28. Ann M. Little, "A "Wel Ordered Commonwealth': Gender and Politics in New Haven Colony, 1636–1690" (Ph.D. diss., University of Pennsylvania, 1996), 180–94.

29. For evidence of the state's drive to bring more properly trained house-wives into Canada, see, for example, the correspondence of Governor Frontenac and Minister Colbert, *Rapport de L'Archiviste de la Province de Québec* (Québec: Ls-A. Proulx, 1927), 7:44, 60, 65–66, 82 (1673–74); and the correspondence of Governor Frontenac and Intendant Bochart Champigny to the Minister, 8:351, 359, 377 (1697–98). Copies of other official correspondence between Québec and Paris are in the Francis Parkman Papers of the Massachusetts Historical Society, Boston. See for example, lettre de M. du Chesneau, November 10, 1679, 1:56; lettre de Monsieur de Meulles, intendant a Québec, November 12, 1682, 1:94–95, 100; lettre de M. Lefebvre de la Barre, Québec, November 4, 1683, 1:120; lettre de Monsieur de Meulles, intendant à Québec, November 12, 1684, 1:197–98; lettre de Champigny, November 16, 1686, 2:456; lettre de Champigny et M. de Dénonville, Gouverneur Général, November 6, 1687, 2:572–74, 594–95. More official correspondence on the recruitment of French women and settlement of French families in New France can be found in *Collections de Manuscrits* 1:393 and vols. 1 and 2, passim.

On the question of the famous "filles du Roi" in particular, see Jan Noel, "New France: Les Femmes Favorisées," in *Rethinking Canada: The Promise of Women's History*, 3rd ed., ed. Veronica Strong-Boag and Anita Clair Fellman (Toronto: Oxford University Press, 1997); *Collections de Manuscrits*, 1:195, 206–07, 210.

30. Leslie Choquette, "'Ces Amazones du Grand Dieu': Women and Mission in Seventeenth-Century Canada," *French Historical Studies* 17 (1992): 627–55; Clark Robenstine, "French Colonial Policy and the Education of Women and Minorities: Louisiana in the Early Eighteenth Century," *History of Education Quarterly* 32 (1992): 193–211; Natalie Zemon Davis, "Marie de l'Incarnation: New Worlds," in *Women on the Margins: Three Seventeenth-Century Lives* (Cambridge, Mass.: Harvard University Press, 1995), 63–139; Patricia Simpson, *Marguerite Bourgeoys and Montreal, 1640–1665* (Montreal: McGill-Queen's University Press, 1997); Greer, "Pattern of Literacy."

On the failure to train Indian women, see, for example, lettre de M. Lefebvre de la Barre, Québec, November 4, 1683, 1:120–21; and lettre de Monsieur de Meulles, intendant à Québec, November 12, 1682, 1:94–95 in the Parkman Papers.

31. Moogk, "Manon's Fellow Exiles"; Noel, "New France"; lettre de M. de Meulles, intendant en Canada, Québec, November 12, 1684; lettre de M. de Denonville, Gouverneur général de Canada, Québec, May 8, 1686, both in the Parkman Papers 1:197–98 and 346 (translation by Annette H. Tomarken).

32. Database built from information in Coleman, *New England Captives*, vols. 1 and 2. Following Coleman's practice, this database does not include the soldiers taken captive during King George's War or the Seven Years' War. Furthermore, I have chosen to include only those captives who appear in French notarial records, which is why my estimates of those who remained in Canada from 1689 to 1730 are more conservative than those of Vaughan and Richter in "Crossing the Cultural Divide," especially in tables 6 and 7; as well as those of Ulrich in *Good Wives*, 203.

33. I am indebeted to Laurier Turgeon of Laval University, Québec, P.Q., for this insight about borrowing from Indian practices.

34. William Foster has uncovered an extensive network of elite Montrealers who sponsored the redemption and naturalization of English captives in the late seventeenth and early eighteenth centuries, *Captors' Narrative*, ch. 1.

35. *DCB* 2:565–74; Coleman, *New England Captives*, 1:316–17, 330–31, 356–57, 425–35, 2:44–58, 147, 390–91; SC1 45X, Massachusetts Archives Collection, 51:212–13, and 72:13–15, Massachusetts State Archives, Boston; Demos, *Unredeemed Captive*, 35–36; Ann M. Little, "The Life of Mother Marie-Joseph de L'Enfant Jesus, or, How a little English Girl from Wells became a Big French Politician," *Maine History* (Winter 2002), 276–308.

36. Coleman, *New England Captives*, 2: 320–21, 391, 396; Bunker Gay, *A genuine and correct account of the captivity, sufferings & deliverance of Mrs. Jemima Howe, of Hinsdale in New-Hampshire* (Boston, 1792), 16–18; *DCB* 4:662–74.

37. Coleman, *New England Captives*, 1:121–29; Axtell, *Invasion Within*, 290–91. See also Dechêne's evidence on Montreal, which shows the number of single women over age fifteen eclipsing that of their male cohort by nearly 2:1 in 1713, a pattern that held through 1739, Table A, 292–93.

38. Choquette, "'Ces Amazones du Grand Dieu'"; Davis, *Women on the Margins*; Little, "Mother Marie-Joseph"; Foster, *Captors' Narrative*.

39. The four nuns were Mary Anne Davis, Lydia Longley, Mary Silver, and Esther Wheelwright (Coleman, *New England Captives*, 1:268–71, 283–86, 356–58, 425–35). All were taken during King William's War or Queen Anne's War, within the same span of fifteen years.

40. However, Mary Storer St. Germaine (see below) was apparently offered the opportunity to send her children from Montreal to Boston, presumably to be educated there. She never sent her children to Boston, but there may have been other than religious reasons for declining (Mary Storer St. Germaine to Ebenezer Storer, June 26, 1725, Mary Storer Papers, 1725–64, Massachusetts Historical Society, Boston).

41. Austen, "Captured . . . Never Came Back"; Nash, "Two Stories"; Coleman, *New England Captives*, vols. 1 and 2, passim.

42. John Norton, *The Redeemed Captive* (Boston, 1748), 23–26; Coleman, *New England Captives*, 1:413–25; Axtell, *Invasion Within*, 293–94.

43. Susanna Johnson, *A Narrative of the Captivity of Mrs. Johnson, together with a Narrative of James Johnson*, 3rd ed. (Windsor, Vt., 1814; reprint, Bowie, Md.: Heritage Books, 1990), 89–90; C. Alice Baker, *True Stories*, 35–68; Little, "Mother Marie-Joseph."

44. Nash, in "Two Stories" says that French officials actively opposed Christine Otis's return to New England, since she was a naturalized citizen and a baptized Catholic, 44.

45. Hanson, *God's Mercy*, 7, 14, 35–36; Coleman *New England Captives*, 1:20–21, 2:161–66.

46. Hanson, *God's Mercy*, 37–39; Samuel Penhallow, *The History of the Wars of New-England with the Eastern Indians* (Cincinnati: J. Harpel, 1859), 104.

47. Hanson, *God's Mercy*, 38–39; Coleman *New England Captives*, 2:165–66;

personal communication with Arthur Worrall, May 2001 on the Dover Monthly Meeting (men's meeting), July 20, 1728.

48. Coleman, *New England Captives*, 1:255–61; Nathaniel Bouton, ed., *Collections of the New-Hampshire Historical Society* vol. 8 (Concord: McFarland & Jenks, 1866), 146–48; Ulrich also cites domestic violence as a reason why Willey might have wanted to remain in Canada, *Good Wives*, 209. Coleman cites another woman, Isabella McCoy, who might have returned "not too willingly" to New England after her 1747 captivity because her husband was "a man of rather rough and violent temper." However, she cites no colonial sources as evidence of this (Coleman 2:197–98). On domestic violence in early America, see Ann Taves, ed., *Religion and Domestic Violence in Early New England: The Memoirs of Abigail Abbot Bailey* (Bloomington: Indiana University Press, 1989), and Christine Daniels and Michael V. Kennedy, eds., *Over the Threshold: Intimate Violence in Early America* (New York: Routledge, 1999).

49. Cornelia Hughes Dayton, *Women Before the Bar: Gender, Law, and Society in Connecticut, 1639–1789* (Chapel Hill: University of North Carolina Press, 1995), ch. 3; Nancy Cott, "Divorce and the Changing Status of Women in Eighteenth-Century Massachusetts," *William and Mary Quarterly* 3rd ser., 33 (1976): 586–614; Peter Moogk, *La Nouvelle France: The Making of French Canada—A Cultural History* (East Lansing: Michigan State University Press, 2000), 229–33.

50. Coleman *New England Captives* 1:255–61. Edouard de Flecheur may well have spoken English, as the record of their marriage states that his mother was one "Marie Hannesson citizen of the town of Narez in old England," reproduced in Coleman 1:258.

51. Evidence taken from Coleman, *New England Captives*, vols. 1 and 2, passim. Five captive daughters in Canada received their inheritances, whereas seven didn't; among captive sons, six received their inheritances, and only three were withheld.

52. Coleman, *New England Captives*, 1:234–35, 418–19, 431.

53. Ibid., 1:163–64, 244–45, 391–93, 406–9; *New-England Historical and Genealogical Register* 5 (1851): 186–87.

54. Coleman, *New England Captives*, 1:391–93.

55. Ibid., 1:322–23, 293–97.

56. Demos, *Unredeemed Captive*, 51, 177–80, and ch. 9. Demos suggests that an October 12, 1743, gift of nearly thirteen pounds by the Massachusetts General Court "Tarragie (an Indian of the Cagnawaga Tribe who hath marryed an English Woman), His Wife, and Children, now in Town," with a further annual allowance of seven pounds, ten shillings if they should move to Massachusetts, was probably intended for Arosen and A'ongote, who were then visiting Boston. Demos says that Tarragie was one of Arosen's aliases, 208–9, 301–2.

57. Another example of an English colony offering little incentive for women to move there can be found in David Ransome, "Wives for Virginia, 1621," *William and Mary Quarterly*, 3rd ser., 48 (1991): 3–18.

58. Coleman, *New England Captives*, 1:419.

59. Mary Storer Papers, Massachusetts Historical Society, Boston, Mass. All letters cited below are in this collection.

60. Coleman, *New England Captives*, 1:413–25. Jeremiah Storer, Priscilla's and Rachael's father, wrote a will in 1729 that included Rachael but not Priscilla, although both women were living at the time of his death.

61. Mary Storer St. Germaine (hereafter MSS) to Ebenezer Storer (hereafter ES), June 29, 1725 (from Newport, R.I.); MSS to ES, June 26, 1725 (from Newport, R.I.).

62. MSS to Seth Storer, June 29, 1725 (from Newport, R.I.).

63. Coleman, *New England Captives*, 1:418–19. Other family members besides parents could effectively force a disinheritance even where one never existed on paper. Mary Scammon's father, who died the same year she did, left her several lots according to a will that had been drawn up before her marriage to Louis-Joseph Godefroi, Sieur de Tonnancour, but her husband and heirs never received her portion from her New England family (Coleman, 2:151).

64. MSS to ES, July 13, 1725 (from New York). Moogk claims that families in New France were characterized by fierce loyalty and protectiveness, especially on the part of parents toward their children, *La Nouvelle France*, ch. 8.

65. MSS to ES, July 17, 1727.

66. MSS to ES, July 17, 1727; May 2, 1728; May 26, 1730; June 1, 1732; April 19, 1733.

67. MSS to ES, April 19, 1733.

68. MSS to Hannah Storer, April 1733.

69. ES to MSS, May 24, 1733.

70. Coleman, *New England Captives*, 1:418–19.

71. MSS to ES, September 22, 1739. Quotations here are from the contemporaneous English translation found alongside the French original, which was apparently prepared for Ebenezer's convenience.

72. Jean St. Germaine (JS) to ES, March 20, 1748. Mary Storer St. Germaine had died August 25, 1747. (Translation by the author.)

73. JS to ES, June 15, 1749; JS to ES, April 17, 1750. The quotations above are taken from the apparently contemporaneous English translation included with the French original.

74. ES to JS, 1750.

Chapter 5

1. Kenneth Lockridge, *Literacy in Colonial New England* (New York: W. W. Norton, 1974); Ross W. Beales, Jr., "Studying Literacy at the Community Level: A Research Note," *Journal of Interdisciplinary History* 9 (1978): 93–102; Allan Greer, "The Pattern of Literacy in Québec, 1745–1899," *Histoire Sociale/Social History* 11 (1978): 295–335; E. Jennifer Monaghan, "Literacy Instruction and Gender in Colonial New England," *American Quarterly* 40 (1988): 18–41.

2. For a comprehensive analysis and lively narrative of the Seven Years' War, see Fred Anderson, *Crucible of War: The Seven Years' War and the Fate of Empire in British North America, 1754–1766* (New York: Alfred A. Knopf, 2000).

3. While English scholars have emphasized the emergence of masculinities built around secular ideals in the eighteenth century, some still see Protestant piety as a major factor in English manhood. See, for example, Jeremy Gregory, "*Homo Religiosus*: Masculinity and Religion in the Long Eighteenth Century," in *English Masculinities, 1660–1800* (London: Longman, 1999), 85–110; and Stephen H. Gregg, "'A Truly Christian Hero': Religion, Effeminacy, and Nation in the Writings of the Society for Reformation of Manners," *Eighteenth Century Life* 25 (2001): 17–28.

4. Examples of sermons using the phrase "Christian soldier": Joseph Parsons, *Religion Recommended to the Soldier* (Boston: B. Green and Co., 1744); Samuel Cooper, *A Sermon Preached to the Ancient and Honourable Artillery Company* (Boston: J. Draper, 1751); Thomas Barnard, *A Sermon Preached to the Ancient and Honourable Artillery Company* (Boston: Edes and Gill, 1758). Examples of sermons based on or citing Exodus 15:3: Thomas Ruggles, *The Usefulness and Expedience of Souldiers* (New London, Conn.: T. Green, 1737); Isaac Stiles, *The Character and Duty of Soldiers Illustrated* (New Haven, Conn.: James Parker, 1755). The Parsons sermon noted above cites 2 Samuel 17:8: "And thy Father is a Man of War."

On English nationalism, misogyny, and anti-Catholicism, see Anne McLaren, "Gender, Religion, and Early Modern Nationalism: Elizabeth I, Mary Queen of Scots, and the Genesis of English Anti-Catholicism," *American Historical Review* 107 (2002): 739–67; and Michèle Cohen, *Fashioning Masculinity: National Identity and Language in the Eighteenth Century* (London: Routledge, 1996).

5. In *A People's Army: Massachusetts Soldiers and Society in the Seven Years' War* (Chapel Hill: University of North Carolina Press, 1984), Fred Anderson examines the providentialism of the sermons preached to provincial soldiers of the Seven Years' War (ch. 7 and app. D).

6. Sermons based on or citing 2 Samuel 1:18: John Davenport, *A Royall Edict for Military Exercises* (London, 1629); Oliver Peabody, *An Essay to revive and encourage Military Exercises, Skill and Valour among the Sons of God's People in New-England* (Boston: T. Fleet for J. Eliot and J. Philips, 1732); Ruggles, *Usefulness and Expedience of Souldiers.*

7. Sermons based on or using Genesis 14:14: Joshua Moodey, *Souldiery Spiritualized, or the Christian Souldier Orderly, and Strenuously Engaged in the Spiritual Warre* (Cambridge, Mass.: Samuel Green, 1674); Samuel Nowell, *Abraham in Arms: or, the first religious General with his Army engaging in a War . . .* (Boston, 1678), reprinted in *So Dreadfull a Judgment: Puritan Responses to King Philip's War, 1676–1677,* ed. Richard Slotkin and James K. Folsom (Middletown, Conn.: Wesleyan University Press, 1978); Peabody, *Essay to revive;* Ruggles, *Usefulness and Expedience of Souldiers;* William Williams, *Martial Wisdom Recommended* (Boston: T. Fleet for Daniel Henchman, 1737); Ebenezer Gay, *Well-accomplish'd Soldiers, a Glory to their King, and Defence to their Country* (Boston: T. Fleet for Daniel Henchman, 1738); Benjamin Colman, *Christ Standing for an Ensign of the People* (Boston: J. Draper, 1738).

Another popular bible verse for artillery sermons was Judges 18:27–28: "And they—came to Laish, unto a people that were at quiet and secure, and smote them with the edge of the Sword, and burnt the city with fire. And there was no deliverer, because they were far from Zidon." For examples, see Charles Chauncy, *The Char-*

acter and Overthrow of Laish considered and applied (Boston: S. Kneeland and T. Green, 1734); and Gay, *Well-accomplish'd Soldiers.* I am indebted to William V. Trollinger of Bluffton University for directing me to this passage of Judges as the inspiration for these sermons.

8. See, for example, Cotton Mather's captivity narrative of Hannah Duston in *Humiliations follow'd with Deliverances* (Boston, 1697); François Seguenot, *A Letter from a Romish Priest in Canada, To One who was taken Captive in her Infancy, and Instructed in the Romish Faith, but some time ago returned to this her Native Country* (Boston: D. Henchman, 1729), 25; Ruggles, *Usefulness and Expedience of Souldiers,* 8; Jonathan Todd, *The Soldier Waxing Strong and Valiant in Fight through Faith, or, Religion Recommended to Soldiers* (New London, Conn.: T. Green, 1747), 38–39.

9. Peabody, *Essay to revive,* 34; Ruggles, *Usefulness and Expedience of Souldiers,* 6–7, 12; Gay, *Well-accomplish'd Soldiers,* 27–28.

10. Nathaniel Walter, *Extraordinary Events the Doings of GOD, and marvellous in pious Eyes,* a thanksgiving sermon for the taking of Louisbourg (Boston: D. Henchman, 1745), 23; the same passage, verbatim, is found in Thomas Prince, *Extraordinary Events the Doings of GOD, and marvellous in pious Eyes* (Boston: D. Henchman, 1747), also on p. 23; Ebenezer Bridge, *A Sermon Preach'd to the Ancient and Honourable Artillery Company in Boston, June 1, 1752* (Boston: S. Kneeland, 1752), 3. Bridge's sermon cites Acts 10:2 on Cornelius: "A devout man, and one that feared God with all his house, which gave much alms to the people, and prayed to God always."

Fred Anderson argues in *A People's Army* that the New England soldiers were democratic in their organization—sometimes to their great disadvantage—and overall very pious, two qualities that distinguished them dramatically from the British Army.

11. Nathaniel Walter, *The Character of a Christian Hero: a Sermon preached before the ancient and honourable Artillery Company* (Boston: J. Draper, 1746), 21.

12. M. La Roche, *A Letter from Québeck, in Canada, to M. L'Maine, a French Officer* (Boston: Thomas Fleet, 1754), 5–6; Joseph Nichols, (Diary of Ticonderoga expedition, 1758), July 6–17, HM 89, Henry E. Huntington Library, San Marino, Calif. A clear suggestion that *A Letter from Québeck* is fraudulent is the choice of the Irish priest's name, "M'Laish." The destruction of the people of Laish, as mentioned in Judges 18:27–28, was a common theme in eighteenth-century artillery sermons (see footnote 7 above.)

13. Cotton Mather, *Things to be Look'd for* (Cambridge, Mass.: Samuel & Barth. Green, 1691), 74; La Roche, *A Letter from Québeck,* 6; SC1 45X, Massachusetts Archives Collection, 73:40, 75:217–20, Massachusetts State Archives, Boston.

14. L. Boitard, "British Resentment at the French Fairly Coopt at Louisbourg" (London, 1755).

15. In *An Unsettled Conquest: The British Campaign Against the Peoples of Acadia* (Philadelphia: University of Pennsylvania Press, 2000), ch. 6, Geoffrey Plank describes a similar continuation of Mi'kmaq warfare in Nova Scotia in between King George's War and the Seven Years' War. For examples of the use of the phrase "Canada Indians," see, for example, SC1 45X, Massachusetts Archives Collection, 51:244, 73:753, Massachusetts State Archives, Boston; Capt. Ami Rushami Cutter to

Samuel Waldo, May 18, 1744, in the Samuel Waldo Papers, Massachusetts Historical Society, Boston (hereafter abbreviated as MHS); Israel Williams to anonymous, 1754, in the Israel Williams Papers, MHS.

16. SC1 45X, Massachusetts Archives Collection, 73:469–70, 707–8, 753, and 74:13, 31, 36, Massachusetts State Archives, Boston.

17. SC1 45X, Massachusetts Archives Collection, 74:45–47, Massachusetts State Archives, Boston.

18. SC1 45X, Massachusetts Archives Collection, 5:486–529 passim, Massachusetts State Archives, Boston; Quotation from 5:527 (Shirley to La Jonquière, October 9, 1750).

19. William Pote, Jr., original ms. journal kept by him 1745–47 during captivity among the French & Indians, Ayer Collection, Newberry Library, Chicago, Ill., 20, 49. Pote had the unusual advantage of the Massachusetts governor's advocacy for his return, SC1 45X, Massachusetts Archives Collection, 5:486, Massachusetts State Archives, Boston.

20. Emma Lewis Coleman, *New England Captives Carried to Canada* (Portland, Maine: Southworth Press, 1925; Bowie, Md.: Heritage Books, 1989), 2:171–385.

21. *The Military History of Great Britain, for 1756, 1757* (London: J. Millan, 1757), 14–15; William Bollan, *The Importance and Advantage of Cape Breton* (London: John and Paul Knapton, 1746), 142.

22. *The Military History of Great Britain, for 1756, 1757*, 7–14. While this English author heaps contempt on the Canadians for being too slavish, he is also wary of Anglo-Americans whose "Notions of Liberty are too extensive, they have run it to a Fault." He does except the men of Massachusetts, whose service in war and refusal to trade with enemy Indians makes them "the Flower of the *British* Colonies in *America*," 17–20.

On *politesse* in French Canada: William J. Eccles quotes Peter Kalm, the Swedish travel writer of the 1740s, as writing that he greatly prefers French Canada to the English colonies, as "the people there [Canada], even the common man, are much more polite than the people in the English provinces, and especially compared to the Dutch. . . . The difference was as great as if one had gone from the Court to a peasant's house," in *The French in North America, 1500–1783*, revised ed. (East Lansing: Michigan State University Press, 1998), 149.

23. Ibid., 64; Gary B. Nash, "Poverty and Politics in Early American History," in *Down and Out in Early America*, ed. Billy G. Smith (University Park: Pennsylvania State University Press, 2004), 1–37. William Foster discusses the particular humiliations of English boys and men working for French Catholic nuns in the eighteenth century in *The Captors' Narrative: Catholic Women and Their Puritan Men on the Early American Frontier* (Ithaca, N.Y.: Cornell University Press, 2003).

24. Pote, 6, 15, 20, 112.

25. *An Authentic Account of the Reduction of Louisbourg* (London: W. Owen, 1758), 58–59; *The Military History of Great Britain, for 1756, 1757*, 47–48. For a detailed reconstruction of mid-eighteenth century Louisbourg, see Christopher Moore and Terry Southerland, *Fortress of Louisbourg Guide* (Louisbourg and Sydney, N.S.: Fortress of Louisbourg Volunteers Association and the College of Cape Breton Press, 1981).

26. See, for example, *Collection de Manuscrits contenant Lettres, Memoires, et Autres Documents Historiques Relatifs a la Nouvelle France* (Québec, 1883–84), II: 430 (Gov. Vaudreuil to Gov. Dudley, March 26, 1705).

27. Seguenot, *Letter from a Romish Priest*, 5–6. Seguenot's historical argument against the Protestant heresy focuses on the scandalous lives of Martin Luther, "for all that he was a Priest and a Monk, and [his wife] *Catharine de Bore* a Nunn," and on Henry VIII and his wife Ann Boleyn, whom he beheaded, "having discovered her unfaithfulness and her intreagues with some Gallants which she had," 6–7. For more on Seguenot and the captive convert he wrote to, Christine Otis Robataille, see Thomas W. Jodziewicz, "An Unexpected Coda for the Early American Captivity Narrative: A Letter from a Romish Priest," *Catholic Historical Review* 81 (1995): 568–87.

28. Colin Haydon, *Anti-Catholicism in Eighteenth-Century England, c. 1714–80: A Political and Social Study* (Manchester: Manchester University Press, 1993).

29. Peter Moogk, *La Nouvelle France: The Making of French Canada—A Cultural History* (East Lansing: Michigan State University Press, 2000), 60–62, 193; Louise Dechêne, *Habitants and Merchants in Seventeenth Century Montreal* (Paris: Plons, 1974; English translation, Montreal: McGill-Queen's University Press, 1992), 274–75.

30. Nathaniel Wheelwright journal, January 7, 1754, MHS; Lorraine McMullen, *An Odd Attempt in a Woman: The Literary Life of Frances Brooke* (Vancouver: University of British Columbia Press, 1983), 77; Ann M. Little, "Cloistered Bodies: Convents in the Anglo-American Imagination in the British Conquest of Canada," *Eighteenth Century Studies* 39 (2006): 187–200.

31. Quoted material from Ruggles, *Usefulness and Expedience of Souldiers*, 9; Silvanus Conant, *The Art of War, the Gift of GOD* (Boston: Edes and Gill, 1759); Todd, *The Soldier Waxing*, 38–39; Nathaniel Appleton, *A Sermon Preached October 9, being A Day of Public Thanksgiving, Occasioned by the Surrender of Montreal, and All CANADA* (Boston: John Draper, 1760), 26.

For other sermons that identify the French as New England's "inveterate enemy," see, for example, Peabody, *An Essay to revive*; Andrew Eliot, *A Sermon Preached October 25th 1759 Being a Day of Public Thanksgiving Appointed by Authority For the Success of the British Arms this Year; Especially In the Reduction of QUÉBEC, The Capital of CANADA* (Boston: Daniel and John Kneeland, 1759); and Thomas Foxcroft, *Grateful Reflexions on the signal Appearances of Divine Providence for GREAT BRITAIN and its Colonies in AMERICA* (Boston: S. Kneeland, 1760).

32. Anonymous, in *Louisbourg Journals 1745*, ed. Louis E. DeForest (New York: Society of Colonial Wars in the State of New York, 1932), 61–66, September 7, 1745; *An Accurate and Authentic Journal of the Siege of Québec* (London: J. Robinson, 1759), 27–28. The account of the priest-led regiment of Canadians who were summarily killed and scalped was also reported in *A Journal of the Expedition up the River St. Lawrence* (Boston: Fowle and Draper, 1759), 16. The two accounts differ slightly in terms of the date and the number of Canadians killed. *An Accurate and Authentic Journal* gives the date of the attack as August 15, 1759, and suggests that there were twenty prisoners taken. *A Journal of the Expedition* records the date as

August 24, and gives the total number of Canadians killed as thirty-one. This higher number may reflect the number killed in the skirmish as well as those executed and scalped.

33. La Roche, *Letter from Québeck,* 5–6.

34. John Gilmary Shea, *History of the Catholic Missions Among the Indian Tribes of the United States, 1529–1854* (New York: E. Dunigan & Brother, 1855), ch. 3; James Axtell, *The Invasion Within: The Contest of Cultures in Colonial North America* (New York: Oxford University Press, 1985), 247–54; "Journal of the Rev. Joseph Baxter, of Medfield, Missionary to the Eastern Indians in 1717," *New-England Historical and Genealogical Register* 21 (1867), 45–60; anonymous letter to Joseph Baxter, ca. 1717, Doggett family collection; Minot Family Correspondence, 1708–1752, Maine Historical Society, Portland.

35. Shea, *History of the Catholic Missions,* 146–48; Samuel Shute to Sebastien Ralé, February 21, 1719, SC1 45X, Massachusetts Archives Collection, 51:306–12, Massachusetts State Archives, Boston; Col. Harmor's & Capt. Heath's letter to Col. Wm. Goffe, January 21, 1721/22, Doggett family collection; Minot Family Correspondence, 1708–52, Maine Historical Society, Portland.

36. Letter of Fr. Pierre Joseph de la Chasse, October 29, 1724, *The Jesuit Relations and Allied Documents,* ed. Reuben Gold Thwaites (Cleveland: Burrows Bros. Co., 1896–1901), 67:233–35; Samuel Penhallow, *The History of the Wars of New-England with the Eastern Indians* (Cincinnati: J. Harpel, 1859), 97–104; Shea, *History of the Catholic Missions,* 150. The sources disagree on the size of the English and Mohawk army that marched against Norridgewock; La Chasse says it was a formidable force of 1,100, while Penhallow suggests a more modestly scaled army of 200. Shea calls it a "small force," but all agree that the Norridgewock Abenaki were badly outnumbered.

37. Colin G. Calloway, *The Western Abenakis of Vermont, 1600–1800: War, Migration, and the Survival of an Indian People* (Norman: University of Oklahoma Press, 1990), 113–31. This violent conflict was affiliated with the 1722–25 Anglo-Mi'kmaq war in Nova Scotia described by Geoffrey Plank in *Unsettled Conquest,* 78–80. (The Mi'kmaq were part of the Abenaki confederacy.)

38. Penhallow, *History of the Wars of New-England,* Benjamin Coleman's preface and 103–4.

39. "The Rebels Reward: or, *English* Courage Display'd, being a full and true Account of the Victory obtain'd over the Indians at *Norrigiwock,* on the Twelfth of *August* last, by the English Forces under Command of Capt. *Johnson Harmon*" (Boston: J. Franklin, 1724), available at the Henry E. Huntington Library, San Marino, Calif.

40. John Minot to Stephen Minot, June 20, 1732, Doggett family collection, Minot Family Correspondence, 1708–52, box 1, folder 9, letter 6, Maine Historical Society, Portland.

41. SC1 45X, Massachusetts Archives Collection, 74:45–47, Massachusetts State Archives, Boston. For information on the vexed diplomacy between the English and the Abenaki, especially the Norridgewock Indians, see *A Journal of the Proceedings of the Commissioners Appointed for Managing a Treaty of Peace* (Boston: John Draper, 1749?), and *A Journal of the Proceedings at Two Conferences . . . between His*

Excellency William Shirley, Esq., and the Chiefs of the Norridgewock Indians . . . and the Penobscot Indians (Boston: J. Draper, 1754).

42. *Martyrology, or, A brief Account of the Lives, Sufferings, and Deaths of those two holy Martyrs, viz. Mr. John Rogers and Mr. John Bradford* (Boston: S. Kneeland and T. Green, 1736); *The Cruel Massacre of the Protestants in North America; shewing how the French and Indians join together to scalp the English, and the manner of their Scalping, &c&c* (London: Aldermary Church, 1760); *The French Convert: Being a true Relation of the Happy Conversion of a Noble French Lady from the Errors and Superstitions of Popery to the Reformed Religion, by Means of a Protestant Gardiner, her Servant* (Philadelphia: W. Dunlap, 1758).

43. Commission from Gov. William Shirley to Ephraim Williams, January 17, 1755, and anonymous letter to Israel Williams, September 25, 1755, both in the Israel Williams Papers, MHS; Anderson, *Crucible of War*, 118–23.

44. Anonymous, "Journal from New England to Cape Breton" (1745), Thursday, July 11, 1745, Henry E. Huntington Library, San Marino, Calif. Information on this diarist's probable regiment and company is from the published edition of the journal by DeForest, *Louisbourg Journals 1745*, 1–54. DeForest thinks the author is a common soldier, but the regularity of his handwriting and spelling mark him as a man of some education. I think he was a lieutenant, as he affects familiarity with men of superior rank but more often works directly with lieutenants. This journal remained unpublished until it appeared in DeForest's volume.

45. Pote, 40.

46. Abijah Willard's "Orderly Book" (1755–59), Henry E. Huntington Library, San Marino, Calif.; Plank, *Unsettled Conquest*, 140–57.

47. New England had attempted a siege of Québec twice before, once in 1691, and again in 1711. Both were utter failures.

48. Benjamin Doolittle, *A Short Narrative of Mischief done by the French and Indian Enemy on the Western Frontiers of the Province of the Massachusetts-Bay* (Boston: S. Kneeland, 1750), 5, 17–18.

49. "Brisk" or "briskly": This was a highly desirable quality in military men, implying bold efficiency and courage. Writing to Samuel Waldo, William Pepperell recommended two officers in the following positive terms in 1744: "there is Likewise Lieut. Thomas Perkins who lives at Arrundel A brisk man . . . there is Mr John Wise of Berwick I mentioned to you before as a brave bold man," Pepperell to Waldo, June 29, 1744, Samuel Waldo Papers, MHS. For examples of the adjective "brisk" or the adverb "briskly" used to describe battles, see: Willard's "Orderly Book," June 8, 1755; Penhallow, *History of the Wars of New-England*, 41–42, 103–4; "The Rebels Reward: or, *English* Courage Display'd"; *A Journal of the Expedition up the River St. Lawrence*, 21–22; Charles Chauncey, *A Second Letter to a Friend; Giving a more particular Narrative of the Defeat of the French Army at Lake-George* (Boston: Edes and Gill, 1755), 7.

"Smart" or "smartly": Nichols's diary, July 7, 1758; "The Rebels Reward: or, *English* Courage Display'd"; Seth Pomeroy to Mary Pomeroy, September 10, 1755, in the Israel Williams Papers, MHS.

"Undaunted courage": Walter, *The Character of a Christian Hero*, 19; Louis Effingham DeForest, *The Journals and Papers of Seth Pomeroy* (New Haven, Conn.:

Tuttle, Morehouse, & Taylor Co., 1926), account of the battle of Lake George, September 8, 1755; Pomeroy also uses the very same expression in the letter to his wife Mary, September 10, 1755, cited in the previous paragraph. "Utmost fury": direct quotation from Nichols's diary, July 6, 1758.

50. *Journals and Papers of Seth Pomeroy*, September 8, 1755; Chauncey, *Second Letter to a Friend*. For another example of a glorious English or New England retreats, see Nichols's description of the Battle of Ticonderoga, July 6, 1758.

51. *Travels in New France by J.C.B.*, ed. Sylvester K. Stevens, Donald H. Kent, and Emma Edith Woods (Harrisburg: Pennsylvania Historical Commission, 1941), 114, 116. This is a translation of the original, *Voyage au Canada dans le nord de l'Amerique Septentrionale, fait depuis l'an 1751 à 1761* (Québec, 1887).

52. James Gibson, *A Journal of the Late Siege by the Troops from North America* (London: J. Newberry, 1745), 40–41; "Journal of Chaplin Stephen Williams," in DeForest, *Louisbourg Journals 1745*, 130.

53. *Travels in New France by J.C.B.*, 120; *Journals and Papers of Seth Pomeroy*; Pomeroy to Col. Israel Williams, September 9, 1755, Israel Williams Papers, MHS. For a discussion of these sieges and battles, see Anderson, *Crucible of War*, 118–23; 400–401.

54. John Norton, *The Redeemed Captive* (Boston, 1748), 21–22, 24.

55. Pote, 168–69.

56. William Clarke, *Observations On the late and present Conduct of the French, with Regard to their Encroachments upon the British Colonies in North America* (Boston: S. Kneeland, 1755), 21; *Journals and Papers of Seth Pomeroy*, 128–129.

57. Anderson, *Crucible of War*, 137–40, 150–57; Peter Way, "Soldiers of Misfortune: New England Regulars and the Fall of Oswego, 1755–56," *The Massachusetts Historical Review* 3 (2001): 49–88.

58. William Williams to Israel Williams, August 30, 1756; William Williams to Col. Partridge, September 4, 1756; and Ebenezer Hinsdale to I. Williams, October 5, 1756, all in the Israel Williams Papers, MHS.

59. *Travels in New France by J.C.B.*, 73, 140. On the meaning of calling a man a dog, see Foster, *Captors' Narrative*, 12.

60. Kirsten Fischer sheds light on the politics of being called an animal in colonial America, as she describes how accusations of bestiality and other close association with animals played a role in the development of both slavery and race in eighteenth-century North Carolina in *Suspect Relations*, 145–58 and ch. 5. See also Philip Morgan, "Slaves and Livestock in Eighteenth-Century Jamaica: Vineyard Pen, 1750–51," *William and Mary Quarterly* 3rd ser., 52 (January 1995): 47–76.

61. Anonymous diary, DeForest, ed., *Louisbourg Journals 1745*, entry for April 30, 1745, 80–96; anonymous "Journal from New England to Cape Breton" (1745), April 3, 1745. The Israel Williams Papers record an insult to an English officer, referring to him as "a Littel Inferior Scurvy Dogg," Col. Cheeny's comments, January 24, 1758, Israel Williams Papers, MHS. Seth Pomeroy confirms the actions of the spy Donahue in a letter to his wife, Mary, April 18, 1745 (*Journals and Papers of Seth Pomeroy*, 58).

62. Penhallow, *History of the Wars of New-England*, 23; Topsham & Brunswick

Proposal to the Massachusetts House of Representatives, July 28, 1715, Coll. S-219, misc. box 7/30, Maine Historical Society, Portland.

63. William Williams to Israel Williams, August 30, 1756, Israel Williams Papers, MHS; *The Journals and Papers of Seth Pomeroy*, entry for April 21, 1745, and letter to Mary Pomeroy, April 6, 1745; *Authentic Account of the Reduction of Louisbourg*, 16–17; "A Court of Enquiry held by Order of Major Henry Gladwin Commandr: Detroit ye 9th Sept. 1763," Jeffrey Amherst Papers, 1758–64, vol. 2, Clements Library, University of Michigan, Ann Arbor.

64. Penhallow, *History of the Wars of New-England*, 36, 98; DeForest, *Louisbourg Journals 1745*, 115–16; *All Canada in the Hands of the English: or, an Authentick Journal of the Proceedings of the Army, under General Amherst* (Boston: B. Mecom, 1760?), 5.

65. Lepore, *Name of War*; Anderson, *Crucible of War*, introduction and chs. 30–46.

66. *Authentic Account of the Reduction of Louisbourg*, 16; *All Canada in the Hands of the English*, 5.

Epilogue

1. Francis Parkman, *France and England in North America* (New York: Literary Classics of the United States, distributed to the trade by the Viking Press, 1983), "Montcalm and Wolfe," 2:829–1510; quotation from 843–44. See Simon Schama's entertaining take on Wolfe, Montcalm, and Parkman's glorification of Wolfe in *Dead Certainties (Unwarranted Speculations)* (New York: Knopf, 1991).

2. Fred Anderson, *Crucible of War: The Seven Years' War and the Fate of Empire in British North America, 1754–1766* (New York: Knopf, 2000), 344–414. Anderson titles his chapter on the Battle of Québec "Dubious Battle."

3. "Québec 1759" (Vancouver, B.C.: Gamma Two Games, Ltd., 1972).

4. Anderson, *Crucible of War*.

5. Sharon Block, "Rape without Women: Print Culture and the Politicization of Rape, 1765–1815," *Journal of American History* 89 (2002): 849–68.

6. Alan Taylor, *Liberty Men and Great Proprietors: The Revolutionary Settlement on the Maine Frontier, 1760–1820* (Chapel Hill: University of North Carolina Press, 1990), 1–3, 115–21, 181–207; Philip J. Deloria, *Playing Indian* (New Haven, Conn.: Yale University Press, 1998), 10–70.

7. Nathaniel Hawthorne, *The Scarlet Letter* (New York: Tiknor, Reed, and Fields, 1850), ch. 3.

Index

Abenaki Indians, 9, 70, 80, 105, 116–20, 155, 159, 176, 188; Eastern Abenaki, 1, 11, 104, 115, 131, 136, 149, 173, 186–91; Western Abenaki, 11, 104, 107, 110, 120, 124–25, 131, 173, 188

African Americans, 27–28, 179

Algonquian Indians, 1, 2, 8, 11, 12, 14, 16, 29–34, 38, 54, 63, 70, 99–102, 112, 166

Algonquin Indians, 149

Amherst, Lord Jeffrey, 196

Annawon, 86–87

antinomians/Antinomian Crisis, 23, 96

Arosen, François-Xavier, 144, 158

Awashunkes, 32–34

Bartlett, Joseph, 67, 70–71, 82, 110, 111

Baxter, Joseph, 186

Ben Uncas, 77

Berger, Jean, 160

Bigot, Vincent, 186

borderlands history, 3, 7

bow and arrow, use of, 22, 37

Bradford, William, 16–18, 47–48, 76

Brooks, Mary, 107

Brown, Thomas, 69, 72, 75, 82, 88

"Canada Indians," 173, 191

Canadian history, 7–8, 205

cannibalism, 73, 121

captivity, 9–10, 64–69, 70–76, 80–94, 96–99, 101–2, 104–29, 133–65, 173–76; captives as substitute wartime Indian economy, 111–13; English captives in Canada, 128–29, 133–39, 142–65; English families imperiled by Indian captivity, 104–9, 173–76; English identification of Indian "masters," 91–93, 109–11, 116–26; English motherhood in Indian captivity, 106–7; Indian exchange of captives with the French, 111–13; Indian perspectives on captivity, 92–93, 115–26; Indian rituals for introducing captives to

the community, 64–69, 70–76; Indian women's importance in rituals of, 71–72, 101–2; naturalization of English captives in Canada, 145; networks of English women captives in Canada, 146–48; political uses of captivity narratives, 93–94, 112–26

Cassicinamon, Robin, 76

Catholicism, 10, 27, 75, 127–29, 130–31, 134–35, 136–37, 145–46; English and Anglo-American anti-Catholicism, 127–38, 166–73, 183–93, 203; missionary efforts to convert Protestants, 133–37, 145–46; Protestant fear and loathing of priests, 134–37, 185–90; religious orders in Canada, 127, 131

Cayuga Indians, 11

Champlain, Samuel de, 30, 38

Church, Benjamin, 31–32, 52–53, 69–70, 86–87

clothing/adornment, 9, 58–90, 122–24, 133, 138, 178, 180; cultural cross-dressing, 58–60, 76–90; English complaints about Indian dress, 72–73; identity and, 59–70, 74–76, 81–90, 180; importance of cloth and clothing among the English, 60–63; importance of clothing and adornment among Indians, 63–69; moccasins, English adoption of, 78–79; versus "nakedness," 69–70, 83–84, 190; stripping of live captives and dead bodies, 9, 13, 59, 70–76, 81–87; use of, in borderlands warfare, 73–78, 81–90

Cromwell, Oliver, memory of among eighteenth-century New Englanders, 171–75

Cronon, William, 113

cultural studies, 8

Dagueil, Jean Baptiste, 147

Davenport, John, 22–23, 168

Davis, Sarah (Marie-Anne Davis de Saint-Benoit), 147–48

Acknowledgments

When you take as long as I have to write this book, you have a lot of friends, mentors, and colleagues to acknowledge, and I gratefully do so here. I had the great luck to attend the University of Pennsylvania and study with Richard S. Dunn, Carroll Smith-Rosenberg, Robert Blair St. George, and Michael Zuckerman, four outstanding scholars who were always generous and patient with their dullest student. Mary Maples Dunn became an unofficial mentor, as she and Richard together offered me hospitality, guidance, and the occasional sinecure to help pay my bills. I remain forever grateful for the wonderful example they were of two renowned historians who were also kind and generous mentors. My friends at Penn helped me more than they will know, especially Rosalind Beiler, John Bezis-Selfa, Sharon Block (although she was a Princetonian by the time I got to Penn), Alison Games, Liam Riordan, and Wayne Bodle.

Two of my former colleagues at the University of Dayton, Bill Trollinger and Amy Morgenstern, went above and beyond the call of friendship in very trying times and are always a source of good humor and intellectual companionship. My colleagues at Colorado State University are all dedicated teachers, top-notch scholars, and, fortunately for me, my friends as well. They all have my gratitude, especially Ruth Alexander, Mark Fiege, Judy Gaughan, Elizabeth Jones, Ginger Guardiola, Janet Ore, Alison Smith, and Greg Smoak. Ruth deserves special credit for enforcing the deadlines that at long last squeezed the final draft of this book out of me.

My friends in Oxford, Ohio, my home for four years, deserve special mention. I didn't realize how lucky I was to live there until I moved away. Drew Cayton, Amy DePaul, Katherine Gillespie, Rodrigo Lazo, and Judith Zinsser welcomed a non-Miami University scholar into their ranks and provided great intellectual companionship (and Rodrigo was also a great companion for running in the Batchelor Woods trails). Down the road at the University of Cincinnati, Geoffrey Plank was a great friend and colleague in early American history. The Dutton, Quantz, and Tomarken families were the best neighbors ever, and Annette Tomarken did me the favor of providing me with excellent translations of some of my French sources. R.I.P. Daniel, Flower, Cheeba, Marbles, Caboose, and Sam.

A few close friends and colleagues deserve recognition and thanks, as I truly cannot imagine myself happy or successful in this profession without them. Sharon Block has been a terrific source of intellectual and social companionship since we started graduate school, and talking to her always lifts my spirits and encourages me to continue my work as a women's historian. When I first met Kirsten Fischer, it felt as though we had already been friends for years, and I always feel inspired to become a better historian after talking to her. Over the years, she has read and commented generously on most of the chapters of this book. John Wood Sweet has been a faithful friend and sounding board, and a font of new ideas and information. I will always feel lucky that Amy Froide and I overlapped both in Oxford and at the Newberry Library and that Judith Zinsser became not just a colleague in women's history and a neighbor but a friend and counselor as well. My life in Colorado would be unimaginable without the friendship and support of Erin Jordan, who has favored me with countless fascinating discussions of women's history and emergency backup babysitting. And a new friend, Dana Rabin, has loaned me enough energy and encouragement to start a new project and finish this book at the same time.

Gail Macleitch, R. Todd Romero, and Heather Kopelson have generously shared their fresh dissertation research with me and have been good companions at several conferences. Emerson Baker has set me straight too many times to count in the details of life on the Maine frontier. And Geoffrey Plank provided guidance on the Canadian history in Chapters 4 and 5. Additionally, a number of women in the historical profession have supported the research and writing of this book. Kathleen Brown, Elaine Crane, Susan Juster, Carol Karlsen, Mary Beth Norton, Nancy Shoemaker, and Marilyn Westerkamp all gave me encouragement at critical times in my career, and although I'm sure they never knew how important it was to me, I would like to thank them here. As series editor at the University of Pennsylvania Press, Kathy Brown deserves extra thanks for her thorough and insightful criticisms of the manuscript. Also at Penn Press, my editor, Bob Lockhart, will have my eternal gratitude for his encouragement and support of this project, and my thanks for the many lunches and dinners he bought me while waiting long years to see a completed manuscript!

In addition to the tremendous support I have had from my friends and colleagues, a number of institutions generously supported the research for this book. The Newberry Library awarded me the Monticello College

Foundation Fellowship and, more important, the means to buy a semester off from my teaching responsibilities. I can say confidently that this book would not have been written without the Newberry's generous support, as the time and friendships I had there convinced me that I could find the evidence and make sense of it. Special thanks to James Grossman, Adam Stewart, and my fellow Newberry-ites Robin Bachin, Terry Bouton, Kirsten Fischer, Amy Froide, Elliott Gorn, Allan Greer, Diana Robin, Helen Tanner, Louise Townsend, and Laurier Turgeon for their friendship and encouragement. The Dean's Office of the College of Arts and Sciences at the University of Dayton, the Liberal Arts Dean's Office at Colorado State University under the leadersihp of Bob Hoffert, The John Nicholas Brown Center, the Massachusetts Historical Society, and the Henry E. Huntington Library also supported this work generously. I'd like to thank the staff of the MHS especially for their assistance and friendship, especially Conrad Wright, Virginia Smith, Ondine LeBlanc, and Len Travers (now of the University of Massachusetts, Dartmouth). The staffs of the Clements Library at the University of Michigan, the Maine Historical Society, the Newberry Library, the Connecticut State Library, the Huntington Library, and the Massachusetts Archives were also very helpful in the course of my research at those institutions, and I am grateful for their assistance. I am especially grateful to the Newberry and the Huntington for their generosity in allowing me to use images from their collections in this book.

Many other institutions have also supported this work by giving it a fair hearing in various seminars and colloquia. I am indebted to the Newberry Early American History Seminar and the Library Fellows Seminar, the Colonial Seminar at the Massachusetts Historical Society, the Michigan Early American Seminar, the Ohio State University Early American Seminar, and the University of Minnesota Early American and Women's History Seminars. They helped me to sharpen my arguments, seek out new and better evidence, and write better too. I am also grateful for the assistance of Linda Smith Rhoads at the *New England Quarterly* for her help with an earlier version of Chapter 2 that was published as "'Shoot that rogue, for he hath an Englishman's coat on!' Cultural Cross-Dressing on the New England Frontier, 1620–1760,'" *New England Quarterly* 74:2 (2001): 238–73.

My family has always supported my education and career, and so it is especially deserving of my gratitude. My late grandmother Thelma Warner was an outstanding example of female feistiness, not that following in her footsteps has always worked to my advantage. I have always had the love and encouragement of my parents, Joan and Tom Little, and I hope I have finally lived down my adolescence and let them know how much I appreciate them. My brother Mark and sister-in-law Susan Nelson Little gave me a place to crash in Philadelphia when I needed to return to Penn and always entertained me generously. My in-laws Wendy and Conner Moore not only have taken me into their family but have also provided room, board, and good company while on research trips to Maine and Massachusetts. Giving my parents and in-laws a granddaughter is just a down payment on my debts. While we are not related in the usual way, I will always consider my two oldest friends, Kathleen Ventre and Britany Orlebeke, part of my family. Finally, Carrie Lovell made having a child and finishing a book possible, and even enjoyable, and I gratefully acknowledge the hard work she does looking after Alice and her parents.

This book is dedicated to my husband, Christopher Moore, as there would be no books without his love and support. The fact that he's a native New Englander and grew up as a part-time Canadian and that he dragged me up into the White Mountains of New Hampshire, sailed me around Vineyard Sound and Cape Cod, introduced me to the mysteries of navigating the streets of Boston, Somerville, and Cambridge, and shared with me his love of his home state of Maine is not entirely coincidental.